Pharmaceutics

Basic Principles and Formulations

Second Edition

Pharmaceutics
Basic Principles and Formulations
Second Edition

D. K. Tripathi
M. Pharm, PhD
Director, Pharmacy
Santosh Rungta Group of Institutions, Bhilai, CG

PharmaMed Press
An imprint of Pharma Book Syndicate
A unit of BSP Books Pvt. Ltd.
4-4-309/316, Giriraj Lane,
Sultan Bazar, Hyderabad - 500 095.

Pharmaceutics Basic Principles and Formulations, ***Second Edition***
by **D. K. Tripathi**

Disclaimer: The authors and the publishers have taken due care to provide the authentic, reliable and up to date information related to the subject. However, neither the authors nor the publisher shall be responsible for any liability for any damage caused as a result of use of this book. The respective user must check the accuracy from other sources too.

Published by

PharmaMed Press
An imprint of Pharma Book Syndicate
A unit of BSP Books Pvt. Ltd.
4-4-309/316, Giriraj Lane, Sultan Bazar, Hyderabad - 500 095.
Phone: 040-23445688; Fax: 91+40-23445611
e-mail: info@pharmamedpress.com
www.pharmamedpress.com/pharmamedpress.net

ISBN: 978-93-91910-64-8

PREFACE TO SECOND EDITION

The book Pharmaceutics – 1 (Basic Principles & Formulations) had been prepared earlier as per the requirement of B. Pharmacy first semester students. There are some unique features of this book such as theory and practical experiments have been provided. The examples of practical experiments are in fact living examples and if someone follows the method, he or she can arrive at the final result. The book has been prepared in very simple language so that the student can easily understand. Meanwhile, the Pharmacy Council of India has prepared the syllabus for B. Pharmacy course. Now the book has been revised accordingly and at the end of each chapter a set of questions along with MCQs have provided.
Fortunately, the book has gained due acceptance.

The author expects that the book does not have any mistake. However, if someone points out any mistake, necessary correction shall be made.

- DK Tripathi

PREFACE TO FIRST EDITION

This book has been written with an idea of introducing pharmacy students of undergraduate level, particularly of first years to the fundamentals of the subject, pharmaceutics. Although the contents have been designed in accordance with the syllabus of Chhattisgarh Swami Vivekanand Technical University, it will mostly cover the syllabus for first year B.Pharm course of other universities. The book contains nine chapters. The first chapter provides information about history of pharmacy, career opportunity in pharmacy, and development of pharmacopoeias, etc. Each of the other five chapters contains preliminary information about each type of the pharmaceutical dosage forms and their manufacture. Chapter 7 contains information about the systems of weights and measure and the chapter 9 deals with the pharmaceutical incompatibiliess. At the end, few annexure have been incorporated to furnish allied information.

Besides theoretical information about each dosage form, some classical examples of each type have been incorporated along with methods of manufacture to practice in the laboratory, so that, the students of higher semesters or years can use the book as the handbook for practical pharmaceutics.

The entire effort has been made to make this book a textbook for first year B.Pharm and practical handbook for all other students. The examples which can be conveniently performed in the laboratory have been provided.

However, the author shall be thankful to those who will communicate their views for further improvement or revision and their valuable suggestions shall be duly acknowledged in the revised edition also.

- DK Tripathi

ACKNOWLEDGEMENTS

The journey of this project was initiated few years back. At different times, different types of obstruction came and the work got detained. Although one of my Student-cum-Colleague, Minaketan Tripathy had been constantly inspiring me to complete the book.

Ultimately, it has been completed. For completion, I must thank the people who helped me for this work. I express my thank to Azajuddin, M. D. Junaid Khan, Mr. Amit Alexander, Mr. Hemant Badwaik and Miss. Rashmi Chaurasia, my colleagues in this institute who helped me at various steps. I am also thankful to Sri Chinta Dilip, my office staff and to my elder son, Nirmalya for his assistance and at last I must name the person without whose cooperation nothing could have been done. She is my wife Bimala.

At last, I express my gratefulness to the management of this Institute under Santosh Rungta Group of Institutions for providing me the facility to complete the pending project.

- DK Tripathi

CONTENTS

Chapter 11

Suppositories

Chapter 12

Pharmaceutical Incompatibilities

Chapter 13

Semisolid Dosage Forms

Abbreviations

mol/l	Concentration, gram molecule of a substance per 1000 ml of solution.
n	Refractive index for electromagnetic radiation in a given medium, dimensionless, ratio of the sine of the angle of incidence of electromagnetic radiation on a medium to the sine of its angle of refraction in the medium.
20 n D	Refractive index, value measured at the wavelength of the sodium D-line (589.3 nm) and at a temperature of 20 ± 0.5°C.
NCIMB	National Collection of Industrial, Food and Marine Bacteria Ltd, 23 St Machar Drive, Aberdeen AB24 3RY, Scotland.
NCTC	National Collection of Type Cultures, Central Public Health laboratory, Colindale Avenue, London NW9 5HT, England.
NCYC	National Collection of Yeast Cultures, AFRC Food Research, Colney Lane, Norwich NR4 7UA, England. Probability of an event in statistical estimations.
pH	Dimensionless, physical quantity expressing the acidity or alkalinity of a solution, measured as the negative logarithm of the hydrogen ion concentration or hydrogen-ion activity expressed in moles per liter. The scale 0 to 7, represents the acidity and 7 to 14, represents the alkalinity. 7 indicates the neutral state. Increase of number indicates the increase of alkalinity.
ρ	Density of a substance at a particular temperature, mass per unit volume.
$ñ_{20}$	Density of a substance at a particular temperature of 20°C. ñ According to the International Pharmacopoeia, grams per millilitre (g/ml).
	Reagent.
R_f	Ratio of fronts, related to fronts. In paper or thin-layer chromatography, ratio of the distance travelled by the substance R to that travelled by the mobile phase.
R_r	In chromatography, ratio of the distances travelled by the substance to that of the reference substance.
RS	Reference substance.
SI	International System.
TS	Test solution.
VS	Volumetric solution.

Chapter 1

Historical Background Development of the Profession of Pharmacy

History of Profession of Pharmacy in India in Relation to Pharmacy Education, Industry and Organization, Pharmacy as a Career

Pharmacopoeias: Introduction to IP, BP, USP and Extra Pharmacopoeia.

Defining the Project

Pharmacy has been a part of everyday life since ancient times. Excavations, such as Shanidar (30000 B.C.E) support this fact. The ancient tribal healers, also called as Shamans often guarded this knowledge of healing properties of certain natural substances. But, the recognition of the medicinal plants was so widespread that it obstructed any necessity for a special class of drug gatherers. Earlier people used to describe diseases in supernatural terms. They believed the beneficial medicines worked in supernatural ways. The magical medicines for curing were part of the duty of Shamans. Usually they were in charge of all supernatural things in a tribe, and hence, they diagnosed and treated most serious and chronic diseases. These remedial medicines connected with supernatural world for thousand years continue to fascinate us all even today. Thus, we can conclude that drugs have a dual heritage, a simple curing tool and special substance with supernatural powers.

Though the ancient people discovered a small number of drugs that heals human diseases, but this discovery can be considered as one of the humanity's greatest advances.

Afterwards, settled cultures provided tools (such as writings, weights, measures) to mushroom this rationale method of medical treatment, without which pharmaceutical sciences may have failed to progress.

Antiquity: The advancement of societies also started influencing the fundamentals of disease and healing. The changes can be verified from the remains of the civilizations of Mesopotamia and Egypt. From ancient records of Egyptian civilization, it can be concluded that pharmaceutical sciences rose greater heights in these times, with more dosage forms compounded from more detailed formula. The Egyptian medical texts show a close connection between supernatural and natural healing. Recipes usually began with a prayer or hymn and ended with plant drugs.

In ancient Greece, there was a similar connection of drugs or *pharmakon*, means magic spell, remedy, poison. Most Greek medicines were prepared from plants and the first great study of plants was done by Theophrastus (370 – 285 BC), a student of Aristotle.

Middle Age: Traditionally, middle Ages refer to the period from the first fall of Rome (400 AD) to the fall of Constantinople (1453). Now the use of drugs went another shift. Rational drug treatment was replaced by Church's teaching that sin and disease were related intimately. Monasteries became centres for healing, both spiritual and physical. Now monks planted gardens to grow medicinal herbs, and inclined to credit their cures to the God, rather to their medical resources.

There were many cultures that dealt with medicines but there was no significant change that occurred in this period.

In Western Europe, teachings of Mohammed were followed. Greek writings in medicines were translated into Arabic. As Arabs conquered this region, they brought new medicines with them. They rejected the idea that foul testing medicines worked best. Arabic culture returned the classical knowledge of medicine to Europe. The debate on medicine among European academics was based on speculation but not on observation.

Hence observation methodology was to be followed to bring down a significant change in the medical practice. This new experimental period was called *Renaissance.*

History of Pharmacy Profession in India

In earlier times vegetables, animal and mineral had been used as a source of drug in India. Few experienced persons called Vaidya used to process and prepare medicines from these materials. The knowledge of collecting, processing and preparing the medicines had been kept secret within the family. No scientific method of standardization of drugs was available. India has been ruled by various invaders. However, the Indian system of medicines was influenced during these rules. For example, during Muslim rule in India the Indian system of medicines declined but, the Arabic or Unani-Tibbi system grew. During the British rule the Allopathic or English system of medicines came to India. In fact, during 19th century this system became more popular. Till early nineteenth century all the drugs had been imported into the country from Europe.

After 1900 the development of the system started. Some facts are mentioned below chronologically for information to the readers.

- In 1901 the Bengal Chemical & Pharmaceutical Works was established in Calcutta by Acharya Prafulla Chandra Roy.
- In 1903 a small factory was set up by Prof. T.K. Gujjar at Parel, Bombay.
- In 1907 Prof. T.K. Gujjar set up Alembic Chemical Works at Baroda.

During World War-I (1914 – 1920) the imports of drugs were cut off. Before that war crude drugs were mostly exported and imported in finished form. Import of drug became regularized after the War. Since there was no check on the quality of the imported drugs, the manufacturers took advantage of the situation and as a result

(i) Foreign manufacturers started dumping the inferior quality and adulterated medicines in India.

(ii) Indian market became full of useless and deleterious drugs and these were sold by unqualified people.

As a result of these conditions (1) poisoning due to quinine, (2) selling of chalk powder in place of quinine, (3) in place oil atropine solution, croton oil was instilled into the eye, and (4) compounds of antimony and arsenic, and digitalis (potent drugs) were dispensed without any standard.

The necessity of controlling such situation was felt and following laws framed earlier were reframed and imposed.

Year	Act	Purpose
1878	Opium Act	To deal with cultivation of poppy and the manufacture, transport, export, import and sale of opium.
1889	Indian Merchandise Act	To misbrand the goods in general
1894	Indian Tariff Act	To levy of customs duty on goods including foods, drinks, drugs, chemicals and medicines imported into India or exported there from.
1898	Sea Customs Act	To prevent Goods with 'false trade description' from importing under this act.
1919	Poisons Act	To regulate the import, possession and sale of poisons.
	Indian Penal Code	To make provision for punishment for intentional adulterations as per Sections of IPC.

Some laws were also imposed at state level as indirect reference to drugs; these laws were too superficial and had very less direct link to drugs. For example;

Year	Act	Remarks
1884	Bengal Municipal Act	
1901	City of Bombay District Municipal Act	Concerned with food
1909	Bengal Excise Act	.
1911	Punjab Municipal Act	
1912	United Provinces (now Uttar Pradesh) Prevention of Adulteration Act	Refers to adulteration of foods and drugs.
1914	Punjab Excise Act	
1916	United Provinces Municipalities Act	Inspection of shops and seizure of adulterated substances.
1919	Bengal Food Adulteration Act	
1919	Bihar and Orissa Prevention of Adulteration Act	
1919	Madras Prevention of Adulteration Act	Chiefly concerned with food adulteration
1922	Bihar and Orissa Municipal Ac	
1922	Central Provinces Municipalities Act	
1925	Bombay Prevention of Adulteration Act	
1929	Punjab Pure Food Act	

To assess the status of the Pharmacy profession in the country the Govt of India appointed a committee under the chairmanship of Late Col. R. N. Chopra and recommend the measures to be taken.

- In 1931 this committee published its report and reported that in the country there was no recognized and specialized profession of Pharmacy. The functions were being done by a group of people known as Compounder. After publication of the said report, Prof. Mahadeva Lal Schroff (Prof. M.L. Schroff) took initiative to start Pharmacy education in the Banaras Hindu University (BHU), Allahabad, U.P.
- In the year 1935 United Province Pharmaceutical Association was established which was later on converted into Indian Pharmaceutical Association (IPA).
- In 1937 the 3-years B. Pharm course was started in BHU under the leadership of Prof. M.L. Schroff who published a journal in name of Indian Journal of Pharmacy in 1939.

- In 1940 the All India Pharmaceutical Congress Association (IPCA) was started and to popularize the profession of Pharmacy as a whole IPCA started holding the pharmaceutical conference at various places in the country. Since then the yearly conference has been held at different parts of the country.
- In 1937, the Govt of India brought 'Import of Drugs Bill' which was later on withdrawn.
- In 1940, to regulate the import, manufacture, sale and distribution of drugs in British India the Govt brought 'Drugs Bill'. This was later on adopted as 'Drugs Act of 1940'.
- In 1941, the Drugs Technical Advisory Board (D.T.A.B.) was constituted under this act.
- In 1945, Central Drug Laboratory was established in Calcutta under 'Drugs Act of 1940'.

The Drugs Act has been modified from time to time and presently the provisions of the Act cover Cosmetics and Ayurvedic, Unani and Homeopathic medicines in certain respects.

- In 1945 to standardize the Pharmacy Education in India the Govt brought the Pharmacy Bill.
- In 1946 the Indian Pharmacopoeial List was published under the chairmanship of late Col. R. N. Chopra. The list contained the drugs used in India at that time but not included in British Pharmacopoeia.
- In 1948, the Pharmacy Act was published and in the same year Indian Pharmacopoeial Committee was constituted under the chairmanship of late Dr. B.N. Ghosh.
- In 1949, the Pharmacy Council of India (P.C.I.) was established under Pharmacy Act 1948.
- In 1954, the Education Regulation came in force in some states but other states lagged behind.
- In 1954, the Drugs and Magic Remedies (Objectionable Advertisements) Act 1954 was passed to stop misleading advertisements such as Cure all pills.
- In 1955, Medicinal and Toilet Preparations (Excise Duties) Act 1955 was introduced to enforce uniform duty for all states for products containing alcohol.
- In 1955 the first edition of Indian Pharmacopoeia was published.
- In 1985, to protect the society from dangers of addictive drugs the Narcotic and Psychotropic Substances Act was enacted.

The price of drugs in India is controlled by Drugs Price Order and the Govt of India changes the price from time to time.

Development of Pharmacy Education

The origin of pharmacy education in India dates back to 1899. At that time, training of pharmacists was mostly conducted at Madras (present name Chennai). In 1928 the State Medical Faculty of Bengal followed this pharmacy training procedure by starting a similar programme. However, this has been mentioned above that in 1937 Prof. M.L. Schroff started 3-year degree course (B. Pharm) in pharmacy at Banaras Hindu University, Allahabad. At that time, the curriculum was a combination of pharmaceutical chemistry, analytical chemistry, and pharmacy. The graduates could work as specialists in quality control and standardization of drugs for pharmaceutical companies, but not for pharmacy practice. Thereafter and before independence 2 more institutions were set up to impart pharmacy degree programs; in 1944, the Punjab University started a pharmacy department and in 1947 L.M. College was established in Ahmadabad. After independence and till 1963 six more states Govt Universities and one private university, Birla Institute of Technology, Pilani started offering the course. Afterwards various institutions across the country have been imparting the education in pharmacy.

This has also been mentioned earlier that in 1949, the Pharmacy Council of India (P.C.I.) was established under the Pharmacy Act 1948. The Govt of India established the PCI with the objective of regulation of

- The Pharmacy Education in the country for the purpose of registration as a pharmacist under the Pharmacy Act.
- Profession and Practice of Pharmacy

Hence the functions and duties of the Pharmacy Council of India are;

- To prescribe minimum standard of education required for qualified pharmacist.
- To frame Education Regulations prescribing the conditions to be fulfilled by the institutions seeking approval of the PCI for imparting education in pharmacy throughout the country.
- Inspection of Pharmacy Institutions seeking approval under the Pharmacy Act, monitoring and grant of approval as per the prescribed norms.
- To withdraw the approval, if the approved course of study or an approved examination does not fulfil the educational standards prescribed by the PCI.
- To approve foreign qualifications granted outside the territories of the Pharmacy Act.
- To maintain Central Register of Pharmacists.

Presently, there are more than 3000 institutions imparting various pharmacy training programmes across the country and about 150,000 students are being enrolled in different courses of pharmacy every year. The pharmacy degree programs offered in India include: Diploma in Pharmacy (D. Pharm), Bachelor of Pharmacy (B. Pharm), Master of Pharmacy (M. Pharm), Master of Science in Pharmacy [MS (Pharm)] and Master of Technology in Pharmacy [M Tech (Pharm)], Doctor of Pharmacy (Pharm D), and Doctor of Philosophy in Pharmacy (PhD). Integration of two courses like B. Pharm + MBA or M. Pharm + MBA has also been initiated by some institutions. There are six National Institutes of Pharmaceutical Education and Research (NIPERs) in India offering MS (Pharm), M. Tech (Pharm), and doctoral-level degrees.

Growth of Pharmaceutical Industry in India

The pharmaceutical education being imparted to students in India focuses towards self-employability, and entry into academia and the pharmaceutical industry. In July 2010, Her Excellency Smt. Pratibha Devi Singh Patil, the former President of India, in a speech on "Recent Trends in Pharmacy Education and Practice", mentioned that the Indian pharmaceutical industry has a wide range of capabilities and is ranked amongst one of the foremost industries of the country. It has grown from a meagre turnover of US$ 0.32 billion in 1980, to about US$ 21.3 billion in 2009-10, and it is poised to grow at a compounded annual growth rate of 19 percent. The growth of the pharmaceutical industry, of course, indicates the employment of able and competent pharmacists, and this seems to be one of the major reasons for the growth of pharmacy colleges in India. However, apart from the pharmaceutical industry-related employment, practicing pharmacists are also supposed to cater to the needs of general public and patients. But the latter aspect is lacking in the country. The medical stores are being handled primarily by diploma holders; but patient counselling or patient-pharmacist interaction is rarely taking place. To bridge this gap, the courses or curriculum needs to be designed accordingly. In addition, the students entering into pharmacy institutions have to expand their areas and look beyond the industrial employment to the wider fields of public healthcare. Already, some institutions have started Pharmacy Practice courses; but this initiative is very less than actual requirement. Expansion of training programmes by the teachers and greater acceptance by the students is necessary to cater to the health care needs of patients.

Code of Ethics

Code of ethics has been drafted by Pharmacy Council of India according to the work being done by the pharmacist such as job, trade, medical profession, and profession. Ethics is defined as code of moral principles. It highlights 'what is right and what is wrong'. It is a noble profession; accordingly, there are differences in code of ethics based on type of work being done.

A young prospective pharmacist should feel no hesitation in assuming the following pharmacist's oath:

- I promise to do all I can do to protect and improve the physical and moral well-being of society, holding the health and safety of my community above other considerations. I shall uphold the laws and standards governing my profession, avoiding all forms of misinterpretation, and I shall safeguard the distribution of medical and potent substances.
- Knowledge gained about patients, I shall hold in confidence and never divulge unless compelled to do so by the law.
- I shall strive to perfect and enlarge my knowledge to contribute to the advancements of pharmacy and the public health.
- I furthermore promise neither to maintain my honour in all transactions and my conduct never bring discredit to myself or neither to my profession nor to do anything to diminish the trust reposed in my professional brethren.
- May I prosper and live long in favour as I keep and hold to this, my Oath, but if violated these sacred promises, may the reverse be my lot.

The goal of medical therapy is to improve the patients' health and quality of life. Optimal medical therapy should be safe, effective and appropriate. Accurate and up to date information are necessary to provide best medical care for the patients as well as for the providers.

The responsibilities of physicians and pharmacists are complementary and supportive to meet the goal of providing optimal medical therapy. This requires communication, respect, trust and mutual recognition of each other's professional competence. During counselling the patients, the physician may focus on the goal of therapy, the risks and benefits and side effects. The pharmacists on the other hand may focus on correct usage, treatment adherence, dosage, precautions and storage information.

Responsibilities of a pharmacist during a medical therapy

1. To ensure safe procurement, storage, adequate dosage and dispensing of medicines as per the prescription
2. To furnish information to the patients, which may include the name of the medicine, its purpose, potential interactions and side effects, correct usage and storage

3. To review prescription orders to identify interactions, allergic reactions, contraindications and therapeutic duplications. Significant matters should be discussed with the prescriber (physician)
4. To consult with the physician for the preparation and revision of therapeutic plans of the treatment with the medicines
5. To discuss medicine related problems or concerns with regard to the prescribed medicines, if requested by the patient
6. To advise patients on the selection and use of non-prescription medicines and how to manage the minor symptoms or ailments
7. To advise the patient where self-medication is not appropriate and the respective physician to be consulted for diagnosis and treatment
8. To report adverse reactions of medicines to health authorities, when necessary
9. To provide and share general as well as specific medicine related information and to advise the public and health care providers
10. To update the knowledge on medical therapy regularly through continuous professional development.

When the pharmacist and physician start exchanging information, each provider can understand other's performance. Such understanding ultimately helps to recognize each other's value, to build mutual trust and to develop satisfaction with the relationship. The net benefit of each exchange among service partners adds value to professional collaboration. Similarly, when expectations are met, the satisfaction with exchange partners may result. The continued meeting of expectations also can contribute to the development of trust.

Apart from the above discussed responsibilities, a pharmacist also coordinates with and assists the nursing staff at different levels or stages of therapy.

1. Proper administration of drugs i.e. to take right drug at right time. Whether the drug has to be administered before or after meals, frequency of administration, and dose of drugs to be administered in emergencies. All these are monitored by the pharmacist along with nurses,
2. A pharmacist also provides information to the nurse about the diet plan which should be followed by the patient during the drug therapy. A pharmacist is the best person who knows about the drug-food interactions and thus, he decides the diet plan which should be advised and monitored by the nurses.
3. The pharmacist also guides the nurses about the safe handling of drugs. He provides information regarding proper dispensing, storage of drugs and disposal of waste containers.

4. The pharmacist assists the nurses in documentation which includes recording of day to day and patient to patient plan of drug administration, recording of drug administered and to be administered. He can also assist in documentation of various clinical parameters at regular interval of time.
5. The pharmacist can also train the nurses about the use and sterilisation techniques of surgical instruments.
6. A pharmacist also acts as an active member of the health care team which includes physician and nurse, which can ultimately provide maximum benefits to the patients.

Pharmacy as a Career

Pharmacy is a word derived from the Greek word *pharmakon* meaning drug. Pharmacy is a branch of science related to healthcare services and Pharmacist is a core healthcare professional. Today, the discipline of pharmacy has made enormous progress and is a distinctly independent discipline, known as pharmaceutical sciences & technology with the wealth of knowledge, research and art of technology. Unlike other curricula, pharmacy is a product as well as service-related discipline. Pharmacist works in all stages related to drug, starting from drug discovery, development, safety, quality control, packaging, storage, use, marketing, and sale and also in governing the manufacture, sale, export and import of drugs in the country, i.e. in drug control administration. Precisely, in the real sense, pharmacist is a drug expert.

The position of a pharmacist in health care profession

The Indian pharmaceuticals market is the third largest in terms of volume and thirteenth largest in terms of value, and it accounts for 20 per cent in the volume terms and 1.4 per cent in value terms of the Global Pharmaceutical Industry as per a report by Equity Master. India is the largest provider of generic drugs globally with the Indian generics accounting for 20 per cent of global exports in terms of volume. Of late, consolidation has become an important characteristic of the Indian pharmaceutical market as the industry is highly fragmented.

India plays an important role in the global pharmaceuticals sector. The country also has a large pool of scientists and engineers who have the potential to move the industry ahead to higher level. Presently over 80 per cent of the antiretroviral drugs used globally to combat AIDS (Acquired Immuno Deficiency Syndrome) are supplied by Indian pharmaceutical companies.

The UN-backed Medicines Patent Pool has signed six sub-licences with Aurobindo, Cipla, Desano, Emcure, Hetero Labs and Laurus Labs, and allowed them to make generic anti-AIDS medicine Tenofovir Alafenamide (TAF) for 112 developing countries.

Indian pharmaceutical sector is estimated to account for 3.1 – 3.6 per cent of the global pharmaceutical industry in value terms and 10 per cent in volume terms. It is expected to grow to US$100 billion by 2025. The market is expected to grow to US$ 55 billion by 2020; thereby emerging as the sixth largest pharmaceutical market globally by absolute size, as stated by Mr Arun Singh, Indian Ambassador to the US.

Branded generics dominate the pharmaceuticals market, constituting nearly 80 per cent of the market share (in terms of revenues). The sector is expected to generate 58,000 additional job opportunities by the year 2025.

According to the report given by the Pharmaceuticals Export Promotion Council of India (PHARMEXCIL), India's pharmaceutical exports stood at US$ 16.8 billion in 2016-17 and are expected to grow by 30 per cent by next three years to reach US$ 20 billion by 2020.

Indian companies received 305 Abbreviated New Drug Application (ANDA) approvals from the US Food and Drug Administration (USFDA) in 2017. The country accounts for around 30 per cent (by volume) and about 10 per cent (value) in the US$ 70-80 billion US generics market.

India's biotechnology industry comprising bio-pharmaceuticals, bio-services, bio-agriculture, bio-industry and bioinformatics is expected grow at an average growth rate of around 30 per cent a year and reach US$ 100 billion by 2025. Biopharma, comprising vaccines, therapeutics and diagnostics, is the largest sub-sector contributing nearly 62 per cent of the total revenues at Rs 12,600 crore (US$ 1.89 billion).

The Union Cabinet has given its nod for the amendment of the existing Foreign Direct Investment (FDI) policy in the pharmaceutical sector in order to allow FDI up to 100 per cent under the automatic route for manufacturing of medical devices subject to certain conditions.

According to data released by the Department of Industrial Policy and Promotion (DIPP), the drugs and pharmaceuticals sector attracted cumulative FDI inflows worth US$ 15.570 billion between April 2000 and September 2017.

Some of the major investments in the Indian pharmaceutical sector are as follows:

- The exports of Indian pharmaceutical industry to the US will get a boost, as branded drugs worth US$ 55 billion will become off-patent during 2017-2019.
- Private equity and venture capital (PE-VC) investments in the pharmaceutical sector have grown at 38 per cent year-on-year between January-June 2017, due to major deals in this sector.
- The Indian pharmaceutical market size is expected to grow to US$ 100 billion by 2025, driven by increasing consumer spending, rapid urbanisation, and raising healthcare insurance among others. Pharma sector's revenues are expected to grow by 9 per cent year-on-year through fiscal 2020.
- Going forward, better growth in domestic sales would also depend on the ability of companies to align their product portfolio towards chronic therapies for diseases such as such as cardiovascular, anti-diabetes, anti-depressants and anti-cancers that are on the rise.
- The Indian government has taken many steps to reduce costs and bring down healthcare expenses. Speedy introduction of generic drugs into the market has remained in focus and is expected to benefit the Indian pharmaceutical companies. In addition, the thrust on rural health programmes, lifesaving drugs and preventive vaccines also augurs well for the pharmaceutical companies.

Career Opportunities

There are various options a pharmacy professional do have for their career growth.

1. Pharmaceutical Industries

    Production – Manufacturing, Packaging, Store & Purchase

    Quality Control & Quality Assurance

    Research & Development

2. Pharmaceutical Marketing

3. Hospital & Clinical Pharmacy
4. Community Pharmacy
5. Regulatory Affairs
6. Academics
7. Consultancy
8. Library Information Service and Pharmaceutical Journalism
9. Opportunities Abroad

1. Pharmaceutical Industries

Manufacturing: Whether it is allopathic, ayurvedic or homoeopathic drug manufacturing unit. Each manufacturing unit comprises various major sections like production, packaging, inventory and purchase. Based on type of dosage forms being manufactured the number of sections vary. A pharmacy professional is most desired technical person for production of bulk drugs, intermediates and formulations. The job is supervisory in nature and the initial designation, chemist, supervisor, executive, etc varies from company to company. Based on efficiency and experience the candidate can become Manager, General Manager, Vice-President and President, the top most position.

In cosmetic, soaps & toiletries industry the pharmacy professionals are also preferred as suitable technical persons. For production of Blood and Plasma products pharmacy professionals are appointed as supervisors.

Packaging of pharmaceutical products is of great importance and requires technical supervision. Similarly store & purchase are two major operations associated with production on which the quality of a product depends. Hence, many pharmaceutical companies appoint pharmacy professional for supervising these activities.

Quality Control and Quality Assurance are two major departments of any manufacturing industry. Of course there are official standards for drugs and drug products with permissible limits of impurities and purities for every raw material and finished product, but most of the pharmaceutical industries have their own internal standards for input materials and products, which are more specific and process based. Hence, it is very essential to adhere to established methods and standards, so that the final quality of the manufactured products is achieved consistently. Highly specialised and trained staff is required to operate most sensitive and sophisticated analytical instruments. In general professionals with M. Pharm or M. Pharm, Ph. D are most preferred.

Research & Development is heart of an industry. For sustenance and growth every industry should have its own R&D department. In pharmaceutical industry it is very much essential, because the discovery of a drug molecule and development of a suitable dosage form are continuous processes as the type of disease and its treatment are changing. Even for better treatment of the existing diseases the development of the drug delivery systems are necessary. Hence, a lot of job opportunity exists in this area and persons having M. Pharm or M. Pharm, Ph. D qualification are most suitable.

2. **Pharmaceutical Marketing**

   Without marketing and sales of its products no business can be viable. The pharmaceutical marketing and sales are highly technical in nature, the prescribing physician needs to be aware of the dose, use and contraindication of every drug product. And this is done by the representative of the manufacturer visiting the doctor. Hence, this is a specialised job and needs a person who is fully aware of the subject. Pharmacy professional can do this successfully. Even the retailer needs to be trained on proper storage of a particular drug product and how the patient should take the preparation. This is field job. Scope of promotion is maximum and within short period one can reach to top position with basic qualification only.

   Product management is another area of marketing where the person having some field experience can do excellently. This is not field job. Great scope of earning exists if the person has innovative ideas.

3. **Hospital & Clinical Pharmacy**

   For pharmacy professionals this is one more opportunity to work as *Registered Pharmacist* in the hospitals or drug store. In fact, in most of the countries abroad this is a prestigious job and the pharmacist is the only authorized person to prescribe a medicine. The physician only diagnoses the disease but cannot prescribe a medicine. This requires the knowledge of drug-drug interaction, drug-food interaction, pharmacokinetics of the drug. After careful consideration of the patient's medical history, disease state, health condition, incompatibility with other medicines, if being taken, etc the pharmacist selects the suitable drug, decides the proper dose and its administration schedule.

4. **Community Pharmacy**

   As such this concept is existing in developed countries. Through the community pharmacy a pharmacist plays a vital role during treatment of a patient. The pharmacist through his service becomes a link between the patient and treating physician, i.e. as a link between the patient and drug. The duties of the pharmacist in a clinical pharmacy are,

- Counselling the patients regarding the use of the drugs and dosage forms,
- Providing up-to-date information about the drug/dosage form to the patient, as well as to the medical staff,
- Maintaining the patient record and disease-treatment history,
- Training of the patient regarding use of self-diagnostic kits for certain disease like diabetes, hypertension, etc.
- Providing supply of Home care dosage forms.

5. Regulatory Affairs

In India Drugs Control Administration is the main regulatory body that governs the manufacture, sale, import and export of drug and drug products. Every state has its own Directorate of Drug Control Administration, over and above there is Central Drug Control Administration. In each set up there are Inspectors of Drugs who visit the retail counters, manufacturing units, etc and draw samples for quality check. The state directorate is headed by State Drugs Controller and the central administration is headed by the Drugs Controller of India. In between the Director and Drug Inspector, the Deputy Director and Assistant Directors are there. The minimum eligible qualification for such job is B. Pharm.

6. Academics

Excellent opportunity in teaching profession is there throughout the country. There are many Institutions in the country managed by government and private where vacancies at different levels are still in existence. The minimum eligible qualification at lecturer level is M. Pharm and with Ph.D one reach up to Professor level.

7. Consultancy

For highly technical and experienced pharmacy professional this is an ideal opportunity to earn handsomely as a self-employed entrepreneur. There is no age limit for this profession. The consultancy fees depend on the type of service and field, like regulatory affairs, documentation, approval, manufacturing process know-how, analytical technique, research, market survey and sales promotion, information retrieval, data management, turn key project, etc.

8. Library Information Service and Pharmaceutical Journalism

In the recent times the regulatory affairs and patenting processes involve a lot of documentation work to be done and submitted to the concerned Regulatory Authorities within a definite time schedule, for which a special work force is necessary. Hence, most of the large scale companies have separate department for this purpose and pharmacy professional are best suited for such activities.

Similarly, the Research & Development and Q.C departments need to collect technical information across the world. This needs to be regularly updated to match the pace of global competition. So, library information service is another area of growing demand in pharmaceutical industries. Moreover, Bioinformatics and Electronic Data Retrieval systems are also promising area where a pharmacy professional can find growth.

9. **Opportunities Abroad**

   There are golden opportunities for pharmacy professional to work abroad. Countries like USA, Canada, UK, France, Germany, Australia, African countries; Saudi Arabia, Japan, etc still importing pharmacy professionals for different types of jobs like industrial, academics and clinical pharmacy.

   One with B. Pharm degree can pursue higher education in developed western countries and can find highest career growth.

Pharmacopoeia

The term Pharmacopoeia came from two Greek words, *Pharmakon* (means drug) and *Poiein* (means make). In Bergamo, Italy in the year 1580 this term Pharmacopoea was first used for a book on the standards of drugs. Subsequently many countries started using this word for their books on drug standards. Now almost every country of the world has its own national Pharmacopoeia. This is the official book of standards for drugs and their formulations.

Indian Pharmacopoeia

In the year 1833 a committee of the East Indian Company's Dispensary recommended the Publication of a Pharmacopoeia. The Bengal Pharmacopoeia and General Conspectus of Medicinal Plants were published in 1844. This mainly listed most of the commonly used indigenous remedies. In 1868 IP was published. This covered both the drugs of British Pharmacopoeia (BP) 1867 and indigenous drugs used in India. A supplement containing the vernacular names of indigenous drugs and plants was published in 1869. However, from 1885 the BP was made official in India. A drug Enquiry Committee was appointed in 1927 by the government. The committee recommended the publication of a National Pharmacopoeia.

In 1900, the Indian and Colonial Addendum to the British Pharmacopoeia 1898 was published and in 1901, it was published as the Government of India Edition with certain minor modifications. The important articles of this Addendum were subsequently included into the general body of the British Pharmacopoeia 1914. The British Pharmacopoeia Commission also made provision for publication of Supplement or Addenda according to the local requirements and the Indian Pharmacopoeia List 1946 was accordingly prepared to serve as the Indian Supplement to the British Pharmacopoeia1932. After independence, in the year 1948 an Indian Pharmacopoeia Committee was constituted for preparation of the Pharmacopoeia of India (The Indian Pharmacopoeia) 1955. In 1960, a Supplement to it was published. This Pharmacopoeia contained western as well as traditional drugs. The Indian Pharmacopoeia 1966 and its Addenda 1975 were prepared as per the same policy. Next edition of the Pharmacopoeia of India 1985 and its Addenda 1989 and 1991 also did not include the traditional drugs in general. The traditional drugs were considered separately and only those herbal drugs having definite quality control standards were included.

The Government of India Ministry of Health & Family Welfare, vide their Resolution No. X.19020/1/89-DMS & PFA dated 12.8.1991 reconstituted the Indian Pharmacopoeia Committee for a period of five years for preparation of the next edition of the Indian Pharmacopoeia under the Chairmanship of Dr. Nityanand, Ex-Director, Central Drug Research Institute, Lucknow.

To expedite the preparation of the new edition of the Indian Pharmacopoeia, the Committee constituted various Sub-Committees, Working Groups having expert representatives from the Pharmaceutical industries, Drug control laboratories, Research and Teaching Institutions of the country for preparation of draft monographs and appendices, for examination of the comments received on those and for suitable recommendation there on to the Committee.

It was also felt necessary to prepare a Veterinary Supplement to this new edition. Since the drugs for veterinary use needed specialised information, a Group was formed for this purpose.

Accordingly, the Committee finalised the monographs, appendices and general Notices prepared by the Working Groups and in 1996 the Indian Pharmacopoeia was published. For the said purpose other Pharmacopoeias like the British Pharmacopoeia (BP), European Pharmacopoeia (EP), the United States Pharmacopoeia (USP), National Formulary, the Pharmacopoeia of Japan, the Pharmaceutical Codex, the International Pharmacopoeia, the Marck Index and the standards published by the Bureau of Indian Standards were also consulted.

The full name or title of the Pharmacopoeia including Addenda there to, has been changed to Indian Pharmacopoeia 1996 and abbreviated to IP 1996 because of convenience to all and the initial name, Pharmacopoeia of India has been dropped.

Indian Pharmacopoeia (IP) is an official document meant for overall Quality Control and Assurance of Pharmaceutical products marketed in India by way of contributing on their safety, efficacy and affordability. IP contains a collection of authoritative procedures of analysis and specifications for Drugs. The IP, or any part of it, has got legal status under the Second Schedule of the Drugs & Cosmetics Act, 1940 and Rules 1945 there under.

IP prescribes standards for identity, purity and strength of drugs essentially required from health care perspective of human beings and animals. IP standards are authoritative in nature. They are enforced by the Regulatory authorities for quality control of medicines in India. During Quality Assurance and at the time of dispute in the court of law the IP standards are legally acceptable.

The fifth edition of IP was published in 2007 and in 2008 an addendum was published. In 2010 the sixth edition of IP and in 2012 its addendum were published. The seventh edition was published in the year 2014. The current eight edition of IP has been published in 2018 and its addendum is scheduled to be published in 2019.

United States Pharmacopoeia

In January 1817, Dr. Lyman Spalding of New York City of the United States submitted to the Medical society of the Country a proposal to develop a national Pharmacopoeia. He proposed, -

(1) to divide the country into four districts - northern, southern, western and middle, (2) to call for *Convention* in each district with delegates from all medical societies and medical schools of the respective district, (3) to prepare a draft for pharmacopoeia and, (4) to appoint delegates for *General Convention* to be held later in Washington, D.C.

Accordingly, the drafts were submitted only by the northern and middle districts.

In the General Convention held in January,1820 these drafts were thoroughly reviewed and consolidated. In December 1820, the first United States Pharmacopoeia was published in two languages, English and Latin. Latin was the then international language of medicine. It was of 272 pages and 217 drugs were included. The convention also resolved that the USP would be revised every 10 years. Because of the extensive efforts extended for preparing the USP, Dr. Spadling is called as the *Father of the USP*.

In 1900 the Pharmacopoeial Convention decided to issue Supplements to the USP as and when necessary to maintain satisfactory standards. In 1940, the Convention decided to revise the USP every 5 years with periodic issuance of Supplements.

The USP is a non-governmental, non-profit public health organisation which independently works to set scientific and recognized standards.

In more than 130 countries across the globe USP's standards are recognized and used. To ensure quality medicines, food ingredients and other health care products USP establishes documentary and reference standards. These documentary standards and references are used by regulatory agencies and manufacturers of pharmaceuticals, dietary supplements and food ingredients to ensure appropriate strength, quality and purity of the ingredients and the products.

USP develops information relating to various aspects of drug-use and circulates this information to physicians, pharmacists and others who are associated with health care profession.

USP also acts to improve health and promote optimal public health care delivery around the world by running operations at various places like Europe, middle East, Africa, India, China and at brazil.

Since 2002 the USP-NF has been revised and published annually. The current edition of USP, USP33-NF28 shall be published in the year 2010. The current edition of the USP-NF was published in 2017.

National Formulary

Till 1852 the third revision of USP was the only recognized and authoritative book of drug standards in the United States. The drugs having established therapeutic value were included in the USP. Many drugs and formulas being used by the medical practitioners were not included in the USP due to strict selectivity.

Hence, in 1852 the American Pharmaceutical Association (APhA) organised and prepared a Formulary containing some drugs and formulas which were not included in the USP. In 1888 the first edition of the Formulary was published under the title, National Formulary of Unofficial Preparations. The term unofficial indicated a kind of protest and to distinguish it from the USP in which the term official was used. In 1906 the title was changed to National Formulary (NF) and both USP and NF were made legal books of standards as per the first federal Pure Food and Drug Act under the signature of the then president, Theodore Roosevelt. Hence, according to the law the formulations carried the name USP or NF in their labels were bound to conform to the physical and chemical standards mentioned in the respective monographs.

The initial editions of NF provided uniform names of the drugs, their preparations and working directions as a convenient means to the practicing pharmacists and to the small scale manufacturers of popular preparations prescribed by the physicians.

Till 1940, like USP, the NF had been revised every 10 years and thereafter every 5 years with periodical issuance of supplements as and when necessary.

In 1975 both USP and NF were unified and the first combined compendium USPXX-NF XV was published in 1980. The USP section contained all monographs on the drug substances and the NF section contained the monographs on pharmaceutical agents. The USP25-NF20 became an annual publication in 2002. The next edition of USP26-NF21 with about 4000 drug monographs was published and made available in both hard and soft copy.

All the members related to health care including pharmacists, physicians, dentists, veterinarians, nurses, manufacturers and suppliers of bulk drugs, chemicals and pharmaceutical products, public health agencies, drug regulatory and enforcement agencies and others were made responsible to adhere to the norms and standards mentioned in the USP-NF.

Since 2002 the USP-NF has been revised and published annually. The current USP33-NF28 shall be published in the year 2010. In the 2017current 40th edition of the USP-NF was published.

British Pharmacopoeia

Since 1491 – 1547 the regulation of medicinal products had been regulated by officials in the United Kingdom. Physicians of The Royal College, London were empowered to inspect the products of apothecaries in the London area and to destroy the defective stocks. The first list of approved drugs and their manufacturing guidelines was published in London in 1618 as London Pharmacopoeia. In Great Britain, there were three city-pharmacopoeias – the London, the Edinburgh and the Dublin. These were official till the first British Pharmacopoeia (BP) was published in 1864 and all those three pharmacopoeias were merged. In 1907, a Commission was appointed by the General Medical Council and the body was made responsible statutorily under the Medical Act, 1858 to produce a British Pharmacopoeia on national basis. In 1907 the British Pharmaceutical Codex was published with the information and standards for drugs and other pharmaceutical substances not included in the BP.

The 1968 Medicines Act established the legal status of the British Pharmacopoeia Commission and of the British Pharmacopoeia as the standards for medicinal products in the United Kingdom under the section 4 of the Act. Since then, the British Pharmacopoeia Commission continued the work of the earlier Commissions appointed by the General Medical Council and was responsible for preparing new editions of the British Pharmacopoeia and the British Pharmacopoeia (Veterinary) and for keeping those up-to-date. Since 1864, the distribution of BP has grown throughout the world and is now used in more than 100 countries. Australia and Canada have adopted the BP as their national standard and in other countries, e.g. Korea, BP is recognized as an internationally acceptable standard.

The British Pharmacopoeia is prepared by the Pharmacopoeial Secretariat in collaboration with the BP Laboratory, the British Pharmacopoeia Commission and its Expert Advisory Groups and Advisory Panels. The input information is collected from relevant industries, hospitals, academia, professional bodies and governmental sources, inside and outside the UK.

The current edition of the British Pharmacopoeia contains six volumes with about 3000 monographs for drug substances, excipients and formulations along with supporting General Notices, Appendices and Reference Spectra used in the practice of medicines. BP (Veterinary) contains all items used exclusively in veterinary medicines in the UK.

Volume I and II contain medicinal substances, Volume III contains formulations, blood related products, immunological products, radio-pharmaceutical preparations, surgical materials and homeopathic preparations. Volume IV comprises Appendices, Infrared Reference Spectra and Index. Volume V is British Pharmacopoeia (Veterinary), Volume VI contains CD-ROM version of British Pharmacopoeia, British Pharmacopoeia (Veterinary) and British Approved Names.

Till 1996 the British Pharmacopoeia has been revised and published every 5 years. Since 1998 it has been revised and published annually. In 2017 the BP had been published which superseded the BP 2016.

International Pharmacopoeia

The history of the International Pharmacopoeia dates back to 1874. The first conference was called by the Belgian Government in Brussels in 1902 and an Agreement for the Unification of the Formula of Potent drugs which was ratified by 19 countries in 1906.

A second agreement, the Brussels Agreement, was drawn up in 1925 and ratified in 1929. It was resolved that the League of Nations would be responsible for the administrative work to produce a unified Pharmacopoeia, and a permanent secretariat of an international organisation would coordinate the work of National Pharmacopoeial Commissions. General principles for the preparation of galenicals, maximal doses, nomenclatures and biological testing of arsenobenzones were included in the articles of this agreement along with a table of dosage strengths and descriptions for 77 drug substances and preparations.

In response to the repeated calls from pharmaceutical experts in various countries, the health organisation of the League of Nations set up a Technical Commission of Pharmacopoeial Experts in 1937. In 1947, the Interim commission of WHO (World Health Organisation) took over the work of pharmacopoeias and in 1948, the first World Health Assembly approved the establishment of the Expert Committee on the International Pharmacopoeia.

The third World Health Assembly held in May1950 formally approved the publication of the *Pharmacopoea Internationalis*. This was not intended to be legal pharmacopoeia in any country unless adopted by the pharmacopoeial authority of that country. From that time WHO constituted a permanent International Pharmacopoeial Secretariat. Accordingly, the first edition of International Pharmacopoeia was published in 2 volumes, one in 1951 and the other in 1955, In 1959, a supplement was published. These were published in English, French and Spanish, subsequently translated into German and Japanese languages. Altogether, it included 344 monographs on drug substances, 183 monographs on dosage forms and 84 tests, methods and general requirements. A large number of national pharmacopoeias and official lists were examined and assistance from International Pharmaceutical Federation (FIP) was also obtained to select substances and products for their inclusion in the pharmacopoeia.

The second edition was published in 1967, the third edition in 1975, and in 2006 the fourth edition was published. In 2008, a supplement has been published. This is the current edition of the International Pharmacopoeia. It has two volumes and one supplement. This serves as the source material for reference or adaptation by any WHO Member State wishing to establish pharmaceutical requirements. The International Pharmacopoeia published in 2016 is the current edition.

European Pharmacopoeia

In the year 1964, a Convention was organised by the European countries-Belgium, France, Germany, Italy, Netherlands, Switzerland, Luxembourg and United Kingdom under the banner of Council of Europe and decided to prepare a European Pharmacopoeia. The objectives were to make uniform specifications for medicinal substances of general interest to the people of Europe and to prepare the specifications for the growing number of new medicinal substances coming to the market.

Based on these objectives the European Pharmacopoeia was created and published in the year 1967 comprising monographs and became official standards applicable to the territories of the countries which were contracting parties to the convention. The second edition was published in 1980.

On 16th November1989, a Protocol to this Convention was signed in order to enable the European Community to accede to it and since 1st Nov'92 it was entered into force.

In 1996 the European Directorate for the Quality of Medicines & Health Care (EDQM) came into force. It is an organ of the Council of Europe. It consists of the Technical Secretariat of the European Pharmacopoeial Commission, set up in 1964 by the European Pharmacopoeia Convention.

The EDQM is in charge for

- Preparing and publishing adopted text (printed, CD-ROM, and Internet version) and distributing the European Pharmacopoeia and other publications.
- Checking the text experimentally in the laboratory, the laboratory also carries out analytical studies and organises collaborative studies to establish European Pharmacopoeia chemical or biological reference substances or preparations.
- Preparing, managing and dispatching European Pharmacopoeia reference substances.
- Organising regularly congresses on new scientific and technical subjects, as well as seminars and training sessions on subjects related to European Pharmacopoeia.

The European Pharmacopoeia currently has 37 European Members including the European Union (EU). There are 21 observer countries for European Pharmacopoeia including the WHO.

The 2005 edition, the 5th edition, includes 1800 specific and general monographs, including various chemical substances, antibiotics, biological substances; Vaccines for human or veterinary use; Immuno-sera; Radiopharmaceutical preparations; Herbal drugs; Homoeopathic preparations and Homoeopathic stocks. It also contains Dosage forms, General monographs, Materials and Containers, Sutures; 268 General methods with figures or chromatograms and 2210 reagents are described.

The current edition is the 6th edition, published in the year 2008 and consists of a two- volume main edition with supplements.

The texts and monographs of the European Pharmacopoeia form an integral part of the British Pharmacopoeia. The 9th edition published in 2016 is the current edition of European Pharmacopoeia.

Extra Pharmacopoeia

It was published in 1883 under the title, Martindale: *The Extra Pharmacopoeia*. Presently it is being published as Martindale: *The Complete Drug Reference*. It is a reference book with information of about

6000 drugs and medicines, and 146000 proprietary preparations. It also includes 668 disease treatment reviews along with some selected investigational and veterinary drugs, herbal and complementary medicines, pharmaceutical excipients, vitamins and nutritional agents, vaccines, radiopharmaceuticals, diagnostic agents, contrast media, medicinal gases, drugs of abuse, recreational drugs, toxic substances, disinfectants and pesticides.

The purpose of Martindale is to provide information on drugs and related substances reported to have clinical value anywhere in the world. It is also a source of useful information for patients arriving from different country to search their existing medication, available in different brand name; if not available, their substitutes.

The monographs include Chemical Abstract Services (CAS) and Anatomical Therapeutic Chemical Classification System (ATC) numbers, so that a reader can refer to other information system.

Martindale has two main parts, Monographs and Preparations plus two extensive indexes, Directory of manufacturers and General index. The 37th edition of *Martindale: The Complete Drug Reference,* is available in 2 volumes. The beauty of this work is that it is the most stupendously comprehensive work in its field. To provide more up-to-date information, the interval between print editions has been reduced over successive editions, and the book is now produced about every two years.

Exercise

A. Multiple Choice Questions Carrying 01 Mark

1. Opium Act was enacted in the year

   (a) 1878 (c) 1879

   (b) 1880 (d) 1890

2. Poisons Act was enacted in the year

   (a) 1920 (b) 1919

   (c) 1918 (d) 1921

3. Bengal Food Adulteration Act was enacted in the year

   (a) 1915 (b) 1920

   (c) 1919 (d) 1921

4. Drugs Act 1940 was first amended in the year

   (a) 1943 (b) 1944

   (c) 1945 (d) 1946

5. Which statement is correct?
   (a) Pharmacy Council of India was established under Pharmacy Act 1948
   (b) Pharmacy Council of India was established under Pharmacy Act 1945
   (c) Pharmacy Council of India was established under Pharmacy Act 1947
   (d) None
6. Indian Government brought the Pharmacy Bill in the year
   (a) 1942 (b) 1946
   (c) 1940 (d) 1945
7. B. Pharm course was started first in India at
   (a) Birla Institute of Technology, Pilani
   (b) Banaras Hindu University, Allahabad
   (c) Jadavpur University, Kolkata
   (d) Hari Shankar Gaur University, Sagar
8. The first edition of Indian Pharmacopoeia was published in the year
   (a) 1962 (b) 1960
   (c) 1955 (d) 1967
9. Which organisation is responsible to publish IP in India?
   (a) Indian Pharmaceutical Association
   (b) Indian Pharmacopoeia Committee
   (c) Pharmacy Council of India
   (d) None
10. Since which year USP-NF was being published
   (a) 2000 (b) 1990
   (c) 2001 (d) 2002

B. Question Carrying 05 Marks

1. Write down briefly the history of Pharmacy profession during ancient times.
2. How the education in Pharmacy has been developed in India?
3. Write down the code of ethics.

4. Write down briefly the history of the United States Pharmacopoeia.
5. Describe about the British Pharmacopoeia.
6. Describe about the International Pharmacopoeia.
7. Describe brief note on the European Pharmacopoeia.
8. Describe about the Extra Pharmacopoeia.
9. Write a brief note on National Formulary.
10. Write a brief note on Indian Pharmacopoeia.

C. Question Carrying 10 Marks

1. Discuss how the Pharmacy profession has been developed in India.
2. Write down the responsibilities of Pharmacist during medical therapy.
3. Discuss about the career in Pharmacy.
4. Write down the historical development of Indian Pharmacopoeia.
5. Write down the historical development of National Formulary.
6. Write down the historical development of the United States Pharmacopoeia.
7. Describe how the education in Pharmacy has evolved in India.
8. Discuss on Extra Pharmacopoeia and European Pharmacopoeia.

Answers

A. Multiple Choice Questions

1. (a)	**2. (b)**	**3. (c)**	**4. (c)**	**5. (a)**
6. (d)	**7. (b)**	**8. (c)**	**9. (b)**	**10. (d)**

Chapter 2

Dosage Forms

Introduction to Dosage Forms, Classification and Definitions

Introduction to Dosage Forms

Drug is a substance which is used for diagnosis, mitigation, treatment, cure or prevention of a disease in human beings or in the animals.

Drug(s) are as such rarely administered but are administered as a particular form - known as *dosage form*, wherein certain substances which are non-toxic, therapeutically inactive and compatible with the drug(s) substances are mixed with the drugs to prepare the dosage forms. These substances are termed as *excipients or adjuvants or additives*. Each of these has a specific role or function for being used in a particular dosage form.

Hence, the term **Dosage form** may be defined as *a pharmaceutical preparation designed for administration of a drug into the body through a suitable route.*

Each dosage form must have the following **characteristics**:

- Therapeutic effectiveness,
- Physiochemical stability,
- Ability to deliver the correct dose of the drug at the correct site and at the desired time,
- Acceptability to the patient and
- Reasonable cost.

The formulation or dosage form of a drug may be generic or branded. A drug which is (1) no longer under patent protection, which may be produced by any manufacturer following GMP, (2) is sold under the generic name, is called as **generic product** and the label of the product shall mention only the official name of the drug and its formulation. For example, if on the label the name of the product is given, *Paracetamol Tablets IP*, it is *generic*, but if any name other than this, is given to the formulation by the manufacturer for its promotional purpose, and the name of the drug (paracetamol, here) is only known through the composition, it is **branded**.

Advantages of dosage forms:

- Through a dosage form accurate dose of the drug can be administered.
- It can protect the drug from its degradation.
- The unpleasant odour and taste can be masked.
- Depending on the requirement a drug can be formulated as solid, semisolid, liquid or gaseous dosage form.
- The palatability of a liquid dosage form can be improved by addition of suitable excipient.
- The therapeutic action of a drug can be modified through a formulation, e.g. sustained, delayed, controlled release formulation.
- A properly designed formulation can be inserted into any part of the body for desired therapeutic action, e.g. suppositories, inserts, dental cones, etc.
- For dispensing to various category of patients, e.g. children, adult, elderly, bed ridden, a drug can be formulated differently.

Classification of Dosage Form

The dosage forms may be classified on the basis of (1) the routes of administration, (2) physical state and (3) method of manufacture.

(1) Route of administration

Route of administration	Dosage form
Oral	Tablet, Capsule, Granules, Powders, Solution, Syrup, Elixir, Suspensions, Emulsion, Gel.
Parenteral	Injections (in the form of solution, suspension, emulsion), Implant.
Topical	Ointment, Cream, Paste, Lotion, Gel, Solution, Aerosol.
Eye	Solution, Ointment.
Ear	Solution, Suspension, Ointment
Nasal	Solution, Inhalation
Respiratory Tract	Aerosol (in the form of solution, suspension, powder), sprays, Gases, Inhalation
Rectal/Vaginal	Suppositories, Ointment, Cream, Powder, Lotion

(2) Physical state

Physical state	Dosage form
Solid	Tablet, Capsule, Granules and Powder
Semi-solid	Ointment, Cream, Paste, Gel
Liquid	Solution, Suspension, Emulsion
Gas	Inhalations

(3) Method of manufacture

Method of Manufacture	Dosage form
Aseptic	Sterile
Non-aseptic	Non-sterile
Special	Novel Drug Delivery systems

Routes of Drug Administration

The routes through which a drug may be administered are; oral, buccal or sublingual, inhalation, rectal, parenteral, and topical. The route of administration is selected on the basis of necessity and convenience.

Oral Route: This is the most convenient route because a patient does not require anybody to take a dose of a drug. Only a child, very elderly or bed ridden cannot take the drug without the help of anybody. Most of the drugs are capable of reaching systemic circulation adequately within a reasonable time limit and can elicit expected therapeutic effect. Most of the drugs are absorbed from the gastrointestinal tract. However, there are certain exceptions.

Buccal or Sublingual Route: Although by swallowing a dosage form, adequate plasma concentration of a drug is achieved within a reasonable time, sometimes for faster response and to avoid degradation of the drug in the liver, a drug may be given through buccal or sublingual route. For example, in case of angina pectoris a patient can get relief by taking drug through this route and parenteral route may be avoided. Limited drugs are administered by this route.

Inhalation Route: This route is used to deliver either the gaseous or volatile drug substances or through a gaseous or volatile carrier into the systemic circulation; for example, general anaesthetics. The drug is administered through lungs to the alveoli. As the alveolar and vascular membranes are penetrable to the drugs, flow of blood is abundant and the surface area is large, the absorption of drug is also high. Because of certain problems this route is not used largely. It is mostly useful when the drug is supposed to act on the respiratory tract.

Rectal Route: Usually the drugs which are administered orally can be administered rectally also. It has three distinct advantages,

1. the drug administered rectally can exert a direct action on the rectum,
2. it can evacuate the bowel, and
3. can provide a systemic effect.

In earlier days rectal suppositories and retention enemas were more popular, but due to improvement in parenteral preparations their popularity has been decreased. Still with certain limitation this route is in use and, sometimes, very important for administration of drugs, particularly in paediatrics and geriatrics. In some cases, the retention enemas become very useful substitute for oral route.

Parenteral Routes: There are various routes of administration of a drug parenterally. Depending on the need and the drug, the solution of a drug is injected through one of the following parenteral routes.

1. ***Intracutaneous or Intradermal Injection:*** The drug solution is injected into the skin, between the epidermis (outer layer of the skin) and dermis (inner layer). The volume of injection, usually small, 0.1 to 0.2 mL and normally the skin of left forearm is the site. Main purpose of such injection is diagnostic or investigation of immunity or allergy.
2. ***Subcutaneous or Hypodermic Injection:*** This is given under the skin. That is, into the subcutaneous tissue, and the maximum volume of injection is up to 1 mL. Oily solution or suspension in oil or water cannot be given through this route as these cause pain or irritation.
3. ***Intramuscular Injection:*** These injections are given inside a muscle penetrating the subcutaneous tissue and muscle membrane. The common sites are muscles of shoulder, thigh or of buttock. The maximum volume injected is 4-5 mL. As the muscle can tolerate pain, irritation and there is little fear of blockage, the oily solution or suspension in oil or water can be administered through this route in small volumes. The rate of administration should be slow in such cases.
4. ***Intravenous Injection:*** These are given to the vein and hence, directly to the blood stream. This is the route of choice when immediate response is desired. Most common site of injection is the median basilic vein, near anterior surface of the elbow. The volume of injection may rage from 1 mL to 500 mL or more. For immediate therapeutic action the small injections are given. Large volume is given usually for replacement of body fluids or electrolytes.

5. ***Intra-arterial Injection:*** This is almost similar to intravenous injection. This is given when immediate effect is required in peripheral area. For example, in early gangrene when arterial flow is restricted, this injection is given to improve the flow.
6. ***Intracardiac Injection:*** In emergency only, this is made into the heart muscle or ventricle. For example, in cardiac arrest injection of adrenaline or isoprenaline sulphate is given through this route.
7. ***Intrathecal Injection:*** This is given into the subarachnoid space surrounding the spinal cord. That is the space, between arachnoid and pia matter, containing a fluid known as cerebrospinal fluid. Such injection requires special skill so that the injection is made without entering the spinal cord and causing serious damage. The volume injected normally within 20 ml and in extreme cases like in spinal anaesthesia, tubercular meningitis the drug is given in this route. In the same way the cerebrospinal fluid is taken for diagnostic purpose also.
8. ***Peridural Injection:*** The injection is made into the peridural space between the dura matter and the inner aspect of the vertebrae. The peridural space is narrow but extended throughout the spinal column length wise. Hence, a special skill is necessary for injection.
9. ***Intra-cisternal Injection:*** This is another special route and requires special skill, used either to withdraw the cerebrospinal fluid or to inject a dye for investigation purpose, or to administer an antibiotic for treatment. The needle is inserted between the first and second vertebrae, and into the cisterna magna. This is done when intrathecal route is failed.
10. ***Intra-articular injection:*** This injection is made into the synovial fluid that lubricates the articulating ends of bones in a joint. Usually anti-inflammatory drugs are administered through this route.

Topical Route: This route refers to the application of a drug over the skin either for its local effect or for systemic effect. For example, a dermatological preparation is meant for treating skin disorder, the skin is the target organ. A transdermal preparation is intended to deliver the drug to the systemic circulation through the skin; skin is not the target organ.
Some important Compendial Terms

Monographs: The format of the text given in a Pharmacopoeia containing the official title, the primary information and the all the requirements given under the heading, **STANDARDS** for a pharmaceutical ingredient or for a formulation.

General Monographs are the monographs which describe official preparations, requirements of general application and requirements of tests applicable to all monographs for the relevant dosage forms, unless otherwise mentioned in the individual monograph.

Official Standards: It refers to the requirements mentioned in a monograph of the Pharmacopoeia applicable for a substance or its product intended for medicinal use, not for other purpose. A monograph shall be construed according to any general monograph, notice, note, any appendix, or any other explanatory material given in the Pharmacopoeia and those shall be applicable to that monograph.

Under the heading **STANDARDS** in a monograph all the statements shall refer to as standards, if there is no specific general notice indicating otherwise is given and no material can be considered as of *pharmacopoeial quality* unless it comply with all the requirements stated in the monograph. The monograph limits the presence of potential impurities only. Any material, if found to contain any impurity, contaminant or adulterant which cannot be detected by the prescribed tests, cannot be declared as *not of pharmacopoeial quality* unless the nature and amount of such substance is found objectionable under the conditions of use or is incompatible with good pharmaceutical practice.

Usual Strength: In any individual monograph of a preparation the strength is mentioned as general information to the pharmacist or the medical practitioner and does not prevent any manufacturer from manufacture and market the formulation of different strength with the approval of appropriate authority.

Storage: The storage conditions mentioned in a monograph is not mandatory, only an advice type to maintain the appropriate conditions to protect a substance or a product from the effects of atmosphere, moisture, heat, light and to prevent deterioration and contamination. The terms mentioned as storage condition with respect to temperature are;

Cold: Any temperature within the range from 2° – 8°C, a refrigerator is a cold place.

Cool: Any temperature within the range from 8° – 25°C, unless otherwise mentioned, a refrigerator can be used as a cool place.

Room temperature: The temperature prevailing in a particular place of work

Warm: Any temperature within 30° – 40°C.

Excessive heat: Any temperature more than 40°C.

Protection from freezing: Where it is known that freezing may cause breakage of the container, alter the characteristics of the contents in terms of strength or potency or any other, the precautionary note is provided in the monographs.

Storage under non-specific conditions: Where there is no specific storage condition is mentioned in the monograph, the material is to be kept away from moisture, freezing and excessive heat.

Definitions of Various Dosage Forms

The definitions of commonly used pharmaceutical preparations (formulations) are given below.

Tablet

A tablet is a hard, compressed dosage form which may be round, oval or square in shape. It contains unit dose of one or more drug. It is intended for oral administration. Some tablets contain sweetener, flavours and colour to improve organoleptic property of the tablet. There are different types of tablets.

Moulded Tablets

These are small discs usually containing medicament diluted with excipients, e.g., lactose, sucrose, dextrose, mannitol, etc. The mixture is then moistened with alcohol, hydroalcohol or any other suitable solvent. By pressing the moist mass into standardized mould of metal, plastic or rubber these tablets are prepared.

Effervescent Tablet

These tablets are prepared in such a way that when a tablet is put into water, rapid dissolution of the drug takes place with effervescence (evolution of carbon dioxide). These tablets contain an organic acid, e.g., citric acid, tartaric acid, etc. and a base, e.g. sodium bicarbonate, calcium carbonate, etc. in addition to other excipients. When such tablet comes in contact with water, a chemical reaction between acid and base takes place resulting faster dissolution there by faster release of the medicament from the tablet with evolution of carbon dioxide.

Chewable Tablets

These tablets are intended to be chewed in the mouth, not to be swallowed intact. The reason for making these tablets is to provide quick and better therapeutic action of the medicament. For example, chewable antacid tablet when chewed acid neutralization may be better as the antacid activity depends on the particle size. Such tablets do not have any disintegration time limit and contain sweetening agent, colour and flavour to enhance the palatability.

Buccal and Sublingual Tablets

These tablets contain medicaments intended for absorption directly through the oral mucosa. These are held in buccal cavity (buccal tablet) or beneath the tongue (sublingual tablet). These are small, usually flat tablets designed mostly for slow dissolution and for systemic absorption of the drug. When administered by this route the drug is absorbed directly into blood stream through oral mucosa avoiding bypass metabolism.

Dispensing Tablets

As the name implies these are to be added to a desired volume of water of known quality to produce a solution of a given concentration of the drug. These tablets do not contain any excipient that may react with any other ingredient resulting deleterious effect in the intended application of the solution. Water soluble ingredients are to be used for making these tablets.

Hypodermic Tablets

These tablets are formerly used to prepare a solution to be used parenterally. Hence, the tablets contained all water-soluble ingredients including the drug substance. Although to prepare the drug solution sterile water for injection is used but it is very difficult to maintain sterility of the final solution and since, stable parenteral preparations of most of the drugs are available today these tablets have become obsolete.

Depot Tablets

These are alternatively called as **implantation tablets** and meant for subcutaneous implantation in animal or man to provide a prolonged drug action for period from one month to a year. These tablets are small cylindrical or rosette shape. The major problems with their administration are, a surgical technique is required for both administration and for discontinuation, and tissue toxicity in the area of implantation site.

Coated Tablets

Tablets are coated to mask unpleasant taste, odour, to protect the drug from light (photodegradation) and air or from a substance of potentially sensitizing or irritant nature (*protective coating*); to control the rate of release of drug in the body (*sustained release coating*); or to control the site of drug release in the body (*enteric coating*).

Sustained-Release Tablets

These tablets are formulated in such a way that after release of a initial therapeutic dose of the drug further amounts are released slowly to maintain the therapeutic effect of the drug over a period of several hours.

The main advantage of this product is reduction in the frequency of administration but the drug substance is allowed to remain in the body for an unduly extended period after withdrawal of the drug.

Capsules

Capsules are the solid dosage forms in which the drug is enclosed within either a hard or soft soluble container called shell. The shells are prepared from gelatin; however, these can be prepared from starch or other suitable substances. The size of hard-shell capsules may range from No.5 (smallest size) to 000 (largest size). Generally, powder, beads, granules are filled in hard-shell capsules.

Soft Gelatin Capsules

Soft gelatin capsules are prepared with varied proportion of gelatin, glycerine or sorbitol and water. These contain more moisture than hard gelatin capsules and thus, a suitable preservative, e.g. methylparaben or propylparaben is incorporated in these.

The shape of soft gelatin capsule may be oblong, oval or round. These may be of single colour or multi-colour, transparent or opaque, plain or printed.

Dental Cones

These tablets are smaller in size and administered over the socket following tooth extraction to prevent bacterial proliferation or to check bleeding at the extraction site.

These contain active ingredients like antibacterial, astringent or coagulant. Commonly used ingredients are sodium bicarbonate, sodium chloride or an amino acid; but not any material that can accentuate bacterial growth.

Troches and Lozenges

These are another type of solid dosage form. Troches, lozenges and pastilles are synonymous and come under same category. These are usually discoid-shaped solids having the active ingredient (medicinal substance) in a suitably flavoured base. Commonly sugar candy or glycerinated gelatin is used as base. Sometimes a mixture of sugar and adequate amount of mucilage is used as base. These are intended to be sucked by holding in the mouth so that the medicament is released slowly to result a local effect in the mouth or throat. They are usually used for throat sore or cough. The active ingredients in these forms are antiseptic, antibacterial, local anaesthetic, demulcent, astringent or anti-tussive in nature. These do not disintegrate, but either erode slowly or dissolve on sucking.

Oral Powders or Granules

The ingredients, medicament(s) and auxiliary substances, if directed in the form of powders are mixed thoroughly and packed as such in a suitable container, preferably in a wide mouth jar, or the powder mix is converted to granular form and then packed. The drug with a large dose can also be formulated in this form. The powders may be soluble or insoluble in water. Oral powders may be prepared as single dose or multiple doses and contain flavouring and colouring agents, if specified.

Dusting Powders

These are fine, free-flowing powders. These may be medicated and undedicated. These are intended for external application. These are nontoxic preparations, intended for local application, and usually contain mixture of two or more substances in finely powdered form. These should be free from grittiness. The fineness of these powders makes these more effective and less irritant. The powder mixtures are passed through sieve No 80 or 100. These do not have any systemic effect. Dusting powders are applied to various parts of the body for their protective, absorbent, antipruritic, antiseptic, antibromhidrotic, astringent, and antiperspirant effects.

Douche Powders

These are water soluble powders. The solutions of these powders are intended to be used as antiseptics or cleaning agents for body cavity, mostly for vaginal cavity. They may also be prepared for nasal, optic or ophthalmic use. Usually these preparations contain aromatic oils, for which the powders may agglomerate and form lumps. To eliminate the lumps these are screened through a sieve No 40 or 60. By screening through sieve the mixing can also be made more uniform.

Triturations

These are mixtures of a potent drug and a suitable diluent at a definite ratio. When a potent drug is to be diluted in solid state, the drug is mixed uniformly with a suitable nontoxic, inert diluent in a definite proportion by weight, so that the drug content in the diluted mixture remains uniform within the allowable limits. Hence, the dilution should be properly done. Earlier, these were official preparations for dilution of drug from 1 to 10 times. As the name indicates these are prepared by triturating the drug with successive portions of diluent till the drug is mixed with the entire quantity of diluent.

Insufflations

These are mixtures of micronized powders intended for introduction into the body cavity, e.g. nose, throat, tooth-sockets, ear, and vagina. To ensure administration of uniform dose of the drug an efficient insufflator (powder blower) or an aero haler is used. It is very difficult to administer a uniform dose and for this reason the preparation could not become a popular dosage form.

Cachets

These are one type of unit solid dosage form. These also provide a convenient method of administering a drug having unpleasant odour and taste. Cachets are alternatively called wafer capsules. The cachet shells are prepared from rice flour. The flour is mixed with sufficient purified water to make a wet mass and the wet mass is then moulded to different shapes and sizes. The sheets are prepared by passing the wet mass between two hot rollers.

Pessaries

Pessaries are solid preparations having a shape suitable for vaginal administration and contain medicament intended for local actions. These may be prepared by moulding, like suppositories or by compression like tablets.

Moulded Pessaries

These are commonly conical in shape. Theobroma oil, glycerol-gelatin or hydrogenated vegetable oil may be used as base as in the case of a suppository. A base containing gelatin should be heated for one hour at 100°C with simultaneous replacement of water lost by evaporation. Thereafter, other ingredients should be added. The base should be formulated in such a way that the pessaries prepared shall melt at or slightly below 37 °C.

Compressed Pessaries

These are generally prepared by moist granulation, dry granulation or direct compression method as appropriate for the particular drug, and contain the additives like diluents, binder, disintegrant, lubricant, etc. as required to manufacture a tablet. The compressed pessaries are the tablets having the shape of diamond, almond, wedge, disk, or any other.

Pills

These are solid dosage form, intended for oral administration. The shape of pills may be spherical, ovoid; may be sugar coated. These have largely been replaced by tablets.

Suppositories

These are solid preparations of various weights, suitably shaped containing medicaments for introduction into human body cavities such as vagina, rectum, etc. Suppositories are intended for three purposes, - (1) local action, for example, anaesthetics like cinchocaine, benzocaine; astringents like bismuth subgallate, extract of hamamelis or tannic acid and anti-inflammatory like hydrocortisone are administered in the form of suppositories to relieve from pain and irritation of haemorrhoids in the rectum; (2) evacuation of bowel, for example, laxative like glycerol and bisacodyl are used, (3) systemic effect of the drug incorporated in them, for example, few drugs like aminophylline (anti-asthmatic and anti-bronchitic), indomethacin, phenylbutazone (analgesic and anti-inflammatory), etc. are administered in the form of suppositories.

Ointments

These are semi-solid preparations commonly of a medicament or mixture of medicaments either dissolved or dispersed in a suitable basis intended for application over the skin. The basis is usually non-aqueous. The common uses of ointment are to provide, - (1) emollient effect on the skin, (2) protection of the skin, and (3) local medication.

Creams

Creams are semi-solid preparations and are intended for external application. Primarily creams are emulsions and the emulsions are of two types – aqueous and oily. Aqueous creams are oil-in-water and oily creams are water-in-oil emulsions. The oil-in-water creams (aqueous) are relatively non-greasy and most popularly used for application of drug.

Pastes

These are one type of semisolid preparation, the difference between ointment and paste is that the solid content in the latter is high even up to 50%. A large quantity of insoluble solid powder is incorporated into an ointment base for which the paste is found to be stiffer. A paste when spreaded over skin adheres in the form of a thick layer, it forms a protective and soothing coating over the inflamed and affected skin surface. For this these are useful for protecting the face and lips from the sun.

Gels

These are aqueous colloidal suspensions of hydrated forms of insoluble medicaments such as aluminium hydroxide gel, used as an antacid. Gels may be prepared for oral administration or for external application. Oral preparations such as antacid should have acceptable organoleptic properties. Gels which are externally applied do not require addition of sweetener.

Jellies

Jelly is one type of gel with little difference in the matrix structure. The structural coherent matrix of a jelly contains large amount of liquid, usually water. These are like mucilage; with the same gum mucilage as well as a jelly can be prepared. The difference between a mucilage and jelly lies in consistency. Mucilage does not have jelly-like consistency. A whole gum of the finest quality is better than its powdered form to make a clear preparation with uniform consistency.

Ear Drops

These are solutions of drugs intended for instillation into the ear with the help of a dropper.

Nasal Drops

These are solutions of drugs that are instilled into the nose with a dropper. These are usually aqueous because oily drops inhibit movement of cilia in the nasal mucosa and, if used for long periods, may reach the lungs and cause lipoidal pneumonia.

Elixirs

These are attractively colored, pleasantly flavoured, sweetened, clear liquid preparations intended for oral administration of potent or nauseous drugs. Usually these are hydroalcoholic preparations and more stable than the mixtures; but in some cases elixir should be prepared immediately before administration by adding required volume of solvent to the dry granules or powders.

Emulsions

To administer oil, an emulsion is a relatively suitable form to be used. It is a biphasic liquid dosage form intended for oral administration or external application. These may be oil-in-water and water-in-oil types. In oil-in-water emulsion oil is dispersed in water in form of fine globules; similarly, water is dispersed in oil in form of fine globules in water-in-oil emulsion. Water may be simple water or aqueous solution and oil may be simply oil or a solution of active ingredient in oil. Emulsion intended for oral administration must have desired organoleptic properties; that is, it must be suitably coloured, flavoured and palatability. Emulsion intended for external application does not require any sweetening agent. However, suitable colour and flavour are added to provide an aesthetic value.

Microemulsions

These are mixtures of oil and water stabilized by surfactant (amphiphile). These are optically isotropic, thermodynamically stable liquid systems. The average diameter of droplet in a microemulsion may vary from 10mμ to 50 mμ. Type of emulsion o/w or w/o, formed greatly depends on the oil and surfactant used for the preparation. Microemulsion (o/w) of many oils including volatile oils, vitamin A, D, and E oils, can be prepared by using suitable hydrophilic surfactants.

Solutions

Solution preparations contain one or more chemical substances usually dissolved in aqueous vehicle. The solutes are usually non-volatile. For specific therapeutic action of the solute(s) the solution is used. These may vary in terms of composition, method of manufacture, strength, mode of administration and dosage.

Syrups

Syrups may be medicated or non-medicated containing 66.67% of sucrose in water. The non-medicated syrups containing flavouring agent, sometimes colouring agent also, are used as vehicle to prepare medicated oral liquid preparations which may be solution or suspension depending on the solubility and other physicochemical properties of the drug(s). The drugs which are water soluble and stable in the solution state can only be formulated in this form. The non-medicated syrups are also used as drink after diluting with adequate amount of water.

Linctuses

Linctuses are viscous, coloured and flavoured oral liquids containing active ingredients dissolved in a vehicle that usually contains a high proportion of sucrose, other sugars or a suitable polyhydric alcohol or alcohol (ethyl alcohol). They are usually prepared for use in the treatment of or relief of cough. These are commonly sipped or swallowed slowly without addition of water.

Oral Drops

These are meant for administration in small volumes through a dropper. These are generally prepared for paediatric and elderly use.

Suspensions

These contain active ingredient(s) suspended in a suitable vehicle. The suspended solids may deposit on storage but these should be easily redispersed on shaking; so that, the correct dose can be dispensed. These contain suitable colour and flavour to improve organoleptic property of the preparation. These are intended for oral administration.

Enemas

These may be solutions, suspensions, or oil-in-water emulsions of medicaments. These are intended for rectal administration.

Gargles

Gargles are aqueous solutions used to prevent or treat infection in the throat or in oral cavity. These may be used 'as it is' or after dilution with water as directed by the physician. Usually warm water is used for dilution just before use.

Mouthwashes

These are aqueous solutions, sometimes concentrated solutions, commonly used for cleansing and deodorizing the buccal cavity. The solution is swished in the oral cavity and then thrown out.

Mouthwashes are formulated and used for 1) Therapeutic purposes, 2) Diagnostic purposes and 3) Cosmetic use.

Spirits

These are alcoholic or hydroalcoholic solutions. These may contain medicinal substances or flavouring agents, usually of volatile in nature. Aromatic Spirit of Ammonia is prepared by a process of distillation but most other spirits are prepared by the process of simple solution. Concentration of alcohol in spirits is quite high, generally 60% and more.

Collodions

These are fluid preparation. Collodions are used for external application and are applied with the help of brush or rod. The vehicle used for making these preparations being volatile evaporates after application. As a result a flexible and protective film remains over the area of application. The volatile solvents used to prepare collodions are ether, alcohol, etc. These contain pyroxylin (nitrocellulose) which is responsible for making film and castor oil is used to make the film flexible.

Collodions may be medicated as well as unmedicated. Unmedicated collodions are useful for protecting small cuts and abrasions. The medicated collodions are used to keep the drug in contact with affected areas for prolonged time.

Paints

These are liquid preparations for application to the skin or mucous surfaces. These may be aqueous or alcoholic solutions and sometimes, are prepared with a collodion basis. Usually these contain the medicament like antiseptic, astringent, caustic or analgesic properties. Resinous substances like benzoin, prepared storax, or tolu balsam in ethereal solution are used as bases of medicated varnishes.

Extracts

These are concentrated preparations of animal or vegetable drugs. These are manufactured by separating the active constituents of the respective drug with a suitable solvent (*menstruum*), evaporating all or most of the solvent and finally adjusting the residue to prescribed standard. *The process of separation of the active principles from the drug by use of solvent is called* ***extraction***. The insoluble matter of the crude drug left out after extraction is called *marc*. The crude drugs may be organised or unorganised.

Infusion

This is a process of extraction used when the constituents in the crude drugs is readily soluble in the solvent. The process is of short duration and the extract is a dilute solution. Either water or a mixture of water and alcohol is used as solvent and the solvent may be hot or cold. The duration of extraction ranges from 3 – 20 minutes.

Decoction

Decoction is one of the oldest and common process of extraction. Water is the solvent of common choice. In this method crushed drug is put in water and boiled for at least 15 minutes. The water-soluble components are extracted. After extraction the mixture is cooled and strained. The residue is washed with portions of cold water and washings are added to the bulk till the volume is made. This process is applied to drugs whose components are heat resistant. Tea leaves when boiled with water is an example of decoction. In fact, tea leaves should be put in boiling water for 2-3 minutes, this is infusion.

Digestion

This is similar to the maceration process in which extraction is done by applying heat. When the extractable matter does not degrade on heating, the process of digestion is used for extraction. Due to heat the extracting efficiency of the solvent also increases.

Tinctures

These are manufactured either by maceration or percolation. Either from vegetable drugs or from chemical substances, the alcoholic or hydro alcoholic solutions are prepared. The drug content of different tinctures may not be identical but, must be within the limits of established standards. The tinctures of potent drugs usually have the drug content of 10%. The potency is normally adjusted after completion of the test for drug content (assay). There are five methods for preparing a tincture or an extract; maceration, digestion, decoction, infusion and percolation.

Aromatic Waters

Aromatic waters are clear, saturated solution of volatile oils or other aromatic or volatile substances in water. They are also called as *medicated waters.* The odour and taste of the aromatic water is similar to the drug or substance from which it is prepared. There should not be any empyreumatic (smoke-like) and any other foreign odour in these preparations.

Mixtures

A mixture is a liquid medicinal preparation for internal use, of which a single dose or several doses are contained in a single bottle. These contain one or more medicaments either dissolved or suspended in a suitable vehicle. Usually the vehicle is aqueous, sometimes it may be a non-aqueous also. Some preparations cannot be stored for long time and hence, these should be freshly prepared. Thus, all suspensions may be called mixture, but all mixtures are not suspensions.

Injections

These are sterile preparations intended for administration into the body by injection. There are five main types of injections– Injections, Powders for Injection, Intravenous Infusion, Concentrated Solutions for Injection and Implants.

Intravenous Infusions

These are sterile aqueous solutions or emulsions (o/w type), free from pyrogen or bacterial endotoxins, foreign particle visible to the naked eye, intended for intravenous administration. These are isotonic to the blood and do not contain any antimicrobial preservative. Their nominal content is 100 ml or more.

Implants

These are sterile solid preparations of size and size suitable for implantation into the body tissues for release of the drug over an extended period of time. These are usually packed individually in sterile containers.

Liniments

These are either solutions or emulsions of medicinal substances which are applied by rubbing on the skin. Two types of solvents are commonly used to prepare liniments, one is alcoholic and the other is oleaginous. For example, Soap Liniment BPC contains alcohol while, Methyl Salicylate Liniment BPC or Camphor Liniment BP contains oil. The medicinal substances which have analgesic, counterirritant, rubefacient action or which need to penetrate the skin, are prepared in the form of liniment using alcohol or hydroalcohol as vehicle.

Applications

These are either fluid or semi-fluid intended for application over the skin. Generally, these are prepared in the form of emulsion suspensions. Antiparasitic preparations are commonly available applications in the market.

Magmas

According to USP magmas are suspensions of poorly soluble drugs in a water medium and are distinguished from gels mainly in that the suspended particles are larger. Thus, they tend to separate on standing and require a label directing that they be shaken well before each use.

Milk of Magnesia

Magnesium hydroxide is an inorganic compound with the chemical formula $Mg(OH)_2$. As a suspension in water, it is often called **milk of magnesia** because of its milk-like appearance.

The term *milk of magnesia* was first used for a white-coloured, aqueous, mildly alkaline suspension of magnesium hydroxide formulated at about 8% w/v by Charles Henry Phillips in 1880 and sold under the brand name *Phillips' Milk of Magnesia* for medicinal usage.

Glycerites

A glycerite is a fluid extract of an herb or other medicinal substance made with glycerin. According to King's American Dispensatory (1898) a glycerite is Glycerita —Glycerites. This class of preparations is generally understood as solutions of medicinal substances in glycerin, although in certain instances the various Pharmacopoeias deviate to an extent.

Lotion

Lotions are liquid preparations intended for application over the skin. Lotions should be taken on lint or other soft absorbent material and applied without any friction. Most of the lotions are solutions and their main ingredients are simple salts, e.g. copper and zinc sulphates, lead subacetate, etc which are water soluble. For preparing salicylic acid lotion alcohol is used as solvent.

Inhalations

Inhalations are liquid preparations of volatile drug substances. These are intended to be inhaled the vapours so that the substance can reach directly to the lining of the respiratory tract and exerts a quick relief from bronchial and nasal congestion.

Aerosol

Aerosol may be defined as a pressurized package system which is self-propelled through a valve to expel the contents in the form of spray or foam from the container.

Aerosol dosage form is usually considered as gaseous dosage form, as the preparation is dispensed in the form a gas, spray or mist. Sometimes, it is treated as a disperse system. Since, most of the preparations,- a solution, emulsion or suspension of the active ingredient, is dispersed in propellant system.

Ophthalmic Preparation

According to the USP an ophthalmic preparation is defined as sterile dosage forms essentially free from foreign particles suitably compounded and packed for instillation into the eye. It may be a solution, suspension, ointment, gel, and certain solid dosage forms.

Irrigations/Douche solution

These are solutions of medicaments used for the treatment of infections of the bladder, vagina, and sometimes nose. These solutions are administered through thin, soft, rubber or plastic tube known as catheter (bladder) vulcanite or plastic pipe (vagina) or a specially designed glass irrigator (nose). Both solution and the equipment used for irrigation must be sterile.

Exercise

A. Multiple Choice Question Carrying 01 Mark

1. Which statement is correct?
   (a) A product is called generic, which is no longer under patent protection
   (b) A product is called generic, which can be produced by any manufacturer
   (c) The label of which does not mention the brand name.
   (d) All
2. Which of the following does not provide unit dose of a drug?
   (a) Syrup (b) Tablet
   (c) Suppository (d) Capsule
3. Which dosage form is administered rectally?
   (a) Suppository (b) Powder
   (c) Capsule (d) Pellet
4. Which of the following dosage form requires water for injection for manufacture?
   (a) Dextrose 5% solution for iv administration
   (b) Cough syrup
   (c) Linctus
   (d) Tincture
5. Large volume of injection is administered through
   (a) Intracutaneous route
   (b) Intravenous route
   (c) Intramuscular route
   (d) Subcutaneous route
6. Which of the following dosage forms is not administered orally?
   (a) Enema (b) Suspension
   (c) Emulsion (d) Capsule
7. Which of the following preparations is a solution?
   (a) Emulsion (b) Suspension
   (c) Elixir (d) Microemulsion

8. Which of the following preparations belongs to separate class of dosage form?
   (a) Capsule (b) Ointment
   (c) Gel (d) Eye Drop
9. From which of the following preparations the drug can reach to the lungs directly?
   (a) Suppositories (b) Eye lotion
   (c) Cream (d) Aerosol
10. Which of the following preparations is used for local application in the body cavity?
   (a) Mouthwash (b) Linctus
   (c) Coated tablet (d) Capsule
11. Which of the following preparation is orally taken?
   (a) Inhalation (b) Douche solution
   (c) Milk of magnesia (d) Lotion

B. Question Carrying 05 Marks

1. Classify the dosage forms on the basis of routes of administration and physical state.
2. Define the terms; a) Collodions, b) Tincture
3. Classify the dosage forms on the basis of method of manufacture and route of administration.
4. Define three dosage form administered orally.
5. Explain the terms – generic product and branded product.

C. Question Carrying 10 Marks

1. Define the following terms
   (a) Cachet (b) Insufflations
   (c) Triturations (d) Suppositories
   (e) Microemulsion
2. What is a dosage form? Write down the characteristics and advantages of dosage form.
3. Define the terms - Drug and Dosage form. Write the names of six dosage forms administered orally.
4. Define five types of tablets.

Answers

A. Multiple Choice Question

1. (d)	2. (b)	3. (a)	4. (a)	5. (b)
6. (a)	7. (c)	8. (a)	9. (d)	10. (a)
11. (c)				

Chapter 3

Prescription

Definition, Parts of Prescription, Handling of Prescription and Errors in Prescription.

Introduction

During recent years in healthcare system attention has significantly shifted from advancement in technology to patient safety. In 2002, the WHO passed a World Health Assembly Resolution on Patients Safety. This was prompted by the realization that countries have been losing up to $29 billion annually just for health care errors.

The stated role of General Medical Council, U.K., has changed from "Registration of Doctors and Regulating Medical Education", to "Protecting Patients and Guiding Doctors". The U.K. has created a National Patients Safety Agency (NPSA). In Australia there is Australian Patients Safety Foundation; and India has established the National Institute for Patients Safety (NIPS). In short, patients' safety has become the primary focus in therapeutic medicine.

Medication errors play an important role in adverse drug reactions (ADRs). About 19.3% of all cases handled by the Medical Protection Society in the UK are due to medication error. This is an organization similar to the Medical Indemnity Insurance in India. In the United States each year approximately 7,000 deaths are caused by medication errors. The most worrying fact is that in the US the medication errors increased 2.6 folds during 1983 to 1993.

In India we do not have the culture to record and publicize our mistakes. Hence, we have no data on this issue.

The Guidelines for prescription writing and handling have been drafted based on existing laws. However, as the regulatory documents do not cover all the aspects, the stakeholders have drawn out guidelines based on legal implications, social and moral principles, and responsibilities of all those involved in prescription writing as well as prescription dispensing.

Definition

Only a Registered Medical Practitioner (R.M.P.) who is registered with the respective State Medical/Dental/Veterinary Council is authorized to prescribe allopathic medicines. An R.M.P. includes an allopathic doctor (Minimum M.B.B.S), a Dentist (minimum B.D.S), a Veterinarian (minimum B.V. Sc).

- A Dentist should prescribe only those medicines which are related to, and needed for his/her profession, and for his/her patients only.
- A Veterinary Doctor should prescribe only those medicines which are related to and needed, for his/her profession, and for his/her veterinary patients only.
- An Ayurvedic doctor, a Homeopathic doctor, a Unani doctor, a Naturopath, etc. are NOT authorized to prescribe or recommend allopathic medicines.
- A Nurse or Pharmacist is not authorized to prescribe allopathic "prescription" medicines to their patients.
- Unqualified persons or persons with doubtful and unauthorized degrees are not recognized by the Govt. of India to prescribe allopathic medicines. Those who do prescribe/recommend allopathic medicines without proper authorization are termed Quacks.

Certain medicines can be prescribed by doctors of a particular specialty only. For example, Sildenafil Citrate can be prescribed only by an Urologist, Psychiatrist, Endocrinologist, Dermatologist or Venerologist. Similarly, Letrozole can be prescribed by a cancer specialist only.

Prescription is defined *as a written directive to the pharmacist from a Registered Medical Practitioner for compounding or dispensing and administration of drugs, or device or other service to a particular patient.*

A prescription is a legal document and it can be produced and challenged in the court of law.

Parts of Prescription

A prescription has various parts; some of them are "mandatory" (as per the Drugs & Cosmetics Act and Rules, or the Medical Council of India), and some of them though not mandatory, important for better understanding of the prescription by the pharmacist and the patient also. Since it is a legal document, it contains necessary information about the physician, patient, date of examination/prescription, and about the drugs or device prescribed.

In general, a prescription has 9 parts

1. Date
2. Name, age, sex and address of the patient
3. Superscription
4. Inscription
5. Subscription
6. Signature
7. Name
8. Address, and Registration Number of the Physician

However, the dosage forms are not being prepared by a dispensing Pharmacist in his/her pharmacy and the physician does not direct the preparation of dosage form. The physicians in recent times write the names of the prepared and marketed dosage forms. Hence, among the parts of prescription, subscription which speaks about the methods of preparation has become outdated or irrelevant.

For the sake of knowledge only all these parts are being explained here. As a reference a typical prescription of old days is also given here along with modern prescription.

A sample of ideal prescription to be used by a private practitioner is shown below. The different parts of the prescription having legal implications are indicated by arrows.

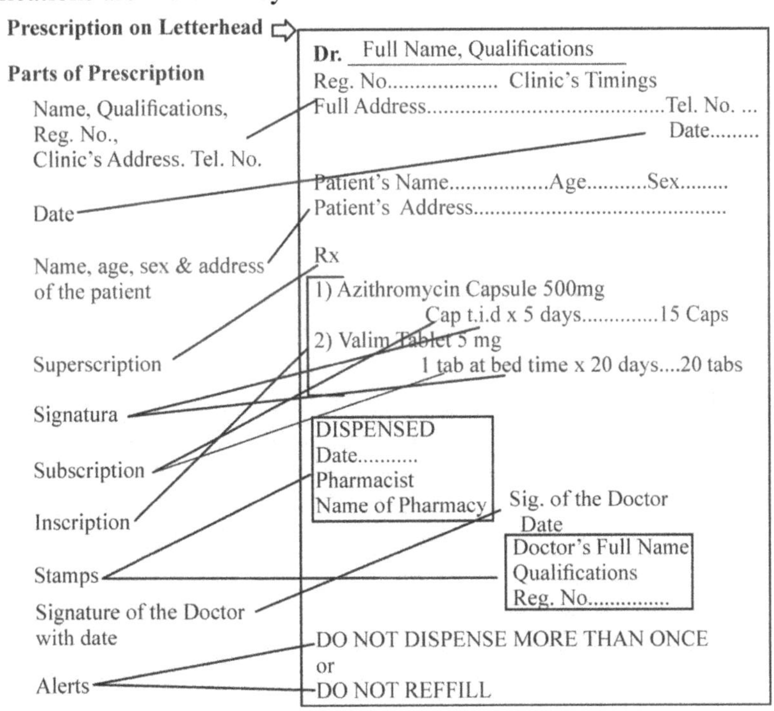

Sample of Modern Prescription

The prescription issued by a physician in a Govt hospital is different from that issued at a private clinic. The prescription issued at private clinic is a letterhead as shown above. The contents of both prescriptions are almost same. A sample prescription issued at the Govt hospital is shown below.

Prescription from a Govt Hospital

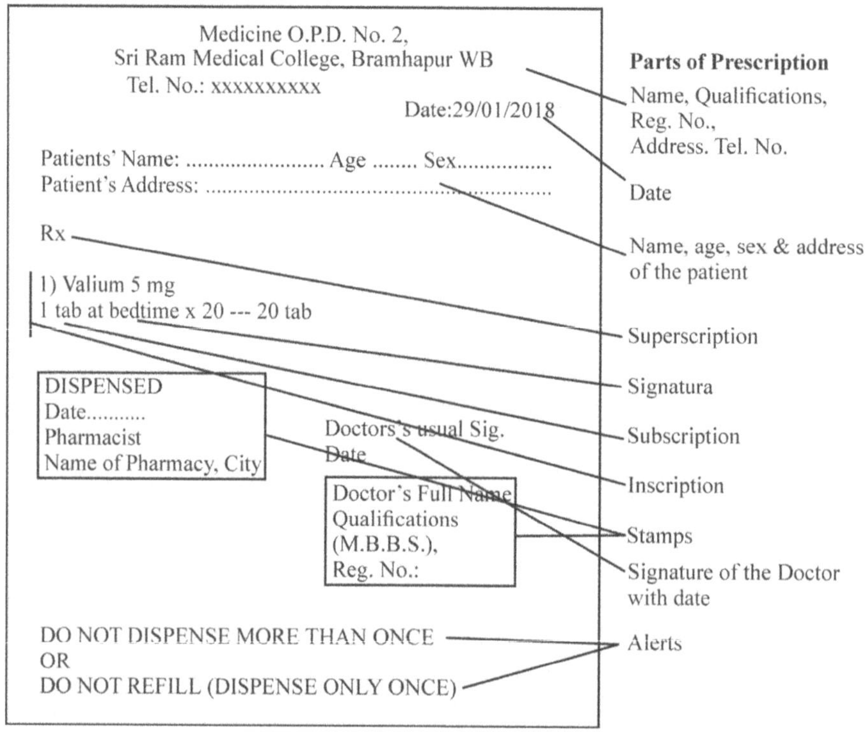

1. *Date:* Every prescription must mention the date on which the medicine and/or other advices have been prescribed. It is legally required. It helps to know the validity of the prescription and to avoid unnecessary refilling of the prescription. In absence of date the pharmacist fails to identify which prescription is previous and which is the current one. If the date is not mentioned the risks of self-medication by repeated, unwarranted usage increases.
2. *Name, age, weight, sex and address of the patient:* For proper identification of a patient his or her full name along with his/her telephone number must be written. A prescription is meant for an individual, and if there are two clients at the pharmacy with the same first or last name the prescriptions may get exchanged. It is legally required. If the name is absent, it cannot be linked to a particular patient with certainty. There is room for error when two patients go to a doctor together. Similarly, prescriptions can get mixed up between

family members when the consult the doctor, as is very common. In case of family members, writing only the surname can cause errors.

Patient's age and weight are to be recorded in the prescription. This information is useful especially for children for whom dose size is calculated on the basis of age or body weight of the child patient. It acts as a safety measure against dosage error. It is not legally required. It helps the pharmacist to confirm the medication; that is dispensing the right drug and right dosage form (medicine).

It is essential to write the sex of the patient. This has no legal requirement; but can help the pharmacist to know or assess correctness for patient, particularly when the handwriting of the physician is illegible or can create confusion between similar brand names. Special precautions are required in pregnancy and breastfeeding.

Sometimes, both males and females may have similar or same names; and hence the pharmacist may not be able to assess whether the name is that of a male or female. This creates confusion or can cause problem to prescribe medicines for gynaecological problems.

3. *Superscription:* This part of prescription is represented by the symbol, Rx. The symbol is written always before prescribing medicines. It has been continuing since long as a matter of practice. It is believed that it's a prayer before Jupiter, the God of healing for quick recovery of the patient. There is another meaning of Rx. It is a symbol of Latin word which means that 'take thou' or 'you take'. It has no legal requirement.
4. *Inscription:* It refers to the body of the prescription. In this part the names of the medicines prescribed are written with mention of strength and potency, and dosage form of each medicine are to be written by the physician. Dosage and dosing instructions along with total quantity of the medicines to be taken (duration) are to be mentioned. These have legal implication. In fact, it is always better to write the generic names of the medicines preferably in capital letters. This will avoid any confusion in understanding the medicine to be given or taken. If felt necessary, the prescriber can write name of the company within bracket. In case of complex prescription, the inscription part can be divided into four parts further:
   - The Basis (active pharmaceutical ingredient, i.e. drug)
   - Adjuvants (inert excipients)
   - Correctives (to reduce the undesirable effect of adjuvants)
   - Vehicle (a solvent used to dissolve a solid substance or used to dilute a preparation)

The ingredients are written one by one in separate line, thereafter the quantity required is written. The last ingredient is usually a vehicle or diluent.

5. *Subscription:* In this part of prescription the physician directs the pharmacist about the type and compounding of dosage form, and number of doses to be prepared. This part of the prescription has also legal implication.
6. *Signatura ('Sig'):* From the patient point of view this part of prescription is important; because in this part the physician writes how and when which medicine is to be taken. Because the patient must know the quantity of tablets/cap/liquid to be taken and how many of times the medicine to be taken in a day. If the patients are orally instructed, the patients are most likely to forget. The pharmacist can also counsel the patient. This part is legally required.
7. *Name, Signature, Address and Registration number of the physician:* Full name of the physician should be printed on the letterhead. Prescription is a legal document and can be produced in the court of law. The printed name of the physician authenticates the prescription before dispensing pharmacist or to anyone. The doctors working in Govt hospitals are not authorized for private practice; such doctors sometimes prescribe on blank paper without mentioning their names and even sometimes do not put their signatures properly. Such a prescription cannot be used as a valid document and no legal action can be taken under any adverse situation.

   The letterhead of a physician must mention the complete address of the physician's clinic with phone number and consultation timings. This is a legal requirement. This helps the patient as well as the pharmacist to contact the doctor for clarification of any doubt or discrepancies.

   On the letterhead the qualification of the doctor such as M.B.B.S./B.D.S./B.V.Sc. must be mentioned after his or name. This has legal requirement. In fact, this indicates the authenticity of the doctor. The basic qualification should be mentioned; because physicians of other systems and sometimes quacks write in their letterheads M.D. which may confuse the patients and others.

   The physician must put his or her usual signature (commonly made) in the prescription with date. This confirms the authenticity of the prescription. In fact, this can avoid misuse of blank or wrong prescription. Legally this is required. If a prescription is typed or printed and is produced as a document by anyone, it cannot be accepted as a valid document unless it is signed by the prescribing physician. Thus, the signature made by the physician on each prescription should be identifiable.

On the letterhead the Registration number of the physician and the name of Registering Authority should be printed. This is legally required. This confirms the authenticity of the doctor further. This also helps to identify the background of the doctor.

Handling of Prescription

After receiving a prescription, the pharmacist starts compounding and then dispenses the medicines as per the instructions given by the physician. These activities are completed by performing the following steps;

1. Receipt of the prescription
2. Reading and examining the prescription
3. Compounding, labelling, and packaging
4. Filling, pricing and delivery of the medicines to the patient.

1. Receipt of the prescription

When a prescription is submitted in the pharmacy, the pharmacist must be present to receive the same; because pharmacist is the authorized person to receive the prescription. The pharmacist reads the prescription thoroughly. The patient is asked to wait in the waiting area. If possible, there should be provisions to educate the patients waiting to improve general knowledge on hygiene, family planning, contagious diseases, and precautions during pregnancy, vaccinations, etc. While examining the prescription the pharmacist should not make any comment or gesture that indicates approval or rejection of the prescription. Even the pharmacist should not change his or her facial expression, so that the patient is either confused or surprised after getting back the prescription.

2. Reading and examining the prescription

The pharmacist must read and examine the prescription carefully, check whether the points which are important with respect to legal aspect and must be mentioned in the prescription are there or not. If any point of such category is found missing, the pharmacist must contact the prescribing doctor to comply the requirement.

The pharmacist remains in a dilemma as to whether the prescription is genuine or from a quack or homoeopathic or ayurvedic doctor. If the prescription is from a hospital, it is not known which of the faculty doctors has prescribed it. Govt. doctors doing private practice most often prescribe without their name, qualification, and other details. In absence of the relevant information, the prescriptions become illegal, and pharmacies are not authorized to dispense them and can be penalized for doing so.

3. **Compounding, labelling, and packaging**

After thorough checking if the prescription is found correct, it should be dispensed. Presently the doctors are not prescribing any medicines to be compounded.

However, for the sake of knowledge following information is provided. The working place for compounding, labelling and packaging must be neat and clean. The equipment and glassware should be thoroughly clean and washed. After compounding the medicines, these should be packed by wrapped with the labels prepared as per the norms. If the compounded medicine is a liquid, it should be filled in a clean and dry bottle. The bottle should be labelled properly. Once the medicines are packed and labelled, the medicines are served to the patient.

4. **Filling, pricing and delivery of the medicines to the patient**

1. Before delivery of the medicine, pricing of the medicine should be done as per the formula given below;

$$\text{MRP} = (\text{MC} + \text{CC} + \text{PM} + \text{PC})\left(1 + \frac{\text{MAPE}}{100}\right) + \text{ED}$$

Where, MRP is the maximum retail price, MC is the cost of all raw materials, CC is the conversion or processing cost, PM is the cost of packaging materials, PC is the cost of packaging, MAPE is maximum allowable post-manufacturing expenses, and ED is the excise duty.

Cost of each raw material used is calculated as per the quantity used in unit dose × number of doses prepared. The cost of all materials are added (MC). CC refers to the sum of cost of manpower + electricity + equipment charges + rent of house.

2. The pharmacist must explain clearly to the patient all the details of the medication such as how, when and which medicine should be taken; how the medicines are to be stored.

For compounding the medicines, the pharmacist must have sufficient expertise and this activity comprises primarily number of operations. The precautions can be categorized into two classes: (a) General precautions and (b) operational precautions.

(a) General Precautions

The precautions to be taken by the pharmacist strictly during compounding are;

1. Compounding should be done using a clean working table

2. The pharmacist must wear the dress (white apron) during working
3. All the ingredients are to be kept orderly and alphabetically on the shelve
4. All the equipment and glass ware should be thoroughly cleaned, washed and dried
5. No container should be kept without label; in fact, two containers without having label should be kept side by side
6. Each container must bear its label
7. At a time only one prescription should be compounded and after completion one, next prescription should be taken up.
8. For convenience the dispensing balance should be placed at the centre of working place and the containers having materials to be used during compounding should be kept at the left side.
9. The label of the container must be read carefully before opening it. After use the container must be closed tightly and for confirmation the label of the container should be read during closing it. To avoid confusion or mistake, after use the containers should be kept at the right hand side.
10. After completion of the medicaments, the containers should be kept on the shelves at their respective places.
11. Each medicament should be compounded as per the direction given by the doctor; in absence of any directive the standard process mentioned in the Pharmacopoeia should be followed.
12. No medicament should be prepared by naked hand; the pharmacist must wear a transparent thin glove before preparing the medicines.
13. Labels should be prepared with all information, cut into suitable size and then pasted on the container.

(b) Operational Precautions

Preparation of a medicine should be done as per the method recommended or approved for a particular type of dosage form. Thus, the pharmacist involved in manufacturing of the preparation must know how to manufacture the medicine and must have required expertise. The manufacture of medicine involves the following operations;

1. **Weighing:** Irrespective of type of medicine prepared or to be prepared, weighing of raw material is essential. Hence a pharmacist must be aware of handling of different types of balances and the basic information related to weighing. Balance may be electrical or electronic single pan balance, dispensing

balance. Specific balance has specific sensitivity and error. Minimum weightable quantity depends on these two criteria as shown below;

$$\text{Minimum weightable quantity (MWQ)} = \text{sensitivity} \times \frac{100}{\text{Error}}$$

Thus, if a balance can weigh 10 mg and its error is ± 10%; then MWQ = 10 × 100/10mg = 100mg.

That is, to weigh accurately minimum 100mg should be weighed.

A sensitive balance is required to weigh small amount of a potent drug. Otherwise for common compounding purpose a dispensing balance is sufficient. Any sensitive balance must be placed over a stable platform and the balance is to be levelled. The levelling can be tested by a spirit level. The sensitivity of a dispensing balance can be checked after levelling it. Once the balance is levelled, it must be checked for oscillation of the beam and for the null point. After levelling the two pieces of white papers are put below the pans and null point is checked for adjustment, if required. Two pieces of butter paper of same size are taken and each of the paper is put over each pan. The oscillating pointer is set at centre. The required weights are taken from the weight box using forceps and put over the paper of left hand pan. If the material to be weighed is powder, then it should be slowly poured over the paper on right hand pan until the oscillating pointer is positioned at centre. During weighing spatula should be used to pour from the container or remove from the pan; forceps is to be used to hold the weights. The balance must be kept in dust free environment. This is most important operation to prepare medicine of accurate strength and potency.

2. **Measuring:** Measuring operation is related to volume, length and area. To measure the length or area the device required is measuring scale, tape or chain. To measure volume of a liquid there are different measuring devices such as micro-pipettes, pipettes, burettes, cylinders, volumetric flasks, etc. Different types of measuring devices have different capacity as well as accuracy. For example, a micropipette can measure 0.01ml to 0.001ml; pipette can measure 0.05 ml to 50ml; while a cylinder can measure 1ml to 1000ml depending on the capacity of the device. Thus, a pharmacist must be aware of the accuracy of each measuring device and he must know which device should be used and where to be used. For example, to measure a volume of a liquid accurately, a pipette should be used; a measuring cylinder can be used where accuracy in volume is not required. Similarly,

to prepare a solution of definite strength or concentration, volumetric flask of required volume can be used. The measuring devices can be certified or uncertified. Accurate measurement requires certified measuring device.

3. **Grinding:** This is also an important operation and commonly performed during compounding of most preparations. Whether a solid or semisolid preparation, the materials are ground in a mortar pestle to make fine powders. The mortar pestle may be made of glass or porcelain. In case of making a powder preparation, various solid materials are mixed together by crushing or grinding in a mortar pestle. While making a semisolid preparation the solid or liquid is pasted with a suitable liquid in a mortar pestle. Sometimes solids are dissolved in a liquid by crushing the solid with the solvent in a mortar pestle. The material of construction of mortar pestle is non reactive.

4. **Solubilization:** This is also a common activity performed for manufacturing of solution, suspension, emulsion, ointment, cream, etc. However, this operation primarily depends on the solubility characteristics of the drug. Based on the solubility characteristics of the drug, the pharmacist can anticipate which type of formulations can be possible and such formulation can be prepared.

5. **Mixing:** Uniformity of drug content in a formulation depends on the success of mixing. How the small amount of drug could be mixed to obtain a homogeneous mixture is a science. Thus, the pharmacist must know the small amount of a component can be mixed with relatively greater amount of other component. Accordingly, the mixtures can be divided into three types – positive, negative, and neutral.

   Positive mixtures are clear preparations obtained by dissolving a soluble solid in a liquid or mixture of liquids. Gentle stirring would be sufficient to dissolve or mix; no external energy is necessary. Thus, such preparations are homogeneous mixtures.

   Negative mixtures are mixture of two or more immiscible liquids or mixture of a poorly soluble solid in a liquid. These mixtures require vigorous stirring to disperse one into other. In most cases once the external energy is removed separation of phases take place. Dispersion of solids in liquid is called suspension and dispersion of one liquid into another liquid is called emulsion. Thus, these systems are heterogeneous and thermodynamically unstable. They require a third substance such as suspending agent, emulsifying agent, flocculating agent, etc. for stabilization.

Neutral mixtures are ointments and solid-solid mixtures. The components of such mixtures mix once external energy is supplied and once mixed, do not separate even the external energy is removed. To prepare such mixture, the ingredients are to be mixed in ascending order.

6. **Filtration:** In case of solution preparation or ointment or creams this activity is necessary. This operation removes the foreign particles from the preparation. There are different types of filtering media and depending on the type of preparation the particular type of filtering medium is selected. For example,

   Muslin, gauze or cotton wool is used to remove large particles from the solution.

   Glass wool is used to remove large particles from oxidising or corrosive liquid.

   Muslin or glass wool are used to remove particles from oleaginous substances such as molten wax (in hot condition). Generally, steam jacketed funnel is used for this purpose.

   Membrane filter (cellulose acetate or nitrate filter) is used to remove fine particles from the solutions. Parenteral solutions are filtered through membrane filter to remove microorganisms.

   Filter paper or sintered glass crucible is used to remove particles from solutions. These are available with different porosity and depending on the type of impurity particular type of filtering media is selected. When the volume of preparation is small, selection of filtering medium and performing filtration become important. The drug content of the preparation and quick filtration are required. Quick filtration means higher rate of filtration. Appropriate filtering media, large surface area, and pressure difference are the factors that influence the rate of filtration.

7. **Filling & Sealing:** These are alternatively called finishing operation. These include making up of volume, weighing of product, selection of appropriate container and closure. Containers may be various types such as glass (colored or colourless), plastic, or metal. Based on the type of product and its stability characteristics the type of container should be selected. Glass is considered non reactive; but based on their reactivity glass is of three types – type I, type II and type III. Type I or borosilicate glass is actually nonreactive, is suitable for storing acids or alkalis. Type II glasses are stable to solutions which are slightly acidic or alkaline; while Type III glasses cannot resist slight acidity or alkalinity.

For example, metronidazole injection is filled in type I glass. Type II glasses or treated soda-lime glasses are used to store regular injections and other solutions. Type III glasses are used store other preparations. Photosensitive materials/preparations are stored in amber color bottle. Plastic bottles or containers have replaced glass bottles or containers extensively. Tablets or capsules can be stored in glass or plastic bottles of wide mouth with pilfer-proof caps.

8. **Labelling:** Labels of medicines are most important; because it contains composition, strength, dose, shelf-life and storage conditions of the medicine. Hence, the pharmacist must know to prepare a correct label.

Errors in Prescription

Prescription errors are considered as an important class of medication errors. Studies have shown that 15 – 21% prescriptions contain at least one prescribing error. In India, there are a few published studies pertaining to medication errors and prescription errors. Most of the published studies have addressed the issue of medication errors in indoor admitted patients. All these studies have been conducted on 300 – 500 subjects. In a survey conducted on 999 OPD prescriptions with the focus mainly on the issue of irrational drug use. This study was planned to initiate the process of identification and subsequent minimization of medication errors. As an initial step, this observational study was planned to look only for errors in prescription writing for OPD patients.

Definition

A prescription error may be defined as a failure in the treatment process that leads to or has the potential to lead harm to the patient.

Prescription errors may be of many types; but commonly following are considered as prescription errors;

- Incorrect doses,
- Illegible details,
- Inappropriate ordering of medications,
- Prescribing of contraindicated drugs that may react with other medications already being taken.

In the UK a study was conducted to develop a definition of prescription errors. The study concluded that followings are the prescription errors;

- Transcription errors,

- Failure to communicate essential information and
- Use of drugs or doses inappropriate for the individual patient

But omissions and deviations from policies or guidelines were not included. Some also define prescribing omissions as errors, for example if a doctor fails to prescribe an antihypertensive drug (ramipril) for someone who could benefit from it.

Classification of Error

- **Type A:** This type of errors is potentially serious to the patient. Such prescription, if dispensed, would be dangerous to the patient.

  Such type of errors includes;

  1. Similarity in the names of the dosage forms
  2. Similarity in the names of the drugs

  For example, (i) if the pharmacist is not able to differentiate between 'Daonil' (Brand name for glibenclamide, a hypoglycemic medicine) and 'Digene' (Brand name of a mixture of antacids and methyl polysiloxone) and dispenses Daonil in place of digene, there may be serious issue; or (ii) if the name of a cardiac drug such as Digoxin is written by the physician in place of Digitoxin, the therapeutic complicacy will arise.

- **Type B:** Serious errors may be found when the prescription does not mention such as;

  1. The type of dosage form,
  2. The strength of the dosage forms, and
  3. The name of the dosage form is not clearly written by the prescriber.

  For dispensing such prescription the pharmacist needs to contact the prescriber in order to know the medicine. For example, if type of formulation prescribed such as conventional tablet or slow release tablet of indapamide is to be dispensed, or the strength of formulation such as aspirin tablets of 75 mg or 150 mg or 325 mg, or Atorvastatin tablets of 10 or 20 mg are to be dispensed, is not mentioned or when the brand name about which the dispensing pharmacist is not aware.

- **Type C:** The errors of this type are not so serious as type A or type B. This type of error can be resolved at dispensary level before dispensing by consulting with other pharmacist to take a professional decision. This type of error includes;

  1. Dosing schedule,
  2. Brand name and
  3. Abbreviations

Although such prescription can be correctly dispensed without contacting the prescriber, such an error causes obstruction in the normal functioning of the dispensary and delays dispensing of medication to the patient. For example, (i) dosing schedules of commonly prescribed medicines like paracetamol, diclofenac is missing, (ii) using brand names of commonly used medicines such as 'Natrilix' for indapamide, 'Tixylix' for promethazine (iii) using abbreviations such as 'NTP' for nortriptyline, 'UDCA' for ursodeoxycholic acid.

- **Type D:** An error of spelling mistake may be sometimes considered as minor; because such errors do not hamper the execution of prescriptions. But omissions of date of prescription, age and/or gender of the patient etc. should not be considered minor. These are legally required to identify the patient.

This has been mentioned earlier that prescription error is a significant problem in health care. In various countries studies have been conducted to categorize such errors. In a report from the United States of America (USA), prescription errors represent 20% of medical errors despite making efforts to minimize such errors. In Australia, the older populations have shown higher rates of medication errors which may be due to higher levels of medication intake and increased likelihood of being admitted to hospital (hospital statistics are the main source of medication incident reporting) than other age groups. In long-term care systems a large number of adverse drug events/ effects (ADE) are caused by preventable errors.

Thus, a pharmacist must know possible sources of errors which can ultimately lead to prescription error and can create problem in dispensing. The most important reasons are summarized below;

1. The limit of tolerance is narrow and ± 10% error is accepted during dispensing
2. The pharmacist must take preventive measures to avoid possible errors due to oversight, carelessness, absentmindedness, and negligence.
3. Each calculation must be rechecked.
4. During making a recipe if conversion from one system to another becomes necessary, it is necessary to check the conversion repeatedly to avoid mistake.
5. At each stage of compounding the label of each ingredient must be checked. For example, before removal of material from a container and at the time of closing it.
6. Writing and decoding the decimal places must be done carefully.

7. The pharmacist must check the accuracy and degree of sensitivity of the balance to be used for weighing. For example, the balance shows movement from the rest point only after a weight of 10 mg is placed over the pan. Thus, any weight less than 10 mg cannot be weighed by using this balance.
8. Say, the sensitivity of the balance is 10 mg and permissible error is ± 2%; then the minimum weightable quantity = $\frac{\text{Sensitivity} \times 100\%}{\text{Error}}$ = $\frac{10 \text{ mg} \times 100\%}{2\%} = 500$ mg.
9. Hence, to weigh 10 mg of a solid material by such balance, the material should be diluted with a suitable inert material so that more than 500mg contains 10mg of the active component. If the active material to be weighed is a liquid, the material is to be diluted with the vehicle accordingly.

Some Latin abbreviations commonly used in writing prescription

Latin Abbreviation	Meaning in English	Latin Abbreviation	Meaning in English
ad.	upto, to	ex. aq.	with water
ad. lib.	at pleasuse, as needed	ft.	make
admove	apply	gr.	grain
agit	shake	gtt	a drop
alt. hor.	alternate hour	hac. noct.	to night
a.a.	of each	h.s.	at bed time
a.	before	In.d.	daily
a.c.	before meals	i.c.	during meals
aq.dest.	distilled water	Inj.	an injection
aq.bull.	boiling water	un.	a liniment
a.d.	right ear	liq.	solution
a.l.	left ear	man.	morning
a.uristill	ear drops	mm.	minimum
b.i.d	twice a day	m.	mix,
Caps.	Capsule	Mistura	a mixture
Capiend	to be taken	Mittee	send
Chart.	Powder	Omni	every
Coch.amp.	Table spoonful	Omni hora	every hour
Coch.Mag.	Table spoonful	o.m.	every morning
CocK parv.	Tea spoonful	o.n.	every night
CocK mm.	Tea spoonful	p.o.	by mouth, orally
Coch.med.	Desert spoonful	p.c.	after meals

Table *Contd...*

Latin Abbreviation	Meaning in English	Latin Abbreviation	Meaning in English
Coch. mod.	Desert spoonful	p.r.m.	when needed
Collunar.	Nose wash	pulv.	powder
Collut.	Mouth wash	q.d.	every day
Collyr.	an eye wash	q.i.d.	four times a day
C	with	quot.	daily
dent.	give, let it be given	Sol.	a solution
div.	divide	Sig.	write
do! urg.	when the pain is severe	S.O.S	when necessary
emul.	an emulsion	tab.	a tablet
e. lact.	with milk	t.i.d.	three times a day

Exercise

A. Multiple Choice Question Carrying 01 Mark

1. Which statement is correct
   (a) Only a Registered Medical Practitioner can prescribe any medicine
   (b) Certain medicines can be prescribed by doctors of respective speciality only
   (c) There is nothing covered in the law regarding prescription writing.
   (d) Doctors can prescribe any medicines
2. Medical Licence is issued by
   (a) The Central Government directly
   (b) The State Government directly
   (c) State Medical/Dental/Veterinary Council
   (d) Medical Council of India
3. Which statement is correct?
   (a) Some parts of a Prescription are mandatory
   (b) All the parts of a Prescription are mandatory
   (c) Prescription is not a legal document
   (d) None
4. Which statement is correct?
   (a) Inscription refers to 'instruction for medication'
   (b) Inscription refers to dose of the drug(s) prescribed

(c) Inscription does not refer to 'signatura' and 'subscription'

(d) Inscription refers to the body of the prescription

5. Which of the following formula is used to calculate MRP of a product?

(a) $MRP = (MC + CC + PM)\left(1 + \frac{MAPE}{100}\right)$

(b) $MRP = (MC + CC + PM + PC)\left(1 + \frac{MAPE}{100}\right)$

(c) $MRP = (MC + CC + PM + PC)\left(1 + \frac{MAPE}{100}\right) + ED$

(d) $MRP = (MC + CC + PM)\left(1 + \frac{MAPE}{100}\right) + ED$

6. Which of the following activities is correct?

(a) Not more than two prescriptions should be handled at a time.

(b) All the equipments and glass wares should be cleaned.

(c) Pharmacist must explain how to handle the prescription.

(d) At a time only one prescription should be handled.

7. Mark the best activity

(a) Weighing balance should be kept over a stable, clean table and should be levelled.

(b) Weighing balance should be kept over a clean table.

(c) Weighing balance should be kept over a table,

(d) None of the above.

8. Less than 0.1 ml of a liquid can be measured accurately using

(a) 50 ml measuring cylinder

(b) 0.1ml micropipette

(c) 50 ml burette

(d) 1 ml pipette

9. Particles less than 1mμ can be eliminated by filtering a solution through

(a) Muslin cloth

(b) Cotton-wool

(c) Filter paper, Whatmann No.1.

(d) Membrane filter

10. What would be maximum limits of tolerance in case dispensing?
    (a) ±15% (b) ±20%
    (c) ±10% (d) ±17.5%

B. Question Carrying 05 Marks

1. Who are health care professionals? Who are licensed to prescribe medication in India?
2. Explain the parts of a prescription which are legally important.
3. Present a sample Prescription and label different parts
4. Explain the parts 'Superscription' and 'Inscription' of a prescription
5. Explain the reasons for which prescription errors make take place.
6. Classify prescription errors.
7. Describe how the weighing operation should be done.
8. Discuss how best mixing of powders should be done to ensure uniform mixing.
9. Explain different types of filters used by the pharmacist to filter different types of solutions.
10. Explain how the liquids should be measured as per the required volume.

C. Question Carrying 10 Marks

1. Briefly explain the various parts of a prescription.
2. Explain briefly the activities to be performed by the Pharmacist after receiving a prescription.
3. Discuss in brief the operational precautions to be taken by the Pharmacist during dispensing a prescription.
4. Classify prescription errors and briefly explain each type.
5. Describe how do the prescriptions errors occur
6. Describe briefly how a prescription should be handled by the Pharmacist.
7. Write down the general precautions to be taken by a Pharmacist during dispensing of drug.
8. Explain the importance of correct weighing and measuring activities during dispensing of drug.
9. Explain the errors caused by Physician and by Pharmacist.
10. Explain the consequences of incorrect handling of prescription.

Answers

1. (d)	2. (c)	3. (a)	4. (d)	5. (c)
6. (d)	7. (a)	8. (b)	9. (d)	10. (c)

Chapter 4

Posology

Definition, Factors Affecting Posology, Paediatric Dose Calculations based on Age, Body Weight and Body Surface Area.

Definition

The term posology has been derived from the Greek words – 'Posos' means how much and 'logos' means science; thus, the term 'posology' means 'dose' of a drug. It is a branch of pharmacology. The dose refers to the therapeutic dose of a drug to be administered for intended therapeutic action.

Therapeutic dose of a drug refers to the amount of a drug that can maintain its minimum therapeutically effective concentration (MEC) in the blood. When the drug concentration crosses the therapeutic level, it results toxic effects; and when the drug concentration is less than therapeutic level, it cannot produce therapeutic effect. The difference between these two concentrations is called therapeutic window. The amount of drug that can produce concentration within the therapeutic window is called dose of the drug. A drug can have two doses – minimum and maximum. However, the doctor can modify the dose depending on various factors.

Factors Influencing Posology (Dose of a Drug)

There are various factors that are considered to calculate the dose of a drug. The factors are;

- **Age:** It is one of the important factors that can influence the dose of a drug to be administered to achieve desired pharmacological action. The physiology of a child is different from that of an adult. The metabolic activity as well as excretion of a drug varies with the ages of a human patient. Thus, the doses of a drug vary with age of the patients.

- **Bodyweight:** It is generally considered that the concentration of a drug at its site of action depends on the ratio between the amount of drug administered and the size of the body; that is on the weight of the patient. Usually the amount of a drug suitable for a patient weighing 70 kg is called adult dose. Thus, the dose of a drug is calculated on the basis of the bodyweight of a patient.
- **Sex:** The weight, general health and certain physiological conditions of male and female are different. Hence the dose of a drug depends on the sex of the patient. In general, if the dose for a male is 1g, for female it would be 0.85g. During menstruation, pregnancy, and lactation the female patient should be given a moderate dose. Under certain physiological conditions of a female, some drugs should be avoided. For example, during menstruation strong purgative or during pregnancy anti-cholinesterase and ergot should not be given, because anti-cholinesterase and ergot stimulate contraction of uterus. Similarly, during lactation tetracycline, antihistamines, morphine should be avoided; because these drugs excrete through milk and the baby shall be unnecessarily receive the drugs. Drugs such as morphine, alcohol, anesthetic gases, barbiturates, etc. can move from mother to foetal circulation and can produce toxic effects on foetus. Hence, such drugs must be avoided during pregnancy.

  Therefore, sex and in case of female patients the dose and drug should be carefully selected.
- **Emotional condition:** The dose of a drug depends on the emotional condition of a patient. In case of psychosomatic disorders this is most applicable. Lesser amount of such drugs is more active in female patients; because compared to male females are more emotional. For early recovery even the personality of a doctor can positively influence. This has been observed that patient's faith in mind can influence the therapeutic efficacy of a drug even in smaller dose. For example, in angina pectoris and in bronchial asthma placebo has been to exert therapeutic effect. Thus, 100mg or even 50mg of chlorpromazine can produce tranquilization in females; while to achieve similar effect 500mg to 1000mg of chlorpromazine may be required for schizophrenic patient.
- **Route of administration:** A drug can be administered through various types of routes such as oral, parenteral, nasal, rectal, etc. Based on the severity of the disease and state of the patient a particular dosage form and route are selected. To achieve immediate therapeutic effect a drug can be administered parenterally, may be through intravenous route (i.v). The rate of absorption of a drug depends on the route of administration as shown below;

Rate of absorption: Oral > sub-cutaneous inj. > intramuscular inj. > rectal > intravenous inj.

The amount of drug or dose would decrease accordingly. If the oral dose of a drug is 30 – 150mg, the same effect would be achieved by administering 5 – 10mg of the drug intramuscularly at every 4 hr and 1 – 3mg by intravenously at every 4hr.

- **Disease state:** Sometimes in disease state a patient can tolerate higher doses, while in normal state the same dose appears to be higher. For example, a patient suffering from fever requires more amount of anti-pyretic drug such as paracetamol to reduce body temperature by 4°C, on the other hand lesser amount of drug can reduce the same degree of temperature when given to a person not suffering from fever. Similarly, a patient suffering from severe headache requires more amount tranquilizer to sleep. Most of the drugs are metabolized in liver and excrete primarily through renal route. Thus, a patient having hepatic and renal disturbances if receives normal dose of a drug, the drug will be accumulated in the body due to hindered metabolism and renal excretion. Such situation is dangerous for the patient; it may be fatal unless the dose is properly adjusted.

- **Time of administration:** Some drugs are absorbed rapidly from empty stomach. If these are taken or administered after food, less therapeutic effect shall be achieved. Hence, these drugs should be taken in empty stomach, not after food. Some drugs if taken in empty stomach may irritate the stomach; such drugs should be taken after breakfast or meal. For example, aspirin, chloroquine phosphate, ibuprofen, etc. should be taken after food.

  The patient must be explained properly, when and how the medicine should be taken to get the desired therapeutic effect. For example, a purgative or laxative should be taken in night after dinner. Therefore, the getting the actual therapeutic effect depends on the time of administration of the drug.

- **Environmental conditions:** The intensity of some diseases depends on the environmental condition. Accordingly, the dose of a drug should be determined. For example, the intensity of headache or migraine is more in daytime than in night. Hence the dose of a tranquilizer that gives relief in night may be insufficient in daytime. The effect of CNS depressant is increased by consumption alcohol. Alcohol makes the hepatic enzymes active and metabolizes certain drugs rapidly. As a result, the liver becomes weak and can increase the sensitivity of those drugs. Thus, the dose of a drug depends on the environmental conditions.

- **Accumulation:** Due to slow excretion, improper degradation or very rapid absorption, the drug may be accumulated in the body. Due to such accumulation, the concentration of the drug in the body increases and exerts toxic effect. For example, emetine, heavy metals, etc. are in this category. If a drug is found accumulated in the body, the dose of the drug should be reduced to provide a maintenance dose. Thus, the prescriber should take appropriate precautions to avoid toxicity.
  - Before prescribing the biopharmaceutical, profile should be known and considered.
  - Liver and kidney functions should be ascertained.
  - Discontinuation of the prescribed drug should be after identification of such situation.
  - Correct form of the drug should be selected.
- **Addiction:** Addiction is defined as the ongoing use of mood-altering substances, such as alcohol and drugs, despite adverse consequences. Genetic, psychosocial, and environmental factors influence the development and manifestations of the disease. To the brain, alcoholism and drug addiction are the same. Continuous use of drugs such as opium, alcohol, morphine, pethidine, cocaine, heroin, etc. results addiction. Hence, special precaution should be taken for such drugs.
- **Antagonism:** When the combined effect of two or more drugs is less than the sum of the individual effect of the drugs, the phenomenon is called antagonism. This is observed when a vasoconstrictor (adrenaline) is administered with a vasodilator (acetylcholine), milk of magnesia administered to neutralize acid (in case of acid poisoning), alkaloid administered with activated charcoal.

Synergism: When two drugs are simultaneously administered, the onset and duration of action of one drug may increase due to the presence of another drug. This phenomenon is called synergism and the drugs are called synergists. In other words, there may be two types of observations:

1. When the total effect of two drugs is equal to the sum of their individual effects, it is called *additive effect*: and
2. When the total effect may be more than the sum of their individual effects, this is type of action is called synergistic action or effect.

For example, procaine and adrenaline when administered together, a synergistic effect is observed. Adrenaline increases the therapeutic action of procaine.

- **Idiosyncrasy:** Usually same drug produces same action in all who take it. But sometimes the same drug when administered to different persons, the persons may respond to the drug differently due to their individual reasons. That is, same dose of a drug is given to different persons and abnormal reaction if observed, it is called idiosyncrasy. For example, a small dose of quinine may produce ringing in the ears of some persons; similarly, small amount of aspirin may cause gastric haemorrhage in some patients. The actual reasons for idiosyncrasy although not fully known; however, this has been found genetically that some people either do not have certain enzymes or if they have, they have in lesser amount. As a result, the drugs are differently metabolised in different systems. For example, primaquine causes haemolysis in some people who have the glucose 6-phosphate dihydrogenase (enzyme) in lesser amount. If idiosyncrasy is observed in a patient, the drug must be withdrawn immediately.
- **Tachyphylaxis:** If the cell receptors are blocked continuously, the pharmacological response to a drug is reduced. This happens when a drug is repeatedly taken at smaller intervals. The reduction of pharmacological action to a drug due to administration of the drug at smaller time interval is called Tachyphylaxis. This is a behavioural aspect of a drug. This cannot be reversed even after increasing the dose. The only measure to this situation is that the drug is to be withdrawn for prolonged period of time to make receptors free, and then the actual dose is administered. Drugs such as amphetamine, ephedrine, cocaine, etc show tachyphylaxis.
- **Hypersensitivity:** When defined dose of a drug is administered, it is expected that the drug will produce desired pharmacological action. If the drug shows enhanced pharmacological action leading to toxic effect of the drug, it is called hypersensitivity. It may be alternatively considered as 'allergic' reactions of the drug. Sometimes, a patient may die due to this hypersensitivity. The reason may be the patient or the drug. The symptoms of drug allergies vary from patient to patient and a single drug may produce different reactions in different patients. In general, the allergic symptoms repeat whenever the patient is given the same drug. For this reason, physician either asks the patient whether he/she has taken the drug known to cause allergy in some patients earlier and has suffered from any allergic reaction. Once the physician is satisfied, he/she prescribes the drug. Sometimes the physician recommends 'skin testing' before prescribing.

  For example, some people are hypersensitive to penicillin; if penicillin is administered to such patient skin rash, diarrhoea, etc. may be observed. Hence, before administration a skin test is conducted to know whether the person/patient is hypersensitive to penicillin.

- **Tolerance:** Sometimes due to various reasons the normal dose of a drug fails to produce desired therapeutic action in some patients. To achieve the expected therapeutic effect large dose is required. This is normally due to the development of resistance to the drug. Such situation is called tolerance. Usually tolerance to barbiturates is observed in treatment of epilepsy. Similarly, larger dose of sedative and hypnotic is required to cause desired level of sedation, if the patient is a smoker or is habitual to the drug. Tolerance may be pseudo or true.

Paediatric Dose Calculations

This has been mentioned earlier that there are various factors that affect the dose of a patient; particularly if the patient is a child. The calculation of dose for paediatric patients depends on the age, body weight, and surface area of the patient. The age of the patient should be less than 12 years.

- **Based on age**

  There are four formulas which can be used to calculate the dose of a drug on the basis of age of the child.

  - **Young's Rule**

    $$\text{Dose of child} = \frac{\text{Age in years}}{\text{Age in years} + 12} \times \text{Adult dose}$$

    For example, the age of the child is 6 years and the adult dose is 500mg,

    Then, the dose of the drug would be $\frac{6}{6+12} \times 500 = \frac{3000}{18} = 166.67$ mg

  - **Dilling's Rule**

    $$\text{Dose of child} = \frac{\text{Age in years}}{20\ dl} \times \text{Adult dose}$$

    For example, the age of the child is 6 years and the adult dose is 500mg,

    Then, the dose of the drug would be $\frac{6}{20} \times 500 = \frac{3000}{20} = 150$ mg.

  - **Cowlings Formula**

    $$\text{Dose of child} = \frac{\text{Age in next birthday}}{24} \times \text{Adult dose}$$

For example, the age of the child is 6 years and the adult dose is 500mg,

Then, the dose of the drug would be $\frac{7}{24} \times 500 = \frac{3500}{24} = 145.8$ mg.

➢ **Fried Rule**

$$\text{Dose of child} = \frac{\text{Age in months}}{150} \times \text{Adult dose}$$

For example, the age of the child is 6 years and the adult dose is 500mg,

Then, the dose of the drug would be $\frac{6yr}{150} \times 500 = \frac{6 \times 10}{150} \times 500$

$$= \frac{36000}{150} = 240 \text{ m}$$

The difference among Formula no. first, second and third is not too much; however, the dose calculated by fourth formula is higher. The dose should be within the therapeutic window.

- **Body weight**

➢ **Clark's Formula**

$$\text{Dose of child} = \frac{\text{Wt. in lb (pound)}}{150} \times \text{Adult dose}$$

For example, the age of the child is 70 pounds and the adult dose is 500mg,

Then, the dose of the drug would be $\frac{70}{150} \times 500 = \frac{70}{150} \times 500 = \frac{35000}{150}$

$$= 233.3 \text{ mg}$$

- **Body surface area**

The dose of a drug can be calculated on the basis of surface area of body. Surface area of the body is one of the factors such as metabolic rate, lean body mass (body weight), age and extracellular fluid volume that can influence the dose of a drug. Catzel, P. Had calculated using the following formula;

$$\text{Percentage of adult dose} = \frac{\text{Surface area of child} \times 100}{\text{Surface area of Adult}}$$

Catzel calculated and correlated the percentage of adult dose with the average age, and published the results in tabular form as shown below;

Average Age	% of adult dose	Average Age	% of adult dose	Average Age	% of adult dose	Average Age	% of adult dose
On birth	12.5	1.5 years	30	10 years	60	16 years	90
2 months	15	3 years	33	11 years	70	20 years	100
4 months	20	5 years	40	12 years	75		
1 year	25	7 years	50	14 years	80		

Dose Calculation

There are various rules for conversion of adult dose to child dose. The rules are given below:

Young's Rule: $\text{Child dose} = \dfrac{\text{Age in year}}{\text{Age} + 12} \times \text{Adult dose}$

Fried's Rule: $\text{Child dose} = \dfrac{\text{Age in month} \times \text{Adult dose}}{150}$

Drilling's Rule: $\text{Child dose} = \dfrac{\text{Age in year} \times \text{Adult dose}}{12}$

Clark's Rule: $\text{Child dose} = \dfrac{\text{Weight in lbs} \times \text{Adult dose}}{150}$

$$\text{Child dose} = \frac{\text{Body surface area of child} \times \text{Adult dose}}{\text{Body surface area of adult}}$$

$$\text{Child dose} = \frac{\text{Body surface area of child} \times \text{Adult dose}}{173\text{M}^2}$$

Example 1: The adult dose of paracetamol is 650 mg. Calculate the dose of the drug for a child whose age is 8 yrs using different formulas.

Solution:

According to Drilling's Rule, Child dose

$$= \frac{\text{Age in year} \times \text{Adult dose}}{12} = \frac{8 \times 650 \text{ mg}}{12} = \mathbf{433.33 \text{ mg}}$$

According to Young's Rule, Child dose

$$= \frac{\text{Age in year}}{\text{Age} + 12} \times \text{Adult dose} = \frac{8}{8+12} \times 650\text{mg} = \mathbf{260mg}$$

According to Fried's Rule, Child dose

$$= \frac{\text{Age in month} \times \text{Adult dose}}{150} = \frac{8 \times 12 \times 650\text{mg}}{150} = \mathbf{416\ mg}$$

Example 2: The adult dose of a drug is 500 mg. Calculate the dose of a child whose body wt is 12 kg.

Solution:

According to Clark's Rule, Child dose

$$= \frac{\text{Weight in lbs} \times \text{Adult dose}}{150} = \frac{26.4 \times 500\text{mg}}{150} = \mathbf{88mg}$$

[1kg = 2.2 lbs, 12kg = 12 × 2.2lbs = 26.4lbs]

Exercise

A. Multiple Choice Question Carrying 01 Mark

1. Which of the statements is correct?
   (a) Dose of a drug refers to its therapeutic dose.
   (b) Dose of a drug refers to its prophylactic dose
   (c) Dose of a drug is the maximum amount of a drug that can be administered to an adult patient.
   (d) Dose of a drug is the minimum amount of a drug that can be administered to an adult patient.
2. The dose of a drug depends on
   (a) Accumulation of drug in the body
   (B) Environmental conditions
   (c) Time of administration
   (d) All
3. Which of the following statements is correct for calculation of dose of a drug
   (a) Disease state of a patient influences the posology
   (b) Age of a patient influences the posology
   (c) Body weight of a patient influences the posology
   (d) All

4. Which of the following statement is not true?
   (a) Same drug administered to different persons may show different actions due to individual reasons.
   (b) Same dose of a drug administered to different persons showing different actions- is called idiosyncrasy.
   (c) Idiosyncrasy is not a factor that influences the dose of a drug
   (d) Idiosyncrasy is a factor that influences the dose of a drug
5. Which one of the following does not influence the dose of a drug?
   (a) Addiction (b) Antagonism
   (c) Hypersensitivity (d) None
6. Which of the following method of calculating the dose of a drug is based on body weight of the patient?
   (a) Young's Formula (b) Clark's Formula
   (c) Dilling's Formula (d) Cowling's Formula
7. To prevent accumulation of drug which of the actions is not correct?
   (a) The correct form of the drug should be selected.
   (b) Liver and kidney functions should be ascertained.
   (c) Before prescribing the biopharmaceutical, profile should be known and considered.
   (d) None.
8. Which action is called synergistic?
   (a) When the total effect of two drugs is equal to the sum of their individual effects.
   (b) When the total effect may be more than the sum of their individual effects.
   (c) When the total effect of two drugs is less than the sum of their individual effects.
   (d) When the total effect of three drugs is equal to the sum of their individual effects.
9. Which of following terms deals with the study of dose?
   (a) Physiology (b) Anatomy
   (c) Psychology (d) Posology
10. Which of the following rule is used to calculate the child-dose of a drug?
   (a) Froed's rule (b) Fried's Rule
   (c) Frank's rule (d) Frink's rule

B. Question Carrying 05 Marks

1. Define the term 'Posology'. Write down the effect of age, bodyweight and sex on the dose of a drug.
2. Write down the effect of emotional condition and environmental condition on the dose of a drug.
3. Write down the effect of addiction, antagonism, and synergism on the dose of a drug.
4. Explain the terms idiosyncrasy and tachyphylaxis.
5. What do you understand by the terms tolerance and hypersensitivity.
6. Write down the Young's formula and Dilling's formula used for calculation of dose.

C. Question Carrying 10 Marks

1. Discuss the effect of emotional condition, environmental condition, route of administration and disease state of the patient on the dose of the drug.
2. Discuss the effect of time of administration, accumulation, addiction, antagonism, and synergism on the dose of the drug.
3. Discuss briefly the factors influencing the dose of a drug.

Answers

A. Multiple Choice Questions

1. (a)	**2. (d)**	**3. (d)**	**4. (c)**	**5. (d)**
6. (b)	**7. (d)**	**8. (b)**	**9. (d)**	**10. (b)**

Chapter 5

Pharmaceutical Calculations

Weights and Measures – Imperial & Metric System, Calculations Involving Percentage Solutions, Allegation, Proof Spirit and Isotonic Solutions based on Freezing Point and Molecular Weight.

Introduction

The history says that till seventeenth century the dimensions of the human body had been used to express short distance units. For example, during the Noah's time, *cubit*, and the *length of a man's forearm* or '*the distance from the tip of the elbow to the end of his middle finger*' was used as length of unit. This proved useful because it was readily available and convenient. However, the problem with this type of measurement was that it was not a positive fixed dimension or a standard. The cubit is not presently used as a unit of measurement. But there are other standards that were originated in about the same way. For example, *inch* was originally interpreted as *the width of a thumb* and this has been mentioned in many languages too. Similarly, *foot* was originally expressed as *the length of a man's foot*. The *foot* varied in length. Three times the length of the foot was the distance from the tip of a man's nose to the end of his outstretched arm. This closely approximates what we call the *yard*. The distance across a man's outstretched arms equalled a fathom or two yards (six feet). Half a yard was a cubit 18 inches and half a cubit was called a *span*, the distance across the hand from the tip of the thumb to the tip of the little finger when the fingers were spread out as far as possible.

All these ancient units could not continue because the dimensions of an adult human body vary greatly.

Weights and Measures

'Metrology' is defined as the science of measurement and 'Legal Metrology' is legislatively and administratively accepted technical procedures. It is established by, or by reference to, public authorities in a regulatory or contractual manner. Legal metrology is implemented on behalf of these authorities to specify and to ensure the appropriate quality and credibility of measurements related to official controls, trade, health, safety, and the environment. The components of legal metrology extend from the Units and Systems of Measurement to the National Institute of Standards and Technology (NIST). The standards used by private and public measurement organizations depend on assigned values and uncertainties are determined and maintained through a measurement system with documented traceability to the NIST. Different nations use different systems of measurement, for example, Metric and English Systems of Measurement. The units associated with the United States Customary Weights and Measures as well as the history, definitions, and values of the International System of Units (SI). The Relationship between "Mass" and "Weight" will also be discussed.

Weights

Minimum Weighable Quantity (MWQ)

A balance must be used within a degree of error tolerable for compounding or manufacturing purpose. USP allows a maximum error of 5% in a single operation. Each balance has range of sensitivity. The percent error depends on the amount of substance being weighed and the error increases as the amount being weighed decreases.

$$\text{MWQ} = \frac{\text{Sensitivity} \times 100}{\text{Error in percent}} = \frac{\text{Sensitivity} \times 100}{\text{Error}}$$

Example 1: What is the MWQ of a balance with 5% error and with sensitivity of 10 mg?

***Solution*:** $\text{MWQ} = \dfrac{\text{Sensitivity} \times 100}{\text{Error}} = \dfrac{10 \times 100}{5} = 200 \text{ mg}$

Example 2: What should be the sensitivity of a balance to weigh 1 mg of a substance with 2% error?

***Solution*:** MWQ = 1 mg and Error = 2%

$$\text{MWQ} = \frac{\text{Sensitivity} \times 100}{\text{Error}} \text{ or } 1 \text{ mg} = \frac{\text{Sensitivity} \times 100}{2}$$

$$\text{Sensitivity} = \frac{2 \times 1 \text{ mg}}{100} = 0.02 \text{ mg}$$

Volume

Measurement of Volume

For measuring the volume of a liquid or solution there are different types of measuring devices. Depending on the type of liquid, quantity and accuracy of the measurement a suitable measuring device should be used. For example, a cylinder is used for measuring a solvent with accuracy up to 0.5 ml, a pipette for a reagent solution with accuracy up to 0.05 ml, volumetric flask for preparing a volumetric solution.

Select the capacity of the measuring device as per the volume to be measured. For accurate measurement, view the meniscus of the liquid or solution horizontally.

For example, if the volume of a solvent to be measured is 10 ml or less, use a cylinder of 10 ml.

To measure 1 ml or less amount of a reagent or volumetric solution, use a pipette of 1 ml, but not more 5 ml.

Imperial System

Imperial system, also called as British Imperial or Exchequer Standard of 1825, is the system of units. It was first defined in the British Weights and Measures Act of 1824. This Act was subsequently refined and reduced. The Winchester Standards were in effect during 1588 to 1825. These standards were replaced by Imperial system. This system was then officially used by the British. The system had been used till late 20th century. In late 20th century most of the countries ruled by the British Empire had officially adopted the Metric system for measurement; but in the United Kingdom, Canada and in other countries some of the imperial units were still in use.

The **Imperial system** is one of the many systems of English or Foot-pound-second units, first defined in the British Weights and Measures Act of 1824. Although most of the units were defined in more than one system, some subsidiary units were used to a much greater extent for different purposes. One of these systems was the US customary system derived from the British units. Units of length and area had been mostly shared between the Imperial and US customary systems. Capacity measures differed mostly due to the introduction of the imperial gallon and the unification of wet and dry measures.

The imperial system was divided into two systems

- Avoirdupois system
- Apothecary system

Avoirdupois System

It is thought that the avoirdupois weight system had come into use in England circa 1300. It was originally used for weighing wool. In the early 14th century several other specialized weight systems were used, including the weight system of the Hanseatic League. According to this system 1 pound was equal to 16 ounces and 7200 grains, 1 mark was equal to 8 ounces. But, for coinage and for everyday use, the main weight system had been used. As per late 16th century, the systems had been used was the avoirdupois system and as per that system the weight unit was pound which was alternatively called as wool pound or, the avoirdupois wool pound. This pound has been known as the today's international pound.

Apothecary System

This is a historical system of mass and volume. **Apothecaries' system** or **apothecaries' weights and measures** were used by the physicians, apothecaries and sometimes by the scientists for preparation of medicaments. The English version of the system is closely related to the English troy system of weights, the definition of pound and grain were being exactly the same in both. It divides a pound into 12 ounces, an ounce into 8 drachms, and one drachm into 3 scruples or 60 grains. The exact system had been extensively used in the United Kingdom. As a result, in some of its former colonies it had been used till the 20th century. The apothecaries' system of measures is a similar system of volume units based on the fluid ounce. For a long time, medical recipes were written in Latin using special symbols to denote weights and measures.

For example, the avoirdupois system was applied only to weights. Later in 1959 some systems were outlawed, and both the US and British yard was defined identically to be 0.9144metres, to match the International yard. The three weight systems are given below.

Weight		**Apothecary Weight**					**Troy Weight**	
		Pound	1				Pound	1
		Ounces	12	1			Ounces	12
1		Drams	96	8	1		Pennyweights	240
20	1	Scruples	288	24	3	1	Grains	5760
480	24	Grains	5760	480	60	20		

Avoirdupois weight

Ton(t)	1						
Hundred weight (cwt)	20	1					
Quarter	80	4	1				
Stone(st)	160	8	2	1			
Pound(lb)	2240	112	28	14	1		
Ounce (oz)	35840	1792	448	224	16	1	
Drachm	573440	28672	7168	3584	256	16	1
Grain	15680000	784000	196000	98000	7000	437.5	27.34

Note: Troy weight, used for precious metals,
Avoirdupois weight, used for most other purposes,
Apothecaries' weight not used because of metric system is in use.

Length:

Units					
League	1				
Mile	3	1			
Furlong	24	8	1		
Yard	5280	1760	220	1	
Foot	15840	5280	660	3	1
Inch	190080	63360	7920	36	12

Maritime units

Nautical mile	1		
Cable	10	1	
Fathom	600	100	1
Foot	6000	600	6 (6.08)

Gunter's survey units

Chain	1		
Pole	4	1	
Foot	66	16.5	1
Link	100	25	1.5151

Area:

Units	In terms of length units	Square miles	Square rods	Square feet	hectare
Perch	1 rod × 1 rod	$\frac{1}{10240}$	1	272.25	0.002529
Rod	1 furlong × 1 rod	$\frac{1}{2560}$	40	10890	0.1012
Acre	1 furlong × 1 chain	$\frac{1}{640}$	160	43560	0.4047

Volume:

Unit	Ounce		Pint		Cubic inch
	Imperial	US	Imperial	US	
Fluid ounce (fl oz)	1	0.96076	$\frac{1}{20}$	0.060047	1.7339
Gill	5	4.8038	$\frac{1}{4}$	0.30024	8.6694
Pint (pt)	20	19.215	1	1.2009	34.677
Quart (qt)	40	38.430	2	2.4019	69.355
Gallon (gal)	160	153.72	8	9.6076	272.42

After completion of legal transition, the use of SI units has become mandated by law for the retail sale of food and other commodities in UK since 1995. However, some people in UK are still using the imperial units.

Example 3: A person can walk 3 miles per hour. If he has walked for 3.5 hr how far he has gone? Express the distance in miles, furlong and in feet.

***Solution*:** Given that in 1hr the person walks 3miles

$$\text{In 3.5hr he walks } \frac{3 \text{ miles} \times 3.5\text{hr}}{1\text{hr}} = 10.5\text{miles}$$

$$1\text{mile} = 24\text{furlong} = 1760\text{yards} = 1760 \times 3 \text{ ft} = 5280\text{ft}$$

$$\text{Hence, } 10.5\text{miles} = \frac{24 \text{ furlong} \times 10.5 \text{ miles}}{1 \text{ mile}} = 252\text{furlong}$$

$$= \frac{5280 \text{ ft} \times 10.5 \text{ miles}}{1 \text{ mile}} = 55\ 440\text{ft}$$

Hence the person has moved a distance of **10.5miles or 525furlong or 55440ft**.

Example 4: The capacity of a vessel is to hold 250gal of water, if 1/4th of its capacity is filled by a liquid how many gallons of the liquid are filled? Express the volume of liquid in imperial pint and in US ounce.

Solution: Given that the capacity of the vessel is 250gal and

$$1/4^{th} \text{ of its capacity} = \frac{1}{4} \times 250\text{gal} = 62.5\text{gal of liquid it is holding}$$

$$1\text{gal} = 153.72 \text{ US oz} = 8 \text{ pint (imperial)}$$

$$\text{So, } 62.5\text{gal} = \frac{153.72 \text{ US0z} \times 62.5 \text{ gal}}{1 \text{ gal}} = 9607.5\text{oz (US)}$$

$$= \frac{8 \text{ pint (imperial)} \times 62.5 \text{ gal}}{1 \text{ gal}} = 500\text{pint}$$

Hence the vessel contains **62.5gal** or **9607.5 oz (US)** or **1250 pint (imperial)** of liquid

Metric System

During the French Revolution in 1790's, the metric system was designed and considered the conflicts and confusions in traditional systems of weights and measures being used in Europe. Before introduction of the metric system, it was common for units of length, area, and weight which vary from one country to another and even from one region to another within the same country. Merchants, scientists, and educated people throughout Europe realized that a uniform system was needed, but it was only in the climate of a complete political upheaval that such a radical change could actually be considered.

The metric units were defined in an elegant way unlike any traditional units of measure. The Earth itself was selected as the measuring stick. The meter was defined to be one ten-millionth of the distance from the Equator to the North Pole. The litre was to be the volume of one cubic decimetre, and the kilogram was to be the weight of a litre of pure water. It did not turn out quite like this, because the scientific methods of the time were not quite up to the task of measuring these quantities precisely, but the actual metric units come very close to the design. The metric system was first proposed in 1791. It was adopted by the French revolutionary assembly in 1795, and the first metric standards (a standard meter bar and kilogram bar) were adopted in 1799. There was considerable resistance to the system at first, and its use was not made compulsory in France until 1837. The first countries to actually require use of the metric system were Belgium, the Netherlands, and Luxembourg in 1820.

Around 1850 a strong movement began among scientists, engineers, and businessmen in favor of an international system of weights and measures. The scientific and technical revolution was well underway, and a global economy was developing. The need for uniformity in measurement was becoming obvious. Furthermore, the metric system was the only real choice available. The only possible competitor, the British Imperial System, was so closely tied to the British Empire it was not even acceptable to the Americans, let alone to non-English speakers. Between 1850 and 1900 the metric system made rapid progress. It was adopted throughout Europe (except in Britain), in Latin America, and in many countries elsewhere. It became firmly established as a key part of the language of science.

In the 1870's, the French made a key decision to turn control of the system over to an international body. In 1875, most of the leading industrialized countries (including the United States, but not Britain) signed the Treaty of the Meter. The treaty established the International Bureau of Weights and Measures*, which has presided ever since over what we now call the International System of Units. It also provided for distribution of copies of the metric standards throughout the world and for continuing consultation and periodic revision and improvement of the system through regular meetings of a General Conference of Weights and Measures. The 21st General Conference met in October 1999.

Most commonly used units as per metric system are:

Weight Unit	Value	Length Unit	Value	Volume Unit	Value
Exagram	10^{18} gram	Exametre	10^{18} metre	Exalitre	10^{18} litre
Petagram	10^{15} gram	Petametre	10^{15} metre	Petalitre	10^{15} litre
Teragram	10^{12} gram	Terametre	10^{12} metre	Teralitre	10^{12} litre
Gigagram	10^{9} gram	Gigametre	10^{9} metre	Gigalitre	10^{9} litre
Megagram	10^{6} gram	Megametre	10^{6} metre	Megalitre	10^{6} litre
Kilogram	10^{3} gram	Kilometre	10^{3} metre	Kilolitre	10^{3} litre
Hectogram	10^{2} gram	Hectometre	10^{2} metre	Hectolitre	
Decagram	10^{1} gram	Decametre	10^{1} metre	Decalitre	10^{1} litre
Gram		Metre		Litre	
Decigram	10^{-1} gram	Decimetre	10^{-1} metre	Decilitre	10^{-1} litre
Centigram	10^{-2} gram	Centimetre	10^{-2} metre	Centilitre	10^{-2} litre
Milligram	10^{-3} gram	Millimetre	10^{-3} metre	Millilitre	10^{-3} litre
Microgram	10^{-6} gram	Micrometre	10^{-6} metre	Microlitre	10^{-6} litre
Nanogram	10^{-9} gram	Nanometre	10^{-9} metre	Nanolitre	10^{-9} litre
Pictogram	10^{-12} gram	Picometre	10^{-12} metre	Picolitre	10^{-12} litre
Femtogram	10^{-15} gram	Femtometre	10^{-15} metre	Femtolitre	10^{-15} litre
Attogram	10^{-18} gram	Attometre	10^{-18} metre	Attolitre	10^{-18} litre

Centimetre-gram-second systems (CGS), Metre-kilogram-second system (MKS) and Metre-tonne-second system (MTS) are the three systems commonly used in metric systems.

However, millimetre-Newton-second system is used in simulation of mechanical systems.

Conversions of weights and measures:

Length	Volume	Weight
1 metre = 39.4 inches	1 fluidounce = 29.6 ml	1 pound avoir = 454 g
1 metre = 3.283 ft	1 pint = 473 ml	1 pound apothecary = 373 g
1 inch = 2.54 cm	1 gallon = 3.79 lt	1 gram = 15.4 grains
	= 4 Quarts = 8 Pints	1 grain = 64.8 mg
	1 Quart = 960 cc = 2 Pints	1 kg = 2.2 lbs
	1 Pint = 480 cc = 16 OZ	1lb = 456 g
	1 OZ = 30 cc	
	1 Teaspoonful = 5 cc	
	1 Wineglassful = 60 cc	
	1 Teacupful = 120 cc	
	1 Tumblerful = 240 cc	

Example 5: A plot of 2 acres measuring 1 furlong by 2 chains is surrounded by a boundary wall. If the cost of making the boundary wall is Rs.200 per sq metre, find out the total cost.

Solution: 1 ac = 1 furlong × 1 chain

= 660 ft × 66 ft [1 furlong = 660ft, 1 chain = 66ft]

= [660× 0.3046 metre] × [66 × 0.3046metre]

= 201.036 metre × 20.1036 [1 metre = 3.283 ft]

= 4041.55sqmt

Given that the cost of construction per 1 sq mt = Rs. 200.00

Hence, for 4041.55 sqm the cost would be $\frac{4041.55 \text{ sqm} \times \text{Rs. } 200.00}{1 \text{ sqm}}$ =

Rs. 808310.00

Thus, the total cost of construction would be **Rs.808310.00**

Calculations Involving Percentage Concentration of Solutions

Percentage concentrations are expressed as follows:

- Percent weight by weight **(%w/w)** is the number of g per 100 g.
- Percent weight by volume **(%w/v)** is the number of g per 100 ml.
- Percent volume by volume **(%v/v)** is the number of ml per 100 ml.
- Percent volume by weight **(%v/w)** is the number of ml per 100 g.

Example 6: A solution contains 10.0 mg of Ephedrine HCl per 5 ml; express the concentration in %w/v.

***Solution*:** Given that each 5ml solution contains 10.0mg of Ephedrine HCl

100 ml of solution contains $\frac{10.0 \text{ mg} \times 100 \text{ ml}}{5 \text{ ml}} = 200\text{mg} = \frac{200 \text{ mg}}{1000} = 0.2\text{g}$

[1g = 1000mg]

So, the concentration of the solution is **0.2%w/v**

Example 7: Each tablet weighing 405mg contains 325mg of Aspirin. Express the amount of Aspirin present in the tablet in %w/w.

***Solution*:** 405mg of tablet contains 325mg of Aspirin

100 mg of tablet contains $\frac{325 \text{ mg} \times 100 \text{ mg}}{405 \text{ mg}} = 80.25\text{mg}$

So, Aspirin content of the tablet is **80.25%w/w**

Example 8: To prepare 500lts of 7.5%w/v glycerine solution how many litres of glycerine would be required? Specific gravity of glycerine is 1.283 at 25°C.

Solution: 7.5%w/v solution of glycerine contains 7.5g in 100ml of its solution.

To make 500 L $\frac{7.5\text{ g} \times 500 \times 1000\text{ ml}}{100\text{ ml}}$ = 37500g of glycerin would be required

Specific gravity of glycerine is 1.283 means; 1ml of glycerine weighs 1.283g

37500g of glycerine measure $\frac{37500\text{ g}}{1.283\text{ g/ml}} = 29228.4\text{ml} = \frac{29228.4\text{ ml}}{1000} =$ 29.23lts.

So, 29.23lts of glycerine would be required.

Example 9: A bottle contains 450ml of 2M solution of sulphuric acid, express the concentration in terms of percentage concentration (%v/v). Density of sulphuric acid is 1.184g/ml at 25°C.

Solution: 1M solution of sulphuric acid contains 98g of sulphuric acid in 1000ml.

2M solution of sulphuric acid contains 2×98g = 196g of sulphuric acid in 1000ml.

450ml of 2M solution of sulphuric acid contains $\frac{196\text{ g} \times 450\text{ ml}}{1000\text{ ml}}$ = 88.2g of sulphuric acid.

100ml of 2M solution of sulphuric acid contains $\frac{88.2\text{ g} \times 100\text{ ml}}{450\text{ ml}}$ = 19.6g

Density of sulphuric acid is 1.184g/ml at 25°C.

That is, 1.184g of sulphuric acid weighs measures 1ml

So, 19.6g of sulphuric acid measure $\frac{19.6\text{ g} \times 1\text{ ml}}{1.184\text{ g}}$ = 16.55ml

Thus, 450 ml of 2M sulphuric acid is equivalent to **16.55%v/v** solution.

Example 10: To prepare 150ml of 10%w/v solution of sulphuric acid how much volume (ml) of concentrated sulphuric acid would be taken? Density of sulphuric acid is 1.184g/ml at 25°C.

***Solution*:** 10% w/v solution means 10g of sulphuric acid in 100ml of solution.

For 150ml solution $\frac{10 \times 150}{100\ g}$ = 15g of sulphuric acid would be required.

Density of sulphuric acid is 1.184g/ml at 25°C means that

1.184g of concentrated sulphuric acid measure 1ml

So, 15g of concentrated sulphuric acid measure $\frac{1\ ml \times 15\ ml}{1.184\ g}$ = 12.67ml

Hence to prepare 150ml of 10%w/v solution of sulphuric acid **12.67ml** of sulphuric acid would be required.

Example 11: To prepare 2.0L of 20% w/v solution of sodium hydroxide how many grams of sodium hydroxide to be taken whose purity is 97.89%w/w?

***Solution*:** 20% w/v solution of sodium hydroxide means 20g of sodium hydroxide having purity of 100%w/v should be present in 100ml of its solution.

To prepare 2.0L of 20%w/v solution $\frac{20\ g \times 2000\ ml}{100\ ml}$ = 400g of sodium hydroxide would be required

Purity of sodium hydroxide available is 97.89%w/w

That is, 97.89g of 100%w/w sodium hydroxide is present in 100g of available sodium hydroxide

So, 400g of available sodium hydroxide is present in $\frac{100\ g \times 400\ g}{97.89\ g}$ = 408.62g

Hence, to prepare 2.0lts of 20% w/v solution **408.62g** of sodium hydroxide would be required.

Example 12: To prepare 250 ml of 5% of calcium chloride solution how many grams of calcium chloride dihydrate to be taken? Molecular weights of calcium chloride ($CaCl_2$) and calcium chloride dihydrate ($CaCl_2, 2H_2O$) are 110.98 and 146.98 respectively.

***Solution*:** 5% solution of calcium chloride contains 5g of calcium chloride in 100ml of solution,

For 250ml solution $\frac{5\text{ g} \times 250\text{ ml}}{100\text{ ml}}$ = 12.5g of calcium chloride would be required

Mol. Wt of calcium chloride is 110.98 and that of calcium chloride dehydrate is 146.98, this means that 110.98g of calcium chloride is equivalent to 146.98g of calcium chloride dehydrate

So, 12.5g of calcium chloride is equivalent to $\frac{12.5\text{ g} \times 146.98\text{ g}}{110.98\text{ g}} = 16.55\text{g}$ of $CaCl_2, 2H_2O$

Thus, to prepare 250 ml of 5% of calcium chloride solution **16.55g** of $CaCl_2, 2H_2O$ would be required.

Example 13: In 45 g of a mixture, 9 g of talcum and 36 g of starch are present. Express the % concentration of talcum and starch in the mixture.

***Solution*:** 9g Talcum is present in 45g of the mixture

In terms of ratio strength: $\frac{9\text{g}}{45\text{g}}$ or 1:5

In terms of % w/w: $\frac{9 \times 100}{45} = 20$

Thus, the mixture contains 20%w/w of talcum or at a ratio of 1:5.

Similarly, 36g of starch is present in 45g of mixture

In terms of ratio strength: $\frac{36\text{g}}{45\text{g}}$ or 4:5

In terms of % w/w: $\frac{36 \times 100}{45} = 80$

Thus, the mixture contains 80%w/w of starch or at a ratio of 4:5.

Example 14: How many grams of sodium hydroxide would be required to prepare 75 ml of 12.5% w/v solution?

***Solution*:** 12.5% w/v solution means,

In 100ml solution, sodium hydroxide is present 12.5 g

In 75ml of 12.5% solution sodium hydroxide required to make 75ml =

$$\frac{75 \times 12.5}{100} = 9.375g$$

Hence, to prepare 75ml of 12.5%w/v solution of sodium hydroxide **9.375g** of sodium hydroxide would be required.

Example 15: In 80 ml of a solution 55 g of sucrose is present; express the concentration in terms of percentage.

***Solution*:** 100ml of the solution contains $\frac{55 \times 100}{80}$ g = 68.75g of sucrose

Hence, the concentration of the sucrose solution is **68.75%w/v**.

Example 16: The composition of 100 ml of a tincture is given below:

Extract of crude drug	2 g
Alcohol (70%)	65 ml
Purified water	35 ml

Find out the concentration (%v/v) of alcohol IP in the preparation.

***Solution*:** As per IP the concentration of alcohol is 95% v/v.

As per composition, 65 ml of the alcohol (70%) is present in the tincture.

The volume of alcohol (95%) in 65 ml = $\frac{65 \times 70}{95}$ = 47.89ml.

Hence, the tincture contains 47.89ml of Alcohol IP.

Example 17: In 100mg of Calcium Carbonate Powder, Compound 37.5mg of calcium carbonate and 12.5 mg of magnesium carbonate, heavy are present along with kaolin and sodium bicarbonate. Express the % concentration of calcium carbonate and magnesium carbonate in the mixture.

***Solution*:** 37.5mg calcium carbonate is present in 100mg of the mixture

In terms of ratio strength: $\frac{37.5 \text{ mg}}{100 \text{ mg}}$ or 1:0.375

In terms of % w/w: $\frac{37.5 \times 100}{100} = 37.5$

Thus, the mixture contains 37.5%w/w of calcium carbonate or at a ratio of 1:0.375.

Similarly, 12.5mg of magnesium carbonate is present in 100mg of mixture

In terms of ratio strength: $\frac{12.5 \text{ mg}}{100 \text{ mg}}$ or 1:0.125

In terms of % w/w: $\frac{12.5 \times 100}{45} = 12.5$

Thus, the mixture contains 12.5%w/w of magnesium carbonate or at a ratio of 1:0.125.

Example 18: As per label each tablet contains Paracetamol IP (100%) 500mg. Average weight of the tablets is 635mg. Since the Paracetamol bought is 98.25%; how much amount of Paracetamol should be present in each tablet?

Solution: As per label each tablet contains 500mg of 100% purity

Purity of given Paracetamol is 98.25%

Hence, the amount of Paracetamol to be present in each tablet =

$$\frac{500 \text{ mg} \times 100\%}{98.25\%} = 508.9\text{mg}$$

Method of Allegation

Example 19: At which proportion 20% alcohol is to be mixed with 50% alcohol to make 40% ?

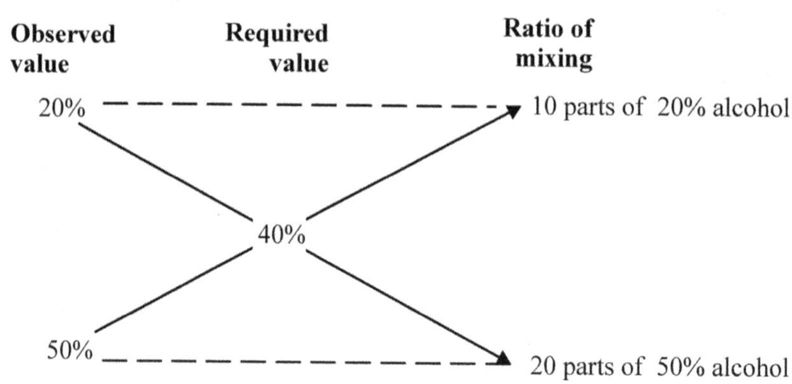

Solution:

Thus, 40% alcohol can be prepared by mixing 10 parts of 20% alcohol and 20 parts of 50% alcohol.

Example 20: For a preparation, 10 ml of a surfactant with HLB value 9 is required. Prepare a mixture of surfactants with HLB values of 8 and 12 to get required HLB for use?

Solution:

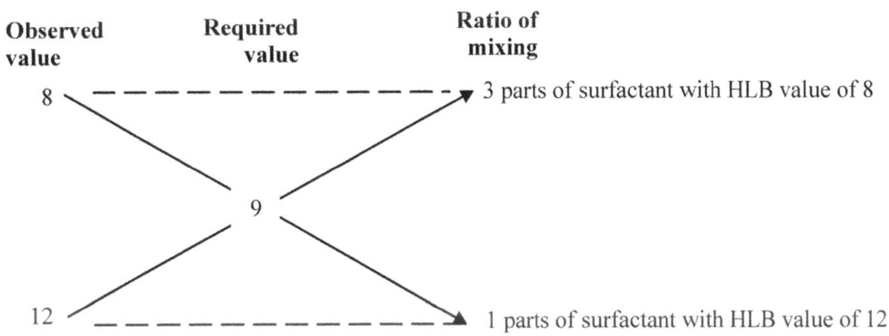

Hence, the two surfactants having HLB values 8 and 12 respectively can be mixed at a ratio of 3:1 to prepare 4 parts of mixture.

To prepare 10ml of the mixture, $\frac{3\text{ ml}\times 10\text{ ml}}{4\text{ ml}}$ = 7.5ml of the surfactant of HLB value of 8 to be mixed with $\frac{1\text{ ml}\times 10\text{ ml}}{4\text{ ml}}$ = 2.5ml of the surfactant of HLB value of 12.

Example 21: A solution is prepared by mixing 70% of sorbitol liquid with water to prepare a mixture containing 45% of sorbitol liquid. Find out the proportion of mixing. How many lts of sorbitol would be required prepare 100lts of 45% sorbitol solution?

Solution:

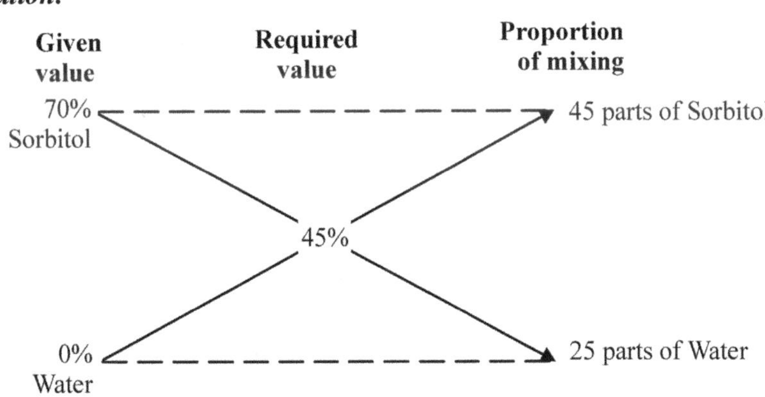

Thus, the proportion of mixing of sorbitol liquid and water would be **45:25 or 9:5**

To prepare 5L of 45% solution of sorbitol, 9L of sorbitol liquid (70%) is to be mixed with 5L of water.

Thus, to prepare 100L of 45% solution of sorbitol $\frac{3 \times 100}{5}$ L = 64.3L of sorbitol would be required.

Example 22: Three paracetamol granules A, B and C having different drug contents recovered during production of three lots are 77%, 74% and 72% respectively. Find out at which proportion these should be mixed to get 75% drug content

Solution:

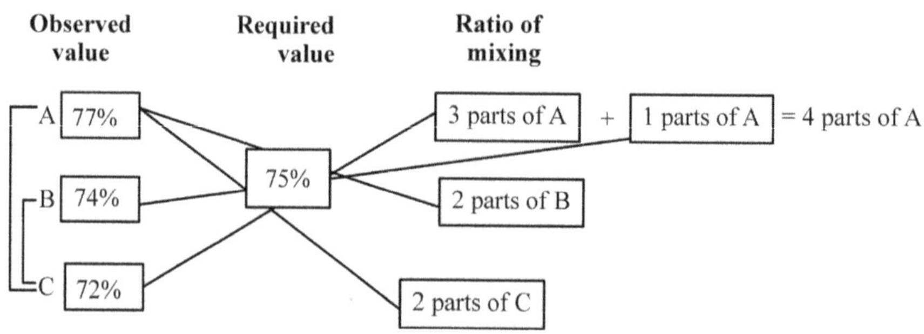

Thus, the proportion of mixing of A:B:C is **4:2:2** or 2:1:1 should be done to prepare a mixture of 75% drug content.

Example 23: The alcohol content of a mixture is 20%. The mixture is prepared by mixing 10%, 30% and 50% alcohol. Find out the ratio of mixing.

Solution:

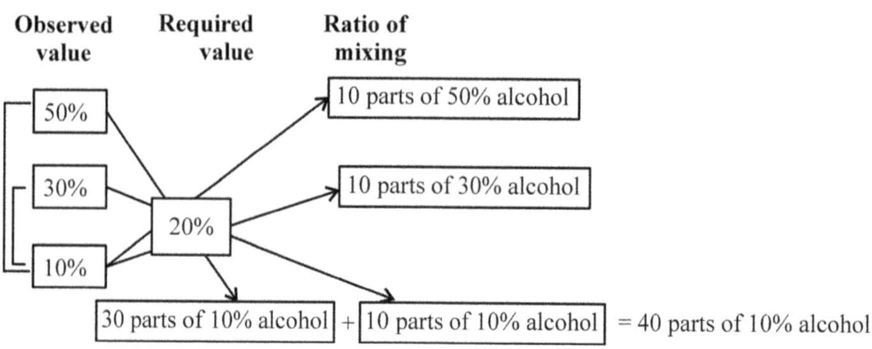

Example 24: Four lots of granules A, B, C, and D having drug content 70.4%, 68.0%, 65.5% and 63.0% respectively are mixed to prepare granules having drug content of 69.2%. Find out the proportion of mixing the granules.

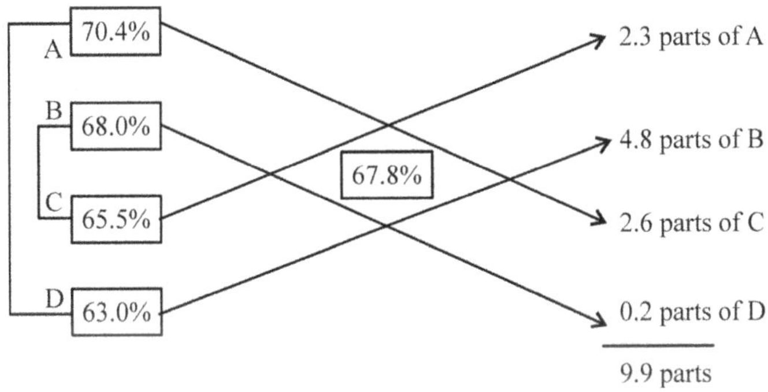

Solution:

Thus, 2.3 parts of A, 4.8 parts of B, 2.6 parts of C and 0.2 parts of D, are to be mixed to produce 9.9 parts of mixture having drug content of 67.8%.

Note: The required value should be placed in between two observed values nearest to the required value to calculate by the method of allegation.

Proof Spirit

In Bonded laboratory (where alcoholic preparations are manufactured under the License of Excise Dept.) the alcohol is called as *spirit*.

The strength or concentration of alcohol is expressed as *Proof degrees* (°). Receipt, Issue and Duty (Tax) are calculated accordingly.

In USA, 100 proof spirit is equivalent 50% v/v or 42.49% w/w of ethyl alcohol (C_2H_5OH) having specific gravity of 0.93426 at 60°F (15.56°C). Thus, 2 proof degree equals to 1% (by volume).

In India, 57.1 volumes of C_2H_5OH (99.8%v/v) is equal to 100 volumes of proof spirit.

That is, 57.1 % v/v of ethyl alcohol is equal to 100° proof.

So, 1volume of 57.1% ethyl alcohol = $\frac{100}{57.1}$ = 1.7513 volume proof spirit.

Or, 1% ethyl alcohol = 1.7513° proof

The Proof strength is expressed in two ways:

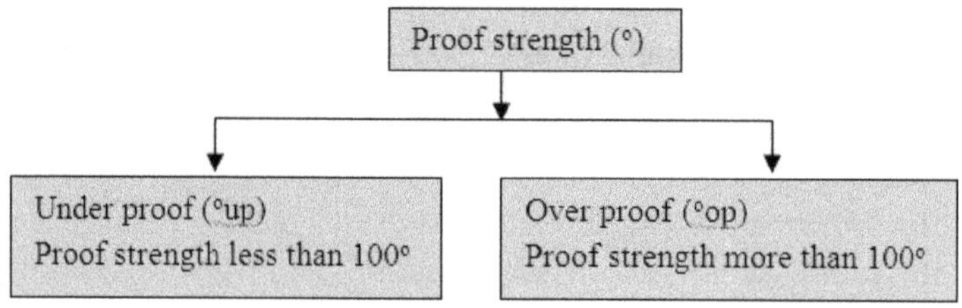

Example 25: What shall be the proof strength (°proof) of 80% v/v and 20% v/v ethyl alcohol?

Solution: 1% of ethyl alcohol = 1.7513° proof

80% of alcohol = 80 × 1.7513 = 140.14° proof, which is more than 100 by 40.14° proof.

So, 80% alcohol is **40.14 ° op.**

Similarly, 20% v/v alcohol = 20 × 1.7513 = 35.03° proof, which is less than 100 by 64.97° proof (100 – 35.03 = 64.97)

So, 20% alcohol is **64.97° up.**

Example 26: Convert 25° up and 30° op into % v/v ethyl alcohol.

Solution: 1% ethyl alcohol = 1.7513° proof

Or 1.753° proof = 1% ethyl alcohol, that is $1^\circ \text{ proof} = \dfrac{1}{1.7513}\% \text{ v/v}$

25° up = 100 – 25 (as it is under proof) = 75° proof

$$75^\circ \text{ proof} = 75 \times \frac{1}{1.7513}\% = 42.82\%\text{v/v}$$

$$130^\circ \text{ proof} = 130 \times \frac{1}{1.7513}\% = 74.23\%\text{v/v}$$

Example 27: A vitamin B-complex preparation contains 10%v/v of ethyl alcohol. Express the alcohol content in terms of proof strength.

Solution: 1% ethyl alcohol is 1.7513° proof

So, 10% ethyl alcohol would be 1.7513 × 10 = 17.51 ° proof

This is less than 100 by (100 – 17.51 = 82.49) 82.49 ° proof.

Thus, the alcohol content of the vitamin B-complex preparation should be expressed as **82.49° up.**

Example 28: As per the label-claim the ethyl alcohol content in the product is 55° up. Calculate the alcohol content in terms of %age by volume.

Solution: 1% ethyl alcohol = 1.7513° proof

Or 1.753° proof = 1% ethyl alcohol, that is $1^\circ \text{ proof} = \frac{1}{1.7513}\% \text{ v/v}$

55° up = 100 – 55 (as it is under proof) = 45° proof

$$45^\circ \text{ proof} = 45 \times \frac{1}{1.7513}\% = 25.69\%\text{v/v}$$

Example 29: A product contains alcohol 55° up. To manufacture 3000lts of the product how many litres of alcohol 97.5% would be required?

Solution: 1% ethyl alcohol = 1.7513° proof

Or 1.753° proof = 1% ethyl alcohol, that is $1^\circ \text{ proof} = \frac{1}{1.7513}\% \text{ v/v}$

55° up = 100 – 55 (as it is under proof) = 45° proof

$$45^\circ \text{ proof} = 45 \times \frac{1}{1.7513}\% = 25.69\%\text{v/v}$$

Total volume of product to be prepared = 3000L

$$\text{So, the volume of alcohol 99.8\% required} = \frac{25.69 \times 3000}{100} = 770.85 \text{ lts}$$

770.85L of 99.8% alcohol would be required.

Say, this is equivalent to x L of 97.5% alcohol,

$$\text{Then, } x = \frac{770.85 \text{ lts} \times 99.8\%}{97.5\%} = 789.03 \text{ lts}$$

So, 789.03L of 97.5% alcohol would be required to prepare 3000L of the product.

Adjustment of Tonicity

When osmotic pressures of two solutions are same, the solutions are called iso-osmotic or isotonic to each other. Osmocity or tonicity of a solution is primarily important when it is intended for intravenous injection. Blood and lacrimal fluid have certain osmotic pressure. Any solution which is mixed with these body fluids should have same osmotic pressure to maintain tonicity. These solutions are called as isotonic solution. On the basis of osmotic pressure, the solutions can be classified into two categories – hypertonic and hypotonic. If the solution is not isotonic to body fluids the tissues may either swell or contract. Solution having osmotic pressure more than that of body fluid is called *hypertonic* solution. If red blood cells of the body are put in a hypertonic solution the cells will *shrink* and become wrinkled or crenated. On the other hand, solution having osmotic pressure less than that of body fluid is called *hypotonic* solution. If red blood cells of the body are put in a hypotonic solution the cells will swell and burst. This will liberate haemoglobin and cause *hemolysis* of the cells. Thus, isotonic solutions must have same osmotic pressure with respect to a particular membrane. If the cells are immersed in a solution containing 0.9g of sodium chloride in 100ml of solution, it is isotonic to body fluids; the cells do not undergo any change. Therefore, 0.9% solution of sodium chloride in water is isotonic to body fluids or living membranes.

The tonicity can be measured by one of the two methods –

1. Haemolytic method based on the effect of various solutions of the drug on the appearance of red blood cells immersed in the solution.
2. Measuring colligative property of the solution. For example, a solution is kept in thermally insulated chamber at constant temperature and measurement of slight difference of temperature due to difference in vapour pressure or by measuring the depression of freezing point of the solution.

There are four methods:

1. Freezing point depression method
2. Sodium chloride equivalence method
3. Molecular concentration method
4. Graphical method utilizing vapor pressure and freezing point data.

The working formulas:

A. When there is no other substance to adjust tonicity, the amount of the substance to be calculated as;

$$\text{The amount required} = \frac{0.52}{x}$$

Where, x is the freezing point depression of 1% solution of the substance.

B. When another substance is required to adjust the tonicity of a solution containing one ingredient,

$$\text{The amount of adjusting substance required} = \frac{0.52 - \text{a}}{\text{b}}$$

Where, a = Freezing point depression of 1% solution of the ingredient, b = Freezing point depression of 1% solution of the adjusting substance.

C. When another substance is required to adjust the tonicity of a solution containing more than one ingredient,

The amount of adjusting substance required = $\frac{0.52 - a}{b}$

Where, a = Sum of freezing point depression of 1% solution of all the ingredients,

c = Sum of concentration of all the ingredients, and

b = Freezing point depression of 1% solution of the adjusting substance

Isotonic Solutions based on Molecular Weight

According to the colligative properties, one gram molecule of a nonionizing solute dissolved in 22.4 litres of water will have osmotic pressure of 1 atm at normal pressure and temperature. In other words, one molar solution of a non-ionizing solute will have osmotic pressure of 22.4 atm.

The osmotic pressure of blood plasma and tear fluids is approximately 6.7 atm.

Or, the concentration of these fluids will be $\frac{6.7}{22.4} = 0.299$ or, 0.3M (approx).

So, 0.3M solution of any non-ionizing solute will be iso-osmotic with body fluids.

For non-ionizing solute the amount required per L = 0.3 × Mol wt.

While for ionizing solute, the amount to be required per litre =

$$\frac{0.3 \times \text{Mol wt}}{\text{Nos. of ions produced per molecule}} = \frac{0.3\text{M}}{\text{N}}$$

Example 30: At which concentrations (%w/v) solutions of dextrose anhydrous would be isotonic with blood plasma? (*Use molar concentration method*)

Solution:

The molecular weight of dextrose anhydrous = 180

Since, this is a non-ionizing solute, the required amount of dextrose anhydrous per litre = 180 × 0.3 = 54 g, or, 5.4 g per 100 ml (5.4% w/v or 5% approx.)

Example 31: At which concentrations (% w/v) the solutions of sodium chloride and calcium chloride would be isotonic with blood plasma? *(Use molar concentration method)*

Solution:

Mol wt of sodium chloride is 58.5 and that of calcium chloride (dehydrate) is 147.

Both of them ionize in water as follows:

$NaCl = Na^{+} + Cl^{-}$, the no. of ions are 2

$CaCl_2 = Ca^{2+} + 2Cl^{-}$, the no. of ions are 3

Hence, the amount of sodium chloride required per litre to make the sol

$$\text{iso-osmotic} = \frac{58.5 \times 0.3}{2} \text{ g/L} = 8.775 \text{ g/L or } 9 \text{ g/L},$$

That is, 0.9g per 100ml, or 0.9 % w/v.

Similarly, the amount of calcium chloride required per Lt to make the solution iso-osmotic

$$= \frac{147 \times 0.3}{3} \text{ g/L} = 14.7\text{g/L or, } 15\text{g/L}$$

That is, 1.5g per 100ml, or 1.5 % w/v.

Isotonic Solutions based on Freezing Point

Freezing point depression method

The blood plasma and tears freeze at -52°C. In other words, the dissolved substances of these fluids can depress the freezing point of pure water by 0.52°C. So, *any solution that can depress the freezing point of pure water by 52°C will have the same osmotic pressure as blood plasma or tears, and thus, will be isotonic to blood plasma or tear fluids* and it is considered that an iso-osmotic solution will be isotonic also. All hypotonic solutions will have higher freezing points. So, to adjust the tonicity of the preparation an adjusting substance is to be added to the solution.

Example 32: What concentration of morphine hydrochloride would be iso-osmotic with blood plasma?

Solution:

The freezing point depression produced by 1% solution of morphine hydrochloride is 0.086°C.

So, the percentage concentration (% w/v) of morphine hydrochloride = $\frac{0.52}{0.086} = 6.046$.

Thus, 6.05% w/v solution of morphine hydrochloride will be iso-osmotic to blood plasma.

Example 33: What concentration of sodium chloride would be iso-osmotic with blood plasma?

Solution:

The freezing point depression by 1% solution of sodium chloride is 0.576°C.

So, the percentage concentration (% w/v) of sodium chloride to be required $\frac{0.52}{0.576} = 0.902$

Thus, 0.9% w/v solution of sodium chloride will be iso-osmotic to blood plasma.

Example 34: How much quantity of sodium chloride would be required to make 1% solution of morphine hydrochloride iso-osmotic to blood plasma?

Solution:

The freezing point depression by 1% solution of morphine hydrochloride is 0.086°C and the freezing point depression by 1% solution of sodium chloride is 0.576°C.

So, % w/v of sodium chloride to be required = $\frac{0.52 - 0.086}{0.576} = 0.753$

Thus, 0.753% w/v solution of sodium chloride is to be added to 1% solution of morphine hydrochloride.

In other words, 1.0 g of morphine hydrochloride and 0.753 g of sodium chloride are to be present per 100 ml of solution.

Exercise

A. Multiple Choice Question Carrying 01 Mark

1. Which one of the following definitions is correct?
   (a) A foot is length of a child's foot
   (b) A foot is length of a man's foot
   (c) A foot is length of a woman's foot
   (d) A foot is one third of a yard

2. Which one of the following statements is correct?
   (a) Metrology does not have any legal implications
   (b) Metrology has legal implication
   (c) Metrology is a local affair
   (d) None of the above
3. Which one of the following statements is correct?
   (a) Sensitivity is the error of a balance
   (b) Sensitivity is the minimum weightable quantity
   (c) Sensitivity of a balance is related to the error of the balance
   (d) None of the above
4. Which one of the following statements is correct?
   (a) Minimum Weightable Quantity is inversely proportional to the sensitivity of a balance
   (b) Minimum Weightable Quantity is directly proportional to the sensitivity of a balance
   (c) Minimum Weightable Quantity is directly proportional to the error of a balance
   (d) None of the above.
5. To measure 10 ml or less of a volumetric solution which one of the following should be used?
   (a) A 10 ml bulb pipette
   (b) A 10 ml measuring cylinder
   (c) A 25 ml measuring cylinder
   (d) A graduated 10 ml pipette
6. To measure 10 ml or less of a reagent solution which one of the following should be used?
   (a) A 100 ml measuring cylinder
   (b) A 250 ml measuring cylinder
   (c) A 10 ml measuring cylinder
   (d) 5 ml bulb pipette
7. What is the value of 1 Teragram?
   (a) 10^{15} gram (b) 10^{9} gram
   (c) 10^{10} gram (d) 10^{12} gram
8. Mark the correct value of 1 ppb
   (a) 10^{8} gram (b) 10^{7} gram
   (c) 10^{9} gram (d) 10^{10} gram

9. Mark the correct answer.
   (a) 1% of ethyl alcohol = 1.7573° proof
   (b) 1% of ethyl alcohol = 1.573° proof
   (c) 1% of ethyl alcohol = 1.7513° proof
   (d) 1% of ethyl alcohol = 1.8135° proof

10. What would be the correct statement?
   (a) Hemolysis is caused by dipping RBC into hypertonic solution
   (b) Hemolysis is caused by dipping RBC into hypotonic solution
   (c) Shrinking of RBCs takes place when RBCs are dipped into hypotonic solution.
   (d) Shrinking of RBCs is called hemolysis.

11. Which solution would be isotonic to body fluids?
   (a) A solution containing 9mg of sodium chloride per 10ml
   (b) A solution containing 90mg of sodium chloride per ml
   (c) A solution containing 0.9mg of sodium chloride per 100ml
   (d) A solution containing 9mg of sodium chloride per ml

12. Osmotic pressure of blood plasma is
   (a) 6.5 atm (b) 6.7 mm of Hg
   (c) 6.7 atm (d) 76cm of Hg

13. Body fluid is iso-osmotic to
   (a) 0.3 M solution of ionizing solute
   (b) 0.3% solution of nonionizing solute
   (c) 0.3M solution of non-ionizing solute
   (d) 3M solution of solute

14. When a solution contains more than one ingredient and another substance is required to adjust tonicity of the solution, the amount of adjusting substance required is equal to
   (a) $\frac{0.52 - a}{b}$ (b) $\frac{0.52 - ac}{b}$
   (c) $\frac{0.52}{x}$ (d) None

B. Question Carrying 05 Marks

1. Explain why metrology is legislatively and administratively accepted.

2. (a) A balance has 5% error and its sensitivity is 1mg. Calculate the minimum weighable quantity.

   Ans. 20mg

   (b) How many grams make 25 Nanogram?

   Ans. 25×10^{-9} grams

3. (a) A balance can weigh minimum 1 mg and the error of the balance 2%; Find out the sensitivity of the balance.

   Ans. 0.02mg

   (b) The dose of suspension is 3tea spoon full a day and the bottle contain 60ml of suspension. How many days it will continue?

   Ans. 4days

4. (a) The volume of a solution prepared was 100ml from which 1ml of the solution was diluted to 100ml; 1ml of this solution is further diluted to 100ml. The concentration of the finally diluted solution was found 1.0376μg/ml. Calculate the concentration of the stock solution in terms of percentage and gram per ml.

   Ans. 1.0376% & 0.010376g/ml

   (b) To prepare 35% alcohol at what proportion 97% of alcohol is to be diluted with water. Calculate by Allegation method.

   Ans. 35 ml of Alcohol is to be mixed 62ml of Water

5. (a) The concentration of a drug solution was 50mg in 100ml. 1ml of this solution was diluted to 100ml and 1ml of this diluted solution was diluted to 50ml and then 2ml of this diluted solution was diluted to 10ml. find out the concentration of final solution in μg/ml and in g/ml.

   (b) Drug content of granules was 65.98%. How much drug having potency 99.68% was mixed to increase the drug content of the mixture to 70.00%? Calculate by Allegation method.

   Ans. 4.02kg of drug was mixed with each of 29.68kg of granules

6. (a) A liquid contains 10%v/v of alcohol (99.8%); convert the alcohol content in terms of ° proof.

   Ans. 82.5 ° up.

   (b) Alcohol content in a product is 35 ° up; convert it into %v/v.

   Ans. 37.11%

7. Alcohol content of a formulation is 45 ° up; Calculate the amount of alcohol (97.5%) would be required to prepare 3000lts of the product.

   Ans. 964.4 lts

8. At which concentrations (% w/v) the solutions of sodium chloride and calcium chloride would be isotonic with blood plasma? (use molar concentration method)

   Ans. 0.9% solution of sodium chloride
   1.5% solution of calcium chloride

9. How much amount of sodium chloride would be required to make100ml of 1% solution of morphine hydrochloride iso-osmotic to blood plasma?

   Ans. 0.753g of sodium chloride

10. (a) The freezing point depression produced by 1% solution of morphine hydrochloride is 0.86°C. What concentration of morphine hydrochloride would be iso-osmotic to blood plasma?

    Ans. 6.05% solution of morphine hydrochloride

    (b) What concentration of sodium chloride would be iso-osmotic to blood plasma?

    Ans. 0.9% solution

Answers

A. Multiple Choice Questions

1. (d)	**2. (b)**	**3. (c)**	**4. (b)**	**5. (d)**
6. (c)	**7. (d)**	**8. (c)**	**9. (c)**	**10. (b)**
11. (d)	**12. (c)**	**13. (c)**	**14. (b)**	

Chapter 6

Powders and Granules

Definition, Classification, Advantages and Disadvantages, Simple & Compound Powders – Official Preparations, Dusting Powders, Effervescent, Efflorescent and Hygroscopic Powders, Eutectic Mixtures, Geometric Dilutions.

Introduction

The powders are mixture of finely divided solids consisting of drug with or without other excipients. These are one of the oldest dosage forms. Originally the crude drugs had been made powder and mixed with other ingredients, and then the mix was divided into single dose packets and dispensed. These became obsolete because of certain limitations, like-

- inconvenience to the patients to take or administer,
- difficulty in dispensing of an accurate dose of a potent drug in this form, and
- less ability to mask the unpleasant odour and taste of the drug,

However, the drugs whose dose is 500 mg or more, slight variation in the dose size does not make any appreciable difference or which are externally used, they are still formulated as powder or granule dosage forms.

Definition

Usually the term powder is used to describe a mixture of two or more powdered medicaments, with or without auxiliary substances, intended for internal administration. Otherwise there are other powders which are externally used. To avoid confusion the former is described as oral powder in the British Pharmacopoeia.

The granules that are used as a dosage form are prepared from powders which are subsequently made aggregated into larger particles.

Classification of Powders

The powders or granules may be classified in terms of their applications.

1. Internal use
   - Bulk powders for single dose
   - Bulk powders for multiple doses
   - Antibiotic syrup to be reconstituted before use,
2. External use
   - Dusting powders
   - Insufflations for ear, nose and throat use,
   - Dentifrices for cleaning of teeth
3. Parenteral use
   - Powders to be reconstituted before injection.

However, there are some products which are manufactured as powder but, dispensed as either an oral liquid preparation by adding sufficient purified water (suspension) or an injection by adding sufficient sterile water for injection.

Powders may be classified on the basis of particle size as follows:

Coarse powder: Mixture of powders of which all the particles pass through mesh no. 10 and not more than 40% can pass through mesh no. 44 is called coarse powder.

Moderately Coarse powder: It is a mixture of powders of which all the particles pass through a mesh no. 22 and not more than 40% pass through a mesh no. 60.

Moderately Fine powder: A mixture of powders of which all the particles pass through a mesh no.44 and not more than 40% pass through a mesh no. 85 is called moderately fine powder.

Fine powder: It is a powder of which all the particles pass through a mesh no. 85.

Very Fine powder: It is a powder of which all the particles pass through a mesh no. 120.

Each mesh has a definite aperture, called as sieve size. The Table 6.1 presents the sieve size with respect to mesh no.

Table 6.1 The sieve size with respect to mesh no.

Mesh No.	Sieve size	Mesh No.	Sieve size
4	4.00 mm	60	250 μm
5	3.35 mm	85	180 μm
6	2.80 mm	100	150 μm
10	1.70 mm	120	125 μm
22	710 μm	150	106 μm
30	500 μm	200	75 μm
44	355 μm		

Advantages of Powders

The powders have the following advantages:

- Powders can be compounded easily with flexibility
- These have greater stability than the liquid dosage form of a drug
- Precise dose can be administered with an option to deviate from conventional dose of the drug
- In powders the ingredients remain in solid forms without presence of moisture; hence no chemical interaction can take place
- Powders contain fine particles of drug(s); hence the drug can dissolve faster and can be absorbed faster
- These can be taken in bulk quantities either with food or with a liquid
- These can be carried easily than a liquid
- The powders do not require many machineries to be prepared; hence these may be economical
- Powders can be administered easily to the elderly and infants who cannot swallow a tablet.

Disadvantages of Powders

Despite having several advantages powders have following disadvantages

- Drugs which are susceptible to air, moisture and light are not suitable for making powder dosage form
- Drugs which are bitter, unpalatable and nauseous are not suitable for making powder dosage form
- Drugs which are volatile are not suitable to be dispensed in form of powders dosage form
- Drugs which absorb moisture, leave moisture, and oxidize are not suitable for making powder dosage form

- Number of manufacturing steps in manufacturing powders are not too less; hence cannot be manufactured quickly
- Powders intended for external administration contain powders of finest particle size; hence this dosage form would not be so economic as expected.

Simple Powders

Simple powders contain only one component. The substance may be originally crystalline or amorphous powder which is subsequently reduced to fine powders, weighed accurately and supplied in a separate packet. Packet is made by single wrapping of the powders or by double wrapping. This is done according to the stability of the drug. If the drug is resistant to atmospheric conditions, single wrapping may be sufficient. If the drug is susceptible to atmospheric conditions, double wrapping would be necessary.

Example

Paracetamol 325mg per packet

Grind the drug (Paracetamol) in a clean and dry mortar pestle to a fine powder. Weigh accurately 325 mg of the drug and wrap in a butter paper.

Prepare a label and paste over the packet. The label should contain following information;

Name of the Drug dispensed..Dose........................

Name of the Patient.......................................Age..................Sex...............

Name of the Doctor......................................Signature...............................

Date of dispensing...

Name of the Pharmacist................................Signature................................

Direction for use..

Name of the Clinic/Hospital..

Compound Powders

Compound powders contain two or more components; that is, it is a mixture of two or more drug substances. Each drug is powdered finely, and the all the drugs are mixed thoroughly then weighed accurately the total quantity as mentioned in the label. This is done when multiple doses are prepared and supplied. Otherwise, the drugs are ground individually and weighed accurately as mentioned in the prescription, transferred into the pack. Label is written and paste over the envelope or over the individual pack.

Example

Aspirin	150 mg
Paracetamol	250 mg
Caffeine	50 mg

Procedure:

- Take a clean mortar and pestle
- Weigh accurately caffeine and transfer into the mortar,
- Weigh accurately aspirin and transfer into the mortar,
- Accurately weigh paracetamol and transfer into the mortar,
- Powder aspirin, paracetamol, and caffeine to make fine powders
- Transfer the quantity of powders into a clean paper, wrap it properly to make a pack
- Wrap the pack with another paper and label the packet properly.

Note: Specimen of the label shall be similar to that shown in simple powders.

Official Preparations

Dusting Powders

These are nontoxic preparations, intended for local application, and usually contain mixture of two or more substances in finely powdered form. These should be free from grittiness. The fineness of these powders makes these more effective and less irritant. The powder mixtures are passed through sieve No 80 or 100. These do not have any systemic effect. Dusting powders are applied to various parts of the body for their protective, absorbent, antipruritics, antiseptic, antibromhidrotic, astringent, and antiperspirant effects. Talcum, kaolin, starch and other natural minerals are commonly used excipients of this type of preparation and are susceptible to contamination with bacteria like *Cl. tetani, Cl. welchii, B. anthracis*, etc. Hence, before use, these materials should be properly sterilised by heating at 160°C for at least 2 hrs. However, if the final product needs to be sterilised, pre-sterilisation is not necessary. Dusting powders are usually nontoxic. Use of preparation containing boric acid to large areas of abraded skin of infant can cause toxic reactions. Inhalation of powders containing zinc stearate by infants can cause pulmonary inflammation also. Dusting powders should not be applied to open wounds or to raw surfaces of large area.

Containers

Extemporaneous preparations are dispensed in sifter-top containers or pressure aerosols. The pressure aerosol packages are expensive than others, but with such packaging the preparation can be protected better from air, moisture and contamination. These are also convenient to use. Foot powders and talcum powders are available as pressure aerosols. However, these are usually packed in suitable coloured glass or plastic jars, preferably fitted with a reclosable perforated lid, unless otherwise specified in the individual monograph.

Labelling

Along with all relevant information the label should mention clearly, *For external use only.*

Formulations

Product: Chlorhexidine Dusting Powder

Composition

Each gram of powder contains,

Chlorhexidine Hydrochloride	5 mg
Sterilised Maize Starch	995 mg

Standards

Content of Chlorhexidine Hydrochloride: 0.45 – 0.55%,

Sterility: It should comply with the test for sterility.

Use: Antiseptic.

Lot size: 5 g

Manufacturing Formula:

Chlorhexidine Hydrochloride	25 mg
Sterilised Maize Starch	4.975 g

Manufacturing Method

- Take about 6 g of starch, free from gritty particles. Dry at 160°C for 2 hrs.
- Allow to cool,
- Weigh accurately 25 mg of chlorhexidine hydrochloride and 4.97 g of dried starch.
- Transfer the chlorhexidine hydrochloride into a clean, dry mortar, add little starch
  - and mix with a spatula,

- Add starch in portions and continue mixing till entire starch is consumed.
- Mix well to get uniform mixture.
- Pass through mesh No.120
- Determine the content of chlorhexidine HCl.
- Pack the powders in suitable container.
- Label properly.

Product: Talc. Dusting Powder

Composition:

Each gram of powder contains,

Purified Talc, sterilised	900 mg
Starch powder	100 mg

Use: Absorbent.

Lot size: 5 g

Manufacturing Formula

Purified Talc, sterilised	4.5 g
Starch powder	0.5 g

Manufacturing Method

- Take about 6 g of talcum powder and about 1 g of starch separately, dry at 160°C for 2 hrs., allow these to cool, screen separately through a mesh No. 120.
- Weigh accurately each of these, as per formula.
- Transfer these into a clean, dry mortar; mix well with a spatula to make a uniform mixture.
- Pass the mixture through mesh No. 120
- Pack the powder in a suitable container, seal and label properly.

Product: Zinc, Starch and Talc Dusting Powder

Standards for the product: content of zinc oxide: 23.3 – 26.4 % calculated as ZnO.

Acid-insoluble matter: 46.1 – 52.5%

Composition:

Each gram of powder contains,

Zinc Oxide	250 mg
Starch powder	250 mg
Purified Talc, sterilised	500 mg

Use: Astringent, absorbent.

Lot size: 5 g

Manufacturing Formula

Zinc Oxide	1.25 g
Starch powder	1.25 g
Purified Talc, sterilised	2.5 g

Manufacturing Method

- Take about 4 g of talcum powder, dry at 160°C for 2 hrs., allow to cool.
- Take zinc oxide and starch separately and dry at about 105°C for 2 hrs., cool.
- Weigh each of the ingredients according to the formula, transfer into a clean, dry
    - mortar mix thoroughly with a spatula until uniformly mixed.
- Pass through mesh No.120
- Determine the content of zinc oxide and acid-insoluble matter,
- Pack the powder in a suitable container, seal and label.

Effervescent Powders

These are prepared formulations. This type of solid dosage form is intended for oral administration. Before administration the powder is added to some amount of water, the powders effervesce with evolution of carbon dioxide and subsequent dissolution. The solution is then swallowed. The powder contains a mixture of weak acid and weak base along with the medicament. In contact with water, the acid reacts with base and forms carbon dioxide which evolves in the form of bubbles. With the evolution of carbon dioxide, the drug goes into solution or dispersion.

Although these are called powders; these may be in form of granules. It is advisable that the preparation should be taken while effervescing.

The effervescing ingredients are sodium bicarbonate, citric acid, and tartaric acid. Sodium bicarbonate reacts with citric acid and tartaric acid when comes in contact with water. The amount of acid is taken slightly more than what is required stoichiometrically. Because effervescent preparation is more palatable if it is slightly acidic. Tartaric acid is anhydrous but citric acid is hydrous. Citric acid has one molecule of water as water of crystallization, about 9.375% of its molecular weight. The relative proportion of two acids is based on the amount of water required to make the mixture sufficiently coherent powders or granules. On heating some amount of this water of crystallization is liberated and makes it moist. The moist acid reacts with sodium bicarbonate and produces water. Accordingly, the reaction proceeds.

$$3NaHCO_3 + C_6H_6O_7.H_2O = C_6H_5Na_3O_7 + 3CO_2 + 3H_2O$$

$$2NaHCO_3 + C_4H_6O_6 = C_4H_4Na_2O_6 + CO_2 + 2H_2O$$

Water makes the material coherent. Sources of water are water of crystallization and water produced during reaction. During granulation the weight of the material is reduced by about 14.3% due to the following reasons:

- Evaporation of water from the moist mass, and
- Loss of carbon dioxide

Hence, this should be kept in mind while preparing this powder. Thus, if 100g of mixture of acids and base is processed 85.7g of product would be obtained.

In general, the medicament is an inorganic salt such as magnesium and sodium sulphates, sodium phosphate, etc. which has water of crystallization. Usually these are dried at 100°C before use. But, such drying may not dry the material completely. In such cases the balance water of crystallization will be liberated during granulation and some of the effervescing agents (acid and base) would be consumed. As a result, the effervescing capacity of the product would be lost. Again, the water of crystallization is completely removed; the material may absorb moisture either from citric acid or during granulation. This may cause improper granulation.

Thus, a balance between removal and retention of water of crystallization from the materials used for production of effervescent granules is to be optimized.

Suitable sweetening agent is added to effervescent granules. Usually sucrose and/or other synthetic sweetener are used.

General Method of Manufacture

Weighed amount of citric acid, sodium bicarbonate, tartaric acid, colours, and sweetener are powdered, mixed thoroughly and transferred into the wide mouth porcelain or stainless-steel evaporating dish. The dish is put over a boiling water bath. The dish must be hot enough to remove water of crystallization as early as possible. For this much of the area of the dish should be exposed to steam. the powder mix should be stirred and pressed down with the help of a plastic spatula or non-corrosive stainless-steel spatula. Once a coherent mass is produced, it is removed from the water bath, cooled to room temperature, crushed to make the granules of appropriate size range.

The granules are packed in water vapour resistant, air-tight container with an appropriate label.

Formulations

Product: Compound Effervescent Powder

Composition

Each packet No.1 contains

Sodium Potassium Tartrate	7.5 g
Sodium Bicarbonate	2.5 g

Each packet No.2 contains

Tartaric acid	2.5 g

Standards: Mixture of packet No.1, content of sodium potassium tartrate: 73 – 77%, calculated as $C_4H_4KNaO_6$, $4H_2O$ and sodium bicarbonate: 24 – 26%, calculated as $NaHCO_3$

Use: Antacid.

Lot size: 30 g

Manufacturing Formula

Sodium Potassium Tartrate	18.0 g
Sodium Bicarbonate	6.0 g
Tartaric acid	6.0 g

Manufacturing Method

- Sift the powders individually through mesh No.60, check for black particles,
- Dry sodium bicarbonate at about 100°C for 2 hrs., allow to cool,
- Weigh accurately the required quantity of sodium bicarbonate and sodium
  - potassium tartrate, mix thoroughly,
- Determine their contents in the mixture.
- Pack 10g of this mixture suitably in an air-tight container/ poly pack, seal.
- Pack 2.5g of Tartaric acid in suitable container/ poly pack, seal.
- Label the product appropriately with the *direction of use*.

Storage: Store in cool, dry place.

Efflorescent Powders

There are some crystalline substances which liberate water of crystallization either partly or wholly when exposed to air of humid atmosphere. During trituration these powders become wet and subsequently liquefy. Caffeine, ferrous sulphate, citric acid, atropine sulphate, etc. falls into this category of powders. This problem can be solved either by using their corresponding anhydrous salts or an inert substance may be mixed with efflorescent substance before mixing with other ingredients.

The characteristic properties of efflorescent powders are-

- Efflorescent powder is a crystalline powder that contains water of hydration or crystallization.
- The substance holds the water molecule weakly.
- This water can be liberated either during manipulations or on exposure to a low-humidity environment
- If the water is liberated, the powders become sticky and pasty

Hygroscopic Powders

The characteristic properties of hygroscopic and deliquescent powders are:

- Hygroscopic powders attract and hold moisture from the air like table salt and sugar
- Deliquescent powders absorb moisture from air and will partially or wholly liquefy
- These must be dispensed in air-tight container with desiccant.

The water vapor pressure of the atmosphere is more than that of hygroscopic substance. As a result, hygroscopic substances absorb moisture from the atmosphere. But these substances remain in powder form even after absorption of moisture. Deliquescent substances also absorb moisture; but they liquefy. For this reason, if the drug is mixed with a deliquescent substance the stability of the dosage form becomes a problem particularly when the drug is susceptible to moisture. The stability problem can be reduced by controlling the time of exposure to air. Grinding reduces the particle size and increases the surface area. With increase of particle surface area, the material can absorb moisture greatly. Thus, these products should be prepared as granular form; never be in the powder form.

While making these formulations all the apparatuses and equipment used must be dried and then used. Packaging of hygroscopic and deliquescent products, the containers to be used must be completely dried and air-tight. If packed in paper, double wrapping is necessary.

The general method of manufacture of hygroscopic or deliquescent powders is same. Only difference would be the environmental conditions. These types of products should be prepared under low humidity and at lower temperature. Even during filling or packaging same conditions need to be maintained.

Eutectic Mixtures

Some substances (powders) when mixed liquefy and finally transform into liquid; these mixtures are called Eutectic mixtures. This happens with some drug substances also which when mixed camphor tend to liquefy. Most common examples of eutectic substances are – thymol, phenol, menthol, aminopyrine, chloral hydrate, acetyl salicylic acid, salol and acetanilide. If any two of these substances are mixed, the mixture turns into liquid. The reason for liquefaction is the depression of melting point or freezing point of the mixture. The melting point lowers below the room temperature and this happens because each substance becomes the impurity to other in the mixture.

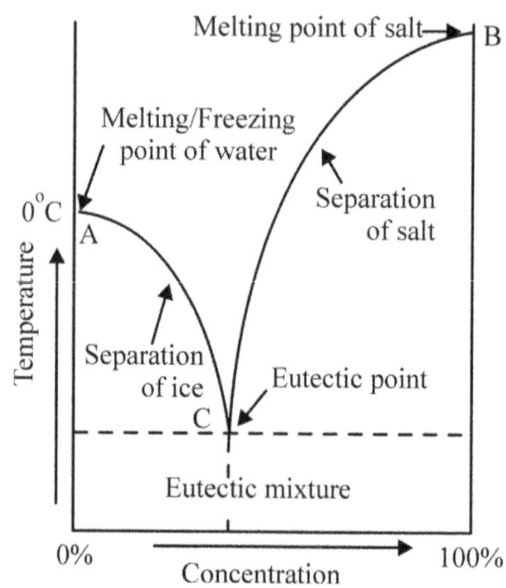

Eutectic mixture is formed from dilute solution of a salt. For example, a dilute solution of potassium iodide when cooled below 0°C (freezing point or melting point of water), pure ice is formed and separates from the solution, because freezing point of a solution is lower than that of pure solvent. As a result, the concentration of the solution with respect to solute (potassium iodide) increases. According to the rule, the freezing point of the solution is lower than that of dilute solution. Hence, freezing point of the solution decreases. If the solution is cooled further, more of ice will form and separates; the solution will become further concentrated. On subsequent cooling the same situation (separation of ice) will take place until a saturated solution is produced which on further cooling will freeze '*en masse*'. As shown in the figure the mixture of water and potassium iodide (*cryohydrate*) at concentration C is called the eutectic mixture and temperature at which this mixture is formed is called eutectic temperature or eutectic point.

Geometric Dilution

It is a method of dilution used to mix a potent drug with large amount of diluent. According to this method, the potent drug is mixed with thoroughly almost equal volume of the diluent. Mixing is done in a clean mortar pestle by trituration. Thereafter a second portion of the diluent equal in volume to the mixture (powder mixture) is transferred into the mortar and mixed thoroughly. Further a third portion of the diluent is added to almost equal volume of the powder-mixture and mixed thoroughly. This process is repeated till the amount of diluent is exhausted. For example, 50mg of drug is to be mixed with 500mg of lactose. Mixing as per geometric dilution should be done as shown below-

50mg of drug + 50mg of lactose = 100mg of mixture

100mg of drug + 100mg of lactose = 200mg of mixture

200mg of drug + 200mg of lactose = 400mg of mixture

400mg of drug + 150mg of lactose = 550mg of mixture

Oral Powders or Granules

The ingredients, medicament(s) and auxiliary substances, if directed in the form of powders are mixed thoroughly and packed as such in a suitable container, preferably in a wide mouth jar, or the powder mix is converted to granular form and then packed.

The drug with a large dose can also be formulated in this form. The powders may be soluble or insoluble in water. Oral powders may be prepared as single dose or multiple doses and contain flavouring and colouring agents, if specified. The single dose can be packed in a sachet or a small vial. For multi-dose powders, it is necessary to provide a suitable measuring device for delivery of required/prescribed quantity of the powder.

Effervescent oral powders need to be dissolved or dispersed before administration. Antacid or laxative powders are sometimes administered in this way.

Storage: These should be stored in tightly closed containers and usually in a cool dry place.

General Standards

Uniformity of content

1. Applicable to single dose containers in which the active ingredient present is either 10 mg or less than 10% of the content.
2. Not applicable when the preparation contains multivitamins and trace elements.
3. If the preparation contains more than one active ingredients, the test is to be carried out for each active ingredient.
   - Draw randomly a sample of 10 containers or packets.
   - Open and empty each container and remove the contents as completely as possible.
   - Determine the content of active ingredient(s) in each of 10 containers.
   - Calculate the average content of ingredient(s).

The lot or batch shall pass, if

1. Not more than one value exceeds the limits of ±15% of the av. content,
2. None of the 10 values exceeds the limits of ±25% of the av. contents.

If the lot or batch deviates from the above limits, repeat the test with another 20 containers. Calculate the average value for 30 containers.
The lot will pass, if

1. Not more than 3 individual values exceed the limits of ±15% of the av. content,
2. Not more than 1 individual value exceeds the limits of ±25% of the av. content.

Uniformity of weight: This test is not applicable, if uniformity of content is carried out.

Exercise

A. Multiple Choice Question Carrying 01 Mark

1. Powders are the intended for
   (a) Oral and external uses
   (b) Oral administration only
   (c) Only for external use
   (d) Preparation of sterile solution only

2. Granules are
   (a) Powders divided into fines
   (b) Not prepared from powders
   (c) Prepared from powders by processing
   (d) Simple mixture of powders
3. Which one is the complete and correct statement?
   (a) Powders used for internal use are called insufflations
   (b) Powders used for ear, nose and throat use are called insufflations
   (c) Powders administered through nasal route are called insufflations
   (d) Powders used for throat use are called insufflations
4. It is a coarse powder, if
   (a) All the particles of the mixture pass through mesh no. 44
   (b) All the particles of the mixture pass through mesh no. 10
   (c) All the particles of the mixture pass through mesh no. 10; but not more than 40% can pass through mesh no. 44
   (d) None of the particles of the mixture can pass through mesh no. 44
5. Fine powder is a powder, if all the particles can pass through mesh no.
   (a) 200 (b) 100
   (c) 120 (d) 85
6. Which of the following statements is correct?
   (a) Bitter drugs can be formulated as powders
   (b) Drugs cannot be taken as bulk
   (c) Drugs which are not susceptible to moisture, air and light are suitable for making powders
   (d) All drugs can be formulated as powders
7. Which of the following statements is correct?
   (a) Drugs which oxidise in presence of even slight moisture can be prepared as powders
   (b) Drugs which do not oxidise in presence of moisture can be prepared as powders
   (c) Volatile drugs are formulated as powders
   (d) None of the above

8. Which of the following statements is correct?
   (a) Simple powders contain one drugs with or without any excipients
   (b) Simple powders contain two drugs, but not any other excipient
   (c) Simple powders contain two drugs with or without any other excipients
   (d) None of the above
9. Compound powders are prepared from
   (a) One drug
   (b) More than one drug
   (c) One drug and two excipients
   (d) One drug and three excipients
10. Effervescent powders contain
   (a) Drug that effervesces
   (b) Drug with a strong acid and strong base
   (c) Drug with effervescing agent
   (d) Drug with a strong acid and weak base
11. Efflorescent powder is
   (a) Crystalline powder containing water of hydration or crystallization.
   (b) Anhydrous powder
   (c) Amorphous powder
   (d) None of the above
12. Deliquescent powders
   (a) Release water to air and become dry
   (b) Absorb water from the atmosphere and liquefy
   (c) Neither absorb nor release water
   (d) None of the above
13. After liberation of water from deliquescent powders
   (a) The powders become anhydrous
   (b) The powders become sticky and pasty
   (c) The powders become amorphous
   (d) None of the above

14. Eutectic mixtures are formed
    (a) When any two substances are mixed
    (b) When two substances are mixed at a particular ratio
    (c) When a mixture of two substances liquefy and finally transform into liquid
    (d) None of the above
15. Geometric dilution is used generally for
    (a) Mixing of small quantity of a potent drug with any substance of larger quantity
    (b) Mixing of any two powders
    (c) Mixing of any two or more drugs in powder forms
    (d) Heterogeneous mixing of powders

B. Question Carrying 05 Marks

1. What do you understand by powders and granules? Give two examples of powders and mention their uses,
2. Classify powders on the basis of their intended applications and particle size.
3. What are advantages and limitations of powders
4. Explain in short the Simple and Compound powders
5. Write down the composition and manufacturing method of Dusting powder.
6. What is Effervescent powder? Write down the general method of its manufacturing.
7. Write a note on Efflorescent powders
8. Write a note on Hygroscopic powders
9. What is meant by Eutectic mixture? How it is formed?
10. Explain the method of geometric dilution.

C. Question Carrying 10 Marks

1. Explain in brief the different types of powders on the basis of their application and on the basis of the particle size.
2. Define Simple and Compound powders. Write down their manufacturing methods of manufacture with an example.
3. What is Dusting powder? Why it is used and how it is prepared? Answer with the help of an example.

4. What is Effervescent powder? Describe how this type of preparation is prepared with reference to an example.
5. Write notes on Hygroscopic and Efflorescent powders.
6. What is a Eutectic mixture? Describe how a small amount of potent drug can be mixed with large amount of a diluent.

Answers

A. Multiple Choice Questions

1. (a)	**2. (c)**	**3. (b)**	**4. (c)**	**5. (d)**
6. (c)	**7. (b)**	**8. (a)**	**9. (b)**	**10. (c)**
11. (a)	**12. (b)**	**13. (b)**	**14. (c)**	**15. (a)**

Chapter 7

Liquid Dosage Forms

Advantages and Disadvantages of Liquid Dosage Forms, Excipients used in Formulation of Liquid Dosage Forms, Solubility Enhancement Techniques.

Introduction

Children, infants, elderly patients and bed-ridden patients prefer liquid dosage form, because they cannot swallow tablet and capsule. Liquid dosage forms are relatively more palatable. However, liquid dosage forms are not as stable as solid dosage forms.

Liquid dosage forms are prepared either by dissolving or dispersing the drug substances in suitable vehicle – aqueous or nonaqueous solvent or mixture of solvents.

Liquid dosage form intended for oral administration contains other excipients which improve colour, taste, and odour.

Advantages of Liquid Dosage Form

The liquid dosage forms have certain advantages. The advantages are;

- There is no problem of drug dissolution; hence, drug is readily available for absorption.
- This type of dosage forms are most preferred by infants, children, elderly and the patients who cannot swallow solid dosage form.
- Drugs such as iodides or bromides, which cause gastric irritation are most suitable for preparing liquid dosage form.
- This type of preparations provides uniformity of dose; because these are homogenous preparations.
- As per the treatment requirement the dose size can be varied.
- Bitter and obnoxious drugs can be formulated as liquid dosage form by using colour, flavour, and sweetening agent.

- Hygroscopic and deliquescent drugs are difficult to be formulated as solid dosage form; but such drugs can be formulated as liquid dosage form.
- These formulations have good aesthetic properties; thus, they have desired psychological effect and good appeal.

Disadvantages of Liquid Dosage Form

Despite various advantages liquid dosage forms have certain disadvantages also. These are:

- The volume of the liquid dosage forms being greater than that of solid dosage form; hence these are not convenient to carry.
- The stability of drugs in aqueous medium is lesser than that in the solid dosage form; hence formulation of drugs which are susceptible to hydrolysis becomes a challenge.
- Incompatible drugs cannot be mixed and given in liquid dosage form; but these can be prepared as solid dosage form and can be given to the patients with safety.
- Liquids are usually good medium for microbial growth; hence require effective preservative system.
- The dose size depends on how the liquid dosage form is being measured; the capacity of spoon used for administration normally varies. Hence, dose of the drug varies without any intention.
- Although rare, children may take overdose of the drug because of the good palatability; for this reason, a general warning is given on the label: Keep away from children.
- It may be lost partially or wholly due to breakage of the container for any accidental reason.
- In case of suspension and emulsion liquid dosage forms additional additive such as suspending agent, emulsifying agent, flocculating agent, etc. are required to make a stable formulation.
- Liquid dosage form containing sugar is not suitable for diabetic patient; hence synthetic sweetener is required.

Excipients used in Formulation of Liquid Dosage Forms

The type of excipients to be used in a particular liquid dosage form depends primarily on the type of the liquid dosage form or its intended application. For example, suspension or solution may be used for parenteral, oral or external application. Similarly, a liquid to be applied over the skin or may be used as enema. Both are liquid and they are prepared for external application. But, the excipients required to prepare these would be different. However, we shall discuss the commonly used excipients in liquid dosage form.

Before knowing about different excipients used let us know about different types of liquid dosage forms usually prepared.

Classification of Liquid Dosage Form

- On the basis of phases

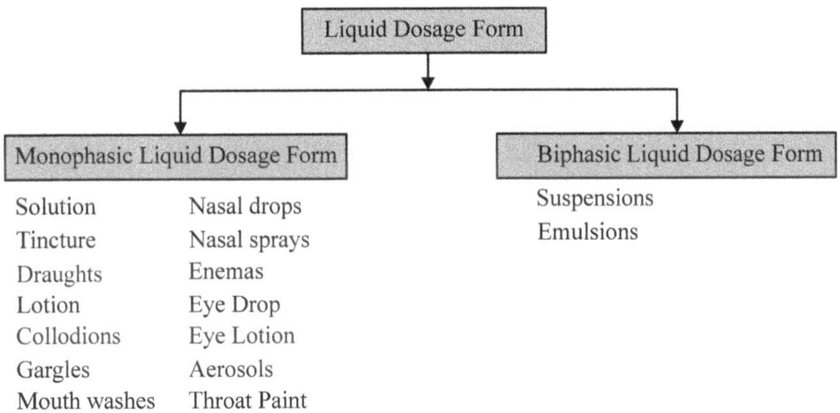

- *On the basis of their application*

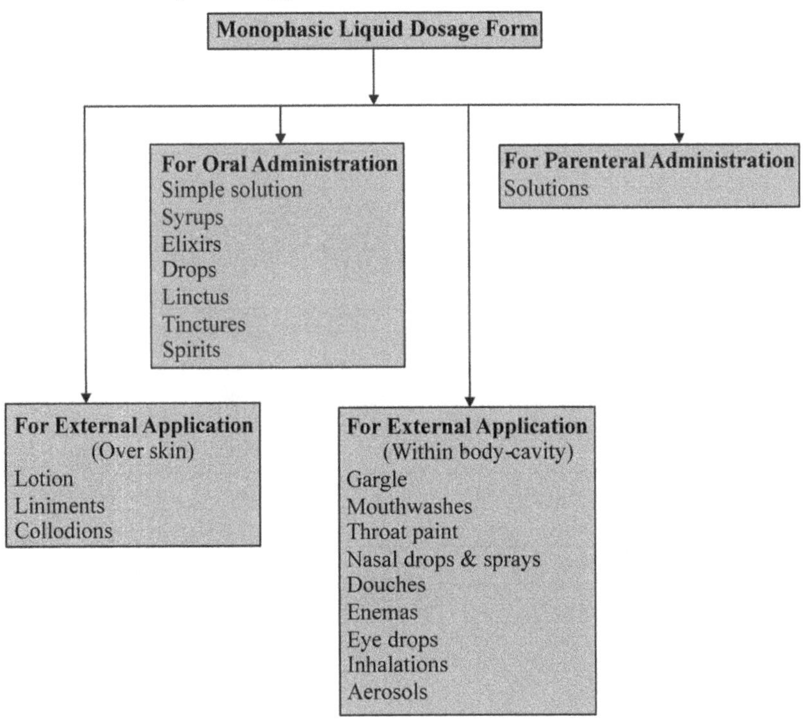

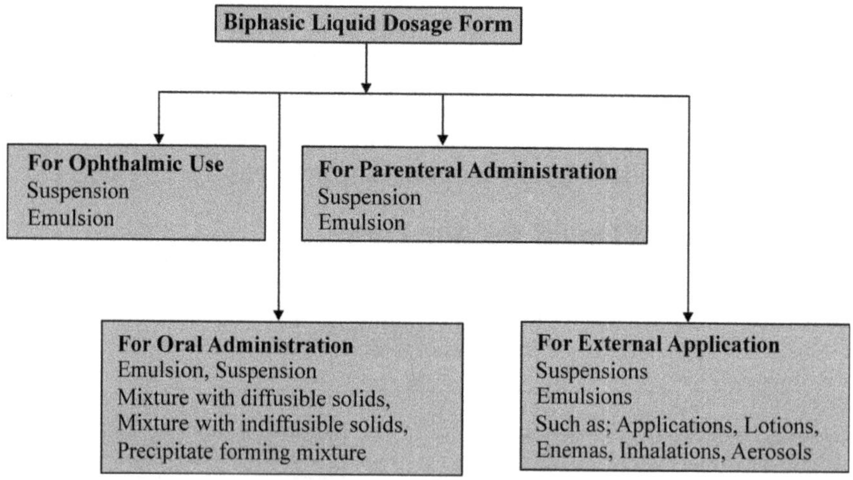

Type of excipients used in liquid dosage forms

The excipients used in oral liquids will not be same used in liquids for external application or for injections. Types of excipients commonly used in different liquid dosage forms are mentioned in tabular form.

Oral liquids	Liquids for external use	Parenteral liquids	Ophthalmic liquids
Solvent	Solvent	Solvent	Solvent
Cosolvent*	Cosolvent	Cosolvent*	Cosolvent
Solubilizer*	Solubilizer	Solubilizer*	Solubilizer
Viscosity Enhancer	Viscosity Enhancer		Viscosity Enhancer
Buffers	Buffers	Buffers*	Buffers
Preservatives	Preservative	Preservative *	Preservative
Chelating agent		Chelating agent*	Chelating agent
Density modifiers	Density modifiers		
Emulsifiers	Emulsifiers	Emulsifiers*	
Suspending agent*	Suspending agent	Suspending agent*	Suspending agent
Emulsion stabilizers*	Emulsion stabilizers	Isotonicity modifiers*	Isotonicity modifiers
Antioxidants	Antioxidants	Antioxidants*	Antioxidants
Sweetening agents			
Flavours	Perfumes		
Colors	Colors		

Note: * not in all preparations

Keeping in view of the three essential criteria of an oral solution product, i.e. palatability, stability and elegance, the excipients should be selected. As shown above there are various types of liquid dosage forms which are intended for different applications.

Selection of excipients for each type varies accordingly. Hence, during formulation development the scientist must select the excipients with scientific and logical justification; so that the product becomes physic-chemically stable and therapeutically effective. For example, a liquid preparation intended for parenteral administration does not require any excipient which improves organoleptic properties of the formulation such as colour, odour and taste. Moreover, preservatives used in parenteral preparations are different from that used in oral preparations.

Therefore, selection of excipients according to type of formulation is most important.

Vehicle

Aqueous vehicles

Water is the universal solvent or vehicle used for liquid formulations. Depending on the source natural water contains dissolved and suspended impurities. Hence, such water cannot be used directly in pharmaceutical formulations. Microorganisms are also present in water. Water is purified as per the requirement. The dissolved impurities present in water are inorganic salts of sodium, potassium, calcium, magnesium, iron, etc. in the form of chlorides, sulphates, bicarbonates. As per the source, water contains various types of microorganisms and various suspended materials. Depending on the uses water is classified as potable or drinking water, purified water, distilled water, water for injection.

The standards of each type of water vary. There are two types of standards according to the use. For example, the standards of potable or drinking water in India are decided by the BIS (Bureau of Indian Standards); while for pharmaceutical applications the standards are given in the Indian Pharmacopoeia.

Parameters	Potable water (BIS)	Purified Water, IP	Water for injection, IP	Sterile Water for injection, IP
Colour	NMT 25 Hz	Colourless		
Odour	No unobjectionable	Odourless		
pH	6.5 – 8.5	5 – 7	5 – 7 (5.4)	5 – 7 (5.4)
TDS	NMT 0.2%			

Table *Contd...*

Parameters	Potable water (BIS)	Purified Water, IP	Water for injection, IP	Sterile Water for injection, IP
Calcium & Magnesium				NIL
Hardness	NMT 600mg/l			
Alkalinity	NMT 600mg/l			
Iron, Fe	NMT 1mg/l			
Manganese	NMT 0.3mg/l			
Sulphates, SO_4	NMT 400mg/l			NIL
Heavy metals		NMT 0.1ppm	NMT 0.1ppm	NMT 0.1ppm
Nitrate, NO_3^-	NMT 100mg/l	NMT 2ppm	NMT 2ppm	NMT 2ppm
Chlorides	NMT 1000mg/l			NMT 0.5ppm
Fluoride, F	NMT 1.5mg/l			
Arsenic, As	NMT 0.05mg/l			
Chromium, Cr	NMT 0.05mg/l			
Aluminium		NMT 10 ppb	NMT 10 ppb	NMT 1 ppb
Copper, Cu	NMT 1.5mg/l			
Cyanide	NMT 0.05mg/l			
Lead, Pb	NMT 0.05mg/l			
Mercury, Hg	NMT 0.001mg/l			
Zinc	NMT 15mg/l			
Conductivity		NMT 5.1 µS/cm at 25°C	NMT 5.1 µS/cm at 25°C	
Volatile substances				
Sterility				
Pyrogen				
Total Coliform Bacteria	NMT 10 Coliform/100ml 95% of samples should not contain Coliform in 100ml			
E. Coliform Bacteria	Nil/100ml			
Microbial contamination		NMT 100cfu/ml (viable count)	NMT 100cfu/ml (viable count)	NMT 100cfu/ml (viable count)
Oxidisable substances		0.05mg/100ml	0.05mg/100ml	0.05mg/100ml

Table *Contd...*

Parameters	Potable water (BIS)	Purified Water, IP	Water for injection, IP	Sterile Water for injection, IP
Bacterial endotoxins		NMT 0.25 Endotoxin Units/ml	NMT 0.25 Endotoxin Units/ml	NMT 0.25 Endotoxin Units/ml
Residue on evaporation				NMT 0.003%
Particulate contamination				NMT 12/ml of 10μm in size NMT 2/ml of 25μm in size

Note: NMT stands for 'Not More Than'
ppm stands for parts per million (10^6)
ppb stands for parts per billion (10^9)

Solvents for Nonaqueous Preparations

Complete solubilization of all ingredients at all storage temperature is not always possible. Even if the drug is stable in aqueous solution, sometimes it becomes necessary to use a nonaqueous system. It seems to be advantageous than an aqueous solution, particularly if the preparation is intended for intramuscular administration. Solution of a drug in oil when administered intramuscularly works as a depot therapy. The solution remains as a discrete entity within the muscular tissue and releases the drug slowly into the surrounding tissue by partitioning.

There are various solvents available for preparation of solutions intended for external use. The number of solvents for oral preparation is less and for parenteral preparation is further less. For selection of a solvent may be for external use the following parameters are to be considered:

- Toxicity,
- Irritancy,
- Skin sensitization,
- Compatibility with other ingredients of the formulation
- Flammability,
- Stability, and
- Cost.

Oils

Oils are primarily of two types- fixed oil and volatile oil. Fixed oil may be vegetable oil and mineral oil. Fixed oils obtained from vegetables consist mainly of glycerides of fatty acids. Arachis oil, almond oil, olive oil, cottonseed oil, soya oil, sesame oil, maize oil and castor oil are widely used as solvent for preparing parenteral formulations. For example, phenol injection is prepared using almond oil, as the aqueous solution of phenol is caustic in nature. Similarly, Dimercaprol injection is prepared with arachis oil. Castor oil is used to prepare miconazole eye drop. Another useful solvent, ethyl oleate is less viscous. It is used to prepare ergocalciferol injection and testosterone propionate injection. Thus, these injections can be easily injected intramuscularly.

Certain oils are tasteless and colourless. These oils are used to prepare oral solution of vitamin A and D. For some antibiotics fractionated coconut oil is also used as solvent. These antibiotics hydrolyze in aqueous medium.

- **Mineral oil (Liquid paraffin)**

  Liquid paraffin is a petroleum product obtained by distillation. This is alternatively known as liquid petrolatum, or white mineral oil. As per pharmacopoeia it is of two grades – light (sp. gravity: 0.818 – 0.880 as per USP) and heavy (sp. gravity: 0.845 – 0.905 as per USP). These are colourless, transparent, tasteless, oily, viscous liquids. These are odourless when cold, on heating a faint odour may be smelt. It is most commonly used in topical formulations, particularly in ointments for its emollient effect. As a solvent it is used in oil-in-water emulsion. In capsules and tablets, it is used as a lubricating agent and in suppositories as mold ejector.

- **Dimethyl sulphoxide (DMSO)**

  DMSO can dissolve various organic compounds like carbohydrates, polymers, peptides, and even many inorganic salts and gases. The unique solvent power of DMSO often allows the reduction of multi-step synthetic schemes. The ability to dissolve charged or ionic materials it has been rediscovered in about 1958 as a super solvent. Since the early 1960s, many important pharmaceutical uses of DMSO have been found. It is less toxic than other members of this class like dimethyl formamide (DMF), dimethylacetamide, etc. It is physico-chemically stable, compatible to environment, recyclable, polar, aprotic, hygroscopic, miscible with water, colourless, and odourless. Its pharmaceutical use has been investigated and recognized. For example, many topical products containing DMSO as an excipient are being marketed in the Europe. It can be used to treat sport related injuries. DMSO is compatible with many drugs and pharmaceutical excipients. The USP-NF 2005 included three monographs of DMSO as Dimethyl sulphoxide gel, Dimethyl sulphoxide irrigation, Dimethyl sulphoxide topical solution. According to ICH (International Council for Harmonization) it is class 3 residual solvent. However, the USP approves DMSO for following purposes:

- Stabilizing formulations as a cosolvent,
- Solution of polymers such as polyvinyl alcohol (PVA) and poly (lactic-co-glycolic acid) (PLGA) in DMSO containing drug and administered into the body for in-situ precipitation of drug and polymer in the body in form of implant. Polymer implants provide a structural support in the body and release impregnated drug in a controlled rate.
- Penetration of drug through skin can be increased by using DMSO up to 70% or more in TDDS.
- In the treatment of intestinal cystitis DMSO has been used.
- Mixing of water with DMSO results the formation of a eutectic mixture. This can depress the freezing point of water significantly. At a ratio of 1:1 the mixture can remain in liquid state at even 280°C and thus the cells are not damaged when preserved in this mixture.

Other Solvents

For external preparations, particularly in cosmetics, isopropyl myristate and isopropyl palmitate are used as solvent. These are preferred for their non-greasiness and low viscosity. For veterinary products dimethyl formamide and dimethylacetamide are used as solvent but for their toxicity these are not used in formulations intended for human use. For preparation of certain insecticides such as pyrethrum and piperonyl butoxide kerosene is also used as solvent.

For parenteral formulation sometimes glycofurol is used as a solvent. Certain ear drops intended for human use are prepared using xylene as solvent.

Cosolvents

Alcohol is commonly used as cosolvent, since it is miscible with water in all proportions. Alcohol contains 95% of ethyl alcohol. It dissolves most of the drugs which are sparingly or poorly soluble in water. It is nontoxic up to a certain concentration. However, its use has been restricted to avoid addiction.

Glycerol is clear, colourless liquid. It is thick, slightly warm and sweet taste. It has syrupy consistency; can absorb water when exposed to air due to its hygroscopicity. It is miscible with water and alcohol in all proportions. It is used as the solvent for various substances. It does not evaporate and does not become rancid. Due to its sweetness it acts as a good flavouring agent. In oral preparations it is used as a cosolvent to increase the solubility in water. It is also used to improve viscosity, taste and flavour, while in external preparations it is used as humectant.

Propylene glycol can be used in various pharmaceutical formulations for multipurpose purposes. Pure propylene glycol has purity of 99.8% and is mono propylene glycol. It is an excellent solvent for many organic substances and an antimicrobial preservative for many systems. It has very less toxicity. It has following applications:

- In flavour-concentrate industries it is used as solvent for aromatics
- For natural gums it is used as wetting agent.
- For preparation of citrus and other emulsified flavours it is used as an ingredient.
- It is used as a solvent in elixirs and other pharmaceutical preparations
- For making lotions, shampoos, creams and other preparations it may be used as coupling agent and solvent.
- In cosmetics and pharmaceutical creams, it is used as emulsifier
- It is an effective humectant, preservative and stabilizer.

Solubilizer

Solubilization of poorly soluble drugs is a major challenge to a formulation development activity. Many drug substances are hydrophobic, are not wetted properly by water; for which they are not soluble in water. Poor wettability and unfavourable interfacial phenomenon play the major role in their solubility. To solve these problems following agents are commonly used:

- **Dispersing agents**

  The substances that can disperse the powders optimally in a suspension is called dispersing agents. Four types of dispersing agents are commonly used on the basis of,

  - Physicochemical properties of the powders,
  - Type of dispersion, and
  - Amount required.

  The four types of dispersing agents are,

  - Wetting agents,
  - Deflocculating agents,
  - Protective colloids,
  - Electrolytes (inorganic).

- **Wetting agents**

  These are surface active agents which reduce the contact angle between the solid-liquid interfaces. Better wetting is achieved when the surfactant is adsorbed maximum onto the liquid-liquid and solid-liquid interfaces. The surfactant may be ionic or non-ionic. For drugs having negative zeta potential anionic surfactant is most effective. Similarly, for drugs having positive zeta potential cationic surfactant is of choice. Non-ionic surfactants are sometimes preferred as they are less toxic and insensitive to pH and electrolyte. Non-ionic surfactants used as wetting agents are of two types – ethoxylate and poloxamer. Usually ethoxylates are preferred, but they form complexes with phenolic/ester preservatives (e.g. parabens) and inactivate.

  High molecular weight poloxamers are synthetic block copolymers and very good viscosity enhancers also. Their molecular weight ranges from 1000 to 150000. Since, the surfactant at higher concentrations can solubilize the drug substance, these develop foam, and spoil the taste and odour; these should be used at minimum required concentration.

  However, alcohol, glycerine and other polyols, e.g. polyethylene glycol, propylene glycol, etc. are sometimes used as wetting agent and these can disperse some powders satisfactorily.

- **Surfactants** work at the surface of the particles or interface between two particles (phases) and are most frequently used in various types of liquid dosage forms. Surfactants or surface-active agents have various applications such as for wetting, emulsification, suspending, dispersing, solubilization, and cleaning (detergent), etc.; these are classified on the basis of their HLB values which ranges from 1 to 40. The surfactants having HLB values less than 10 are hydrophilic in nature and those having HLB values more than 10 are hydrophobic in nature.

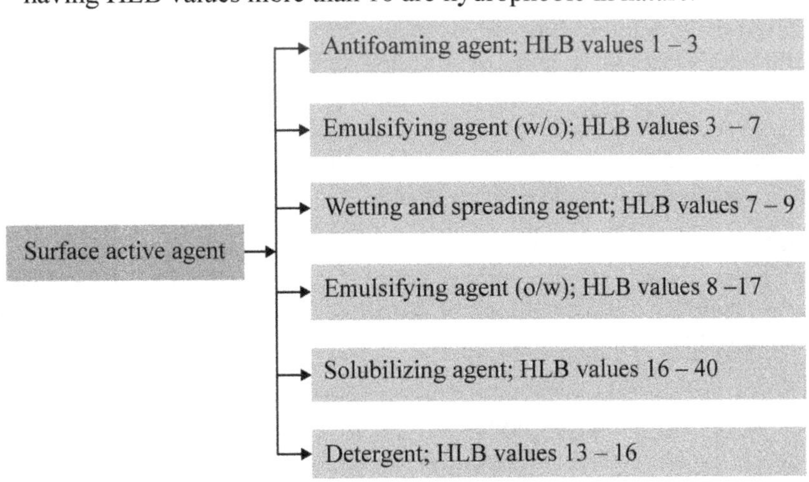

Based on this they may be non-ionic, anionic, cationic and amphoteric. Each surfactant molecule has two ends as shown in the figure.

Non-ionic surfactants contain covalently bonded oxygen-containing hydrophilic groups. These groups are bonded to hydrophobic parent structures. The water-solubility of the oxygen groups is the result of hydrogen bonding. With increasing temperature hydrogen bonding decreases, and therefore, with increasing temperature the water solubility of non-ionic surfactants decrease. These are less sensitive to hard water than anionic surfactants, and they create less strong foam.

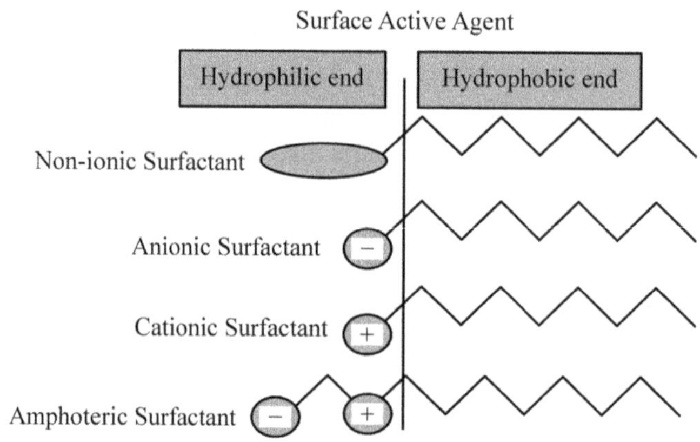

Anionic surfactant contains anionic group such as sulphate, sulphonate, phosphate, carboxylate, etc. at its head. Most common alkyl sulphates include ammonium lauryl sulphate, sodium lauryl sulphate (SLS) and related alkyl-ether sulphate such as sodium lauryl ether sulphate (SLES) and sodium myreth sulphate belong to this group.

Cationic surfactants contain positively charged group (cationic group) on their heads. These dissociate in water into an amphiphilic cation and an anion, mostly halogen type. Most of the cationic surfactants correspond to nitrogen compounds such as fatty amine salts and quaternary ammoniums, with one or several long chain of alkyl groups. The common source of these groups is natural fatty acids. Generally, these surfactants are more expensive than anionics; because the high pressure hydrogenation reaction is to be carried out during their synthesis.

Amphoteric or Zwitterionic surfactant dissociates into a molecule having both anionic and cationic groups. Synthetic products such as betaines or sulphobetaines, and natural substances such as aminoacids and phospholipids belong to this group.

Some amphoteric surfactants are not sensitive to pH, whereas others are cationic at low pH and anionic at high pH, and at intermediate pH these behaves as amphoteric substances. Usually amphoteric surfactants are costly and hence, their use is limited. These are used in cosmetics. These have biological compatibility and low toxicity.

Buffers

Buffers are used to modify and maintain a particular pH. Since drugs are weak organic acids or weak bases, these are best solubilized at particular pH. For this reason, most of the formulations are prepared and maintained a definite pH. A suitable buffer system should be used when –

- The buffer is compatible with drug and excipients
- Capable of maintaining the required pH
- The buffer can provide required solubility of the drug
- Capable of providing desired stability of the product
- pKa value of the buffer and pH of the product are almost equal

The substances most commonly used as buffers for oral liquids are citric acid-sodium citrate, sodium or potassium phosphates, sodium or potassium tartrate-tartaric acid, etc.

Suspending Agent

Suspending agents prevent sedimentation by changing rheological properties of the suspension. The suspending medium should be thixotropic and pseudoplastic also; so that, the product remains as a gel on standing (prevents sedimentation) and becomes fluid on shaking (favours pouring). Thus, it is necessary to select suitable suspending agent for making the suspension structured and flocculated. Based on following criteria the suspending should be selected.

- Ability to form structured vehicle,
- Change of rheological property on shaking,
- Change of rheological property due to change in temperature,
- Ability to retain rheological property within a range of pH,
- Compatibility with electrolyte,
- Compatibility with other excipients,
- Toxicity,
- Yield stress value, and
- Cost.

Hydrocolloids play an important role among the suspending agents. Every hydrocolloid can increase the viscosity of water either by binding with water molecules or by entrapping water molecules inside the intertwined macromolecular chain. Thus, the water molecules cannot move.

The hydrocolloids used in pharmaceutical preparations can be categorized into four classes.

1. Cellulose derivatives,
2. Polysaccharides and gums,
3. Clays, and
4. Synthetic polymers.

Cellulose Derivatives

Sodium carboxymethylcellulose (CMC), microcrystalline cellulose (MCC), hydroxy propyl methyl cellulose (HPMC), ethyl methylcellulose (EMC), hydroxy ethyl cellulose (HEC), hydroxypropyl cellulose (HPC), ethyl cellulose (EC), ethyl hydroxy ethyl cellulose (HEEC), methylcellulose (MC),etc. belong to this class. Some of these are used in oral and some are in topical or parenteral suspensions. These are semi synthetic and generally their properties do not change from batch to batch. These are non-ionic and chemically compatible with most of the excipients. Sodium carboxymethylcellulose is the exception; it is anionic and can form precipitate or gel with other cationic substances like drugs, wetting agents (surfactants), electrolytes, preservatives and flocculating agents. Most of the cellulose derivatives are available in different viscosity grades and exhibit pseudoplastic flow characteristics.

Microcrystalline cellulose is powdered cellulose, insoluble in water but forms dispersions having plastic flow behaviour with yield value. That is why this is used in combination with other polymer such as hydroxy propyl methylcellulose or sodium carboxymethylcellulose. Sodium carboxymethylcellulose although anionic is extensively used in suspensions. It forms structured vehicle and retards sedimentation. It is useful over a wide range of pH (7 – 9) and can show some thixotropic property, if suitable grade is used. If the pH is increased to 10 or more, the viscosity increases and if the pH is reduced to less than 4, the viscosity decreases due to hydrolysis of the polymer. When its solution is exposed to heat for long time, it degrades, and its viscosity is lost permanently.

Hydroxy propyl methyl cellulose (HPMC) swells in water with progressive hydration. Its solution can be prepared by dispersing the powders in hot water at about 80°C; when the powders are completely wetted, cold water is added with continuous stirring until a clear solution is obtained. The apparent viscosity is proportional to its molecular weight. Solution of high molecular weight HPMC exhibits pseudoplastic flow property.

Polysaccharides and Gums

Acacia, sodium alginates, carrageenan, xanthan gum, tragacanth, etc. belong to this category and are commonly used as suspending agents.

Xanthan gum is an anionic polysaccharide which is used as a suspending agent and hydrocolloid. It contains three different mono-saccharides - mannose, glucose and a salt of glucuronic acid. It is soluble in both hot and cold water. Aqueous solution of Xanthan gum has high viscosity. At lower concentration it is pseudoplastic and at low pH it behaves as a gel. Its gelling, pseudoplasticity and viscosity increase with concentration. Solutions of Xanthan gum show unusual resistance to prolonged shear in comparison to other gums. For example, 1% solution of Xanthan gum, if sheared for 1 hour at rate of 46000 per second does not lose viscosity appreciably. Its viscosity is also not affected by change of temperature. It is a suspending agent of choice for its stability at wide range of temperature and pH (1 – 10), compatibility with cations (-mono, -di, and –trivalent) and cationic drugs, preservatives. It is resistant to enzymatic degradation, but susceptible to microorganisms. Hence, suitable preservative should be used.

Synthetic Polymers

Carbomer, polyvinylpyrrolidone, poloxamer, etc. are the semisynthetic polymers generally used in pharmaceutical formulations.

Carbomers are high molecular weight polymers of acrylic acid. These are available in different grades. Among these different grades suitable carbomer is selected after evaluation. As it possesses a yield value and good consistency, at lower concentration it can satisfactorily suspend the powders. In aqueous medium it shows plastic behaviour even at relatively lower concentration even at 0.25%. Similar suspendibility was observed with 3% solution of polysaccharide gum. When dispersed in water the carbomer swells first, and then gradually the viscosity increases with a yield value. If an acid polymer is used, it should be neutralized with inorganic or organic base to get the desired rheological characteristics. In fact, each carbomer should be neutralized. For desired suspendibility the yield value of the polymer is important, not the viscosity. The viscosity of the carbomer is affected by temperature and pH. At pH 5.5 the carbomer shows its maximum viscosity. If the pH is lowered the carbomer loses its viscosity and precipitates out. When exposed to higher temperature for short period, the viscosity of the carbomer is not affected. Further exposure results lowering of its viscosity. It is not compatible with electrolyte. A small amount of soluble electrolyte can reduce the viscosity. It is compatible with other common excipients. When exposed to UV light the viscosity of the carbomer reduces. The solution of carbomer is not susceptible to microorganisms. However, the characteristics of the polymer can be modified by modifying the type of cross-linking and levels with hydrophilic characteristics of the co-monomers in the cross-link.

Clays are inorganic substances and swell in water. The commonly used, pharmaceutically important clays are colloidal aluminium silicates, magnesium aluminium silicate (veegum), bentonite, etc..

Magnesium aluminium silicate (veegum) is obtained from natural smectite clays. Because of its colour and uniformity, it is considered better than other clays. There are different grades of veegum with difference in viscosity, particle size, salt stability and alkalinity. Suitable variety needs to be selected among these different grades. It is stable at wide range of pH, 6 to 11. The aqueous dispersion when exposed to high temperature for long time the viscosity increases. Presence of electrolyte increases both viscosity and yield value of the dispersion of veegum. It is compatible with most of the excipients including anionic and cationic substances like drugs, preservatives and hydrocolloids. When mixed with carboxymethylcellulose (CMC) or xanthan gum (XG), a synergistic effect is observed. The most suitable proportion of veegum and CMC ranges from 9:1 to 2:1.

Deflocculating Agents

Proper wetting makes the particles deflocculated. Polymerized organic salt of sulphonic acid are true dispersing agents or deflocculant. The sulphonic acid may be either aryl-alkyl type or alkyl-aryl type and can alter the charges through physical adsorption. These are polyelectrolytes. The most important disadvantage of these is that they are not safe to be used internally. Lecithin is another deflocculating agent commonly used.

Protective Colloids

Hydrophilic colloids act as protective colloids after certain concentration. These are adsorbed on the hydrophobic dispersed particles. The strength of the double layer increases due to their hydrogen bonding, as a result the molecular interaction is reduced, and the dispersed particles do not coagulate. That is why such colloids are called protective colloids. For example, acacia, albumin, gelatin, tragacanth, etc. are used as protective colloids. The protective activity of these colloids is expressed in terms of *gold number. If 1 ml of 10% solution of sodium chloride is added to 10 ml of gold sol the colour of the sol changes from red to violet. The minimum amount (in mg) of a colloid required to prevent this colour change is called as its gold number.* The colloids with lesser gold number have greater protective action.

The gold numbers of certain protective colloids are mentioned here in the decreasing order.

Gelatin (0.005-0.01) < Albumin (0.1) < Acacia (0.1–0.2) < Tragacanth (2)

Electrolytes

Certain inorganic salts are frequently added to a dispersion to reduce the apparent zeta potential of the dispersion. This indicates that the electrolytes reduce the electric barrier between the dispersed particles and form a bridge between them. Thus, the electrolytes act as flocculating agent.

Aluminium chloride can make flocculated suspension of sulphamerazine by changing the zeta potential. Further addition of the electrolyte causes the flocs to settle which ultimately turned into cake. The zeta potential beyond certain range (positive or negative) could turn a suspension from non-caking to caking. The efficiency of the electrolytes depends on their size and valence. Commonly used electrolytes are aluminium chloride, sodium chloride, aluminium potassium phosphate (alum), sodium phosphate, etc.

Humectants

Both in oral and topical suspensions, humectant is used. Humectants such as glycerin, sorbitol, and propylene glycol prevent crystallization of dissolved solids. These improve the consistency and taste of the formulation.

Preservatives

Carbohydrates, polysaccharides, gum, cellulose derivatives, clay and electrolytes are used in liquid preparations. Many of these ingredients, favour the growth of microorganisms such as bacteria, yeast or fungi. So, any preparation intended for oral, topical or parenteral administration should contain suitable preservative. Microorganisms do not cause health problems to the patients only; but, also change the stability of the formulation. Physical changes like discoloration, change in taste, odour and viscosity take place. Chemical changes include hydrolysis of drug, preservative and other excipients, change of pH, etc.

Broadly, a preservative may be alcohols, aldehydes, acids, esters, phenol and its derivatives (e.g. halogenated phenols), quaternary ammonium compounds, formaldehyde donors, etc. For topical preparations most frequently used preservative system is combination of formaldehyde donor and parabens. The Table below provides different types of preservatives used in liquid preparations and injections.

Table 7.1 Commonly used different types of preservatives.

Type of preservatives	Examples
Acids and their salts	Benzoic acid and its salt Formaldehyde Sorbic acid and its salts
Ester, Alcohol	Methyl parahydroxy benzoic acid (Methylparaben) Sodium salt of Methyl parahydroxy benzoic acid Propyl parahydroxy benzoic acid (propylparaben) Sodium salt of Propyl parahydroxy benzoic acid Butylparaben Benzyl alcohol
Quaternary ammonim compounds	Benzalkonium chloride Cetylpyridinium chloride Benzethonium chloride Ottasept
Phenol Formaldehyde & formaldehyde donor Alcohol	Bronopol Ucarcide Ethyl alcohol

Antioxidants

The drug or certain excipients of a polydispersed formulation may be susceptible to oxidation, and these degrade on storage. As a result, the therapeutic efficacy and/or physicochemical changes of the product take place. None of the two is desirable. The physicochemical changes can be detected by observing the changes in colour, odour, taste, consistency (viscosity). Some pharmaceutical ingredients are prone to auto-oxidation also. The presence of trace amount of metal ion or free radical generated through exposure to UV radiation can initiate/catalyze the auto-oxidation reaction. Hence, a suitable antioxidant should be present in the formulation.

Antioxidants are reducing agents and are divided into two major groups–

- Water soluble such as Sodium bisulphate, ascorbic acid, etc. belongs to the first group. These are oxidized and also react with free radicals. Usually these have less redox potential than the drugs or other excipients susceptible to oxidation.
- Oil soluble such as Butylated hydroxyanisole (BHA), tocopherols, alkyl gallates, etc. belong to the second group and they are true antioxidants. They block and break the free radical chain reactions.

An ideal antioxidant should possess following properties:

- ➢ Odourless, colourless and tasteless,
- ➢ Nontoxic and non-irritant,

- Compatible with other excipients of the formulation,
- Stable and effective within a wide range of pH.

Antioxidant should be selected on the basis of their redox potential. If necessary, combination of two antioxidants along with a chelating agent may be useful. However, it is essential to evaluate the efficacy of the antioxidant in the formulation periodically.

Flavours useful for masking of taste are shown below in the Table below

Taste	*Flavour(s) used*
Bitter	Anise, Chocolate, Mint, Wild cherry.
Sweet	Vanilla, Berries, Fruit.
Sour	Citrus fruits, Liquorice, Raspberry
Salty	Butterscotch, Liquorice, Peach, Vanilla

Stabilisation

The stability of liquid dosage forms may be affected by decomposition due to oxidation, which may be prevented by:

- Filling in container under vacuum or with inert gas,
- Storage of the well-closed filled containers at lower temperature,
- Incorporating a suitable reducing agent or antioxidant in the formulation.

Cause of oxidation	*Remedy*
Atmospheric oxygen	
Oxidising agent agent present in formulation	use of a reducing agent
Microbial contamination	use of antimicrobial preservative

Commonly used **stabilising agents** are shown below in the Table below:

Reducing agents	*Common use*
Sodium sulphite	Antioxidant and antimicrobial Preservative in alkaline preparations.
Sodium metabisulphite	Food and pharmaceuticals containing Easily oxidizable substances.
Sodium thiosulphate	Food and pharmaceuticals
Sulphurous acid	Food(fruit) products and pharmaceuticals
Sulphur dioxide	Food(fruit) products and some injections
Dextrose	Food and pharmaceuticals
Catechol	Products containing oils and fats
Gallic acid	- do -
Pyrogallol	- do -

Table *Contd...*

Reducing agents	*Common use*
Ethyl Gallate	Products of oils, fats, food, cosmetic and perfumes.
Propyl gallate	- do -
Octyl Gallate	- do -
Dodecyl Gallate	- do -
Nordihydroguaiaretic acid (NDGA)	Products of oils and fats
Hydroquinone	- do -
Tocopherols	Food products
Butylated hydroxyl anisole (BHA)	Cosmetics and pharmaceuticals containing oils and fats.
Amino and Hydroxy derivative of ρ-phenylamine diamine	- do -
Diphenyl amines	- do -
Caseine and Edestine	- do -
Cysteine hydrochloride	- do -
Monohydric phenol	- do -

Synergists: These are the substances when used with suitable antioxidant, enhance the activity of antioxidants. For this these are called synergists. These may be water soluble or oil soluble. The names of some synergists are given below in the Table below.

Water soluble	Oil soluble
Citric acid Tartaric acid Phosphoric acid Ascorbic acid Carboxymethyl mercapto succinic acid	Ascorbyl palmitate Monostearyl citrate Mono-isopropyl citrate Palmityl phosphate

Solubility Enhancement Techniques

Solubility can be defined quantitatively as the concentration of the dissolved substance (solute) in its saturated solution at a particular temperature and qualitatively as the spontaneous interaction of two or more substances to form a homogeneous molecular dispersion.

Solubility of drug substance is the maximum concentration of the drug solute dissolved in the solvent under specific condition of temperature, pH and pressure. The drug solubility in saturated solution is a static property whereas the rate of dissolution of a drug is its dynamic property and it closely related to the bioavailability of the drug. The solubility of a drug can be described in various descriptive terms as mentioned in Table below.

Descriptive terms	Approximate volume of solvent in millilitres per gram of solute
Very soluble	Less than 1
Freely soluble	From 1 to 10
Soluble	From 10 to 30
Sparingly soluble	From 30 to 100
Slightly soluble	From 100 to 1000
Very slightly soluble	From 1000 to 10,000
Insoluble	More than 10,000

During development of a liquid formulation may or may not be orally administered, solubility of the active pharmaceutical ingredient (API) is one of its most important properties. The term *solubility* refers to the solubility in water, bwecause water is the universal solvent for liquid formulations.

Most of the drugs are either sparingly soluble or poorly soluble compounds and hence many researches have been conducted to solubilize such drugs. Thus, solubilization of an insoluble or poorly soluble active pharmaceutical ingredient (API) becomes the major challenge. Accordingly, various techniques have been developed to enhance solubility of the poorly soluble drug.

However, before knowing the solubilization techniques the knowledge about the following is important. These are the findings of the researches and based on these the techniques have been developed.

- Most of the drugs are either weakly acid or weakly base, and hence polarity of the solvent plays an important role in solubilization of drugs. In other words, dielectric constant of the solvent has major role in solubilization of drugs. Polar compounds are soluble in polar solvents and nonpolar compounds dissolve in nonpolar solvents.
- Water has the highest dielectric constant; hence, it can solubilize most of the polar drugs.
- Solubility is closely related to absorption and subsequently bioavailability of a drug.
- Drugs have been classified into four groups on the basis of solubility and permeability (BCS classification).

Accordingly, various techniques have been developed to improve solubility and dissolution rates of poorly water-soluble drugs. The techniques include:

1. Particle Size Reduction
2. Nanonization
3. Cosolvency

4. Hydrotropy
5. pH Adjustment
6. Sonocrystallization
7. Supercritical Fluid (SCF) Process
8. Solid Dispersion
9. Inclusion Complexation
10. Self-Emulsifying or Self-Micro Emulsifying Systems
11. Liquisolid Methods

In these techniques carrier plays an important role in improving solubility and dissolution rate. Polymers, super disintegrants, surfactants are extensively studied in recent years for improvement of dissolution of drugs.

1. **Particle Size Reduction**

   The solubility of a substance is usually related to its particle size and if the particle is smaller, the surface area to volume ratio increases. The larger surface area allows greater interaction with the solvent which causes an increase in solubility. Thus, traditionally this method has been used for improving of solubility. The methods of particle size reduction are comminution and spray drying.

2. **Nanonization**

   This is a technique used to reduce particle size of the particles in nano size range approximately 100 nm or less. Various nanonization techniques have been developed to increase the dissolution rates and bioavailability of various poorly soluble drugs in water. Different techniques used for nanonization of drug include Wet milling, Homogenization, Emulsification-solvent evaporation, Pear milling, Spray drying etc. There are many examples of nanonization of drugs.

3. **Cosolvency**

   The aqueous solubility of a poorly soluble drug can be increased by using some water miscible solvents such as alcohol, propylene glycol, etc. in which the drug is readily soluble. This process is known as cosolvency and the solvent used in combination with water is known as cosolvent. Cosolvent system works by reducing the interfacial tension between the aqueous solution and hydrophobic solute.

   It is also commonly known as solvent blending.

4. **Hydrotropy**

   Hydrotropy is a solubilization technique in which addition of large amount of a second water soluble solute is used. Second water soluble solute is known as hydrotropic agent such as sodium benzoate, sodium salicylate, urea, nicotinamide, sodium citrate, and sodium acetate, etc. which can enhance the aqueous solubilities of many poorly water-soluble drugs.

5. **pH Adjustment**

   Drugs are mostly either weak organic acids or weak bases. Hence, by changing the pH of water solubility of drug can be increased greatly. Weakly acidic drug solubilizes in alkaline medium while weakly basic drugs in acidic medium.

6. **Sono-crystallisation**

   The particle size can be reduced by recrystallization of poorly soluble materials using liquid solvents and anti-solvents. Such a novel approach for particle size reduction on the basis of crystallization by using ultrasound is called Sono-crystallisation. This method utilizes ultrasonic rays at a frequency range of 20-100 kHz. Thus, this method can be used to enhance aqueous solubility of a drug.

7. **Supercritical Fluid (SCF) Process**

   It has been known for more than a century that supercritical fluids (SCFs) can dissolve non-volatile solvents. It is safe, environmentally friendly, and economical. The low operating conditions (temperature and pressure) make SCFs attractive for pharmaceutical application. A SCF exists as a single phase above its critical temperature (Tc) and pressure (Pc). SCFs have useful properties to process the products. Their properties are intermediate between those of pure liquid and gas. For example, they have liquid-like density, gas-like compressibility and viscosity and higher diffusivity than liquids. The density, viscosity and diffusivity and other physical properties such as dielectric constant and polarity vary considerably with small changes in operating temperature, pressure, or both around the critical points.

   The SCFs have long been recognized and used in the food industry, now are being used in pharmaceutical processing. Commonly used supercritical solvents include carbon dioxide, nitrous oxide, ethylene, propylene, propane, n-pentane, ethanol, ammonia, and water.

   Once the drug particles are solubilized within SCF, recrystallization of very fine particles up to submicron size range takes place. Current SCF processes have the ability to produce nano suspensions of particles 5-2,000 nm in diameter.

8. **Solid Dispersion**

   Solid dispersions have been found a useful technique to increase the dissolution, absorption, and therapeutic efficacy of drugs in dosage forms. The solid dispersion is a group of solid products of at least two different components, usually a hydrophilic matrix and a hydrophobic drug. The most commonly used hydrophilic carriers for solid dispersions include polyvinylpyrrolidone (Povidone, PVP), polyethylene glycols (PEGs), Plasdone- S630. Surfactants like Tween-80, docusate sodium, Myrj-52, Pluronic-F68, and sodium lauryl sulphate (SLS) also find a place in the formulation of solid dispersion. The solubility of celecoxib, halofantrine, and ritonavir can be improved by solid dispersion using suitable hydrophilic carriers like celecoxib with povidone (PVP) and ritonavir with gelucire.

9. **Inclusion Complexation**

   This technique has been used to improve the aqueous solubility, dissolution rate, and bioavailability of slightly or poorly water-soluble drugs. Inclusion complexes are formed when the nonpolar molecule or the nonpolar region of one molecule (known as guest) is inserted into the cavity of another molecule or group of molecules (known as host). For inclusion complexation the major structural requirement is a snug fit of the guest into the cavity of host molecule. The cavity of host must be large enough to accommodate the guest and small enough to eliminate water. The total contact between the water and the nonpolar regions of the host and the guest is reduced.

   Various methods used to prepare inclusion complexes of poorly soluble drugs are;

   - Kneading

     The kneaded mass is prepared by making a paste of cyclodextrin with guest molecules in small quantity of either water or ethanol to form kneaded mass. Kneaded mass can be dried at 45 °C and pulverized.

   - Melting

     Excess quantity of guest is melted, mixed with powdered cyclodextrin, after cooling excess quantity of quest is removed by washing with weak complex forming solvent. The method restricted to sublimable guest like menthol.

- Solution-enhanced dispersion by the Supercritical fluids (SEDS)

  SEDS is novel and single step method. This method can produce solid drug-cyclodextrin complexes. The optimization of processing conditions is essential to achieve the optimum complexation efficiency and to compare with drug-cyclodextrin complexation methods.

  Advantages over other methods are:

  - Preparation of solid-cyclodextrin complexes is a single step process,
  - Higher complexation efficiency (avoidance of excess cyclodextrin in powder) can be achieved.
  - The contact of drug with cyclodextrin during the process is reduced.
  - Increased dissolution rate of the drug.

- Co-evaporation/Solvent evaporation method

  The aqueous solution of host molecule is added and mixed with the alcoholic solution of guest molecule, stirred for sometimes and evaporated at room temp until dried mass is obtained. The dried mass is pulverized and sieved. The fraction is then collected.

- Microwave Irradiation

  This method provides rapid organic synthesis and reactions. The reaction requires shorter time and produces higher amount of product.

- Freeze Drying/Lyophilisation technique

  According to stoichiometry the required quantity of host and guest molecules were added to aqueous solution of cyclodextrin. The suspension is stirred magnetically for 24 hours and the resulting mixture is freeze dried at 60 °C for 24 hours.

- Spray drying/Atomization

  In this method the solution of host molecules is prepared usually in ethanol: water (1:1). To this solution the guest molecule is added, and the mixture is stirred for 24 hr. at room temperature. The solution is spray dried by optimized conditions of air flow rate, atomizing air pressure, inlet temperature, outlet temperature, flow rate of solution etc. Product obtained is passed through 63-160 micrometer granulometric sieve.

10. Self-Emulsifying or Self-Micro Emulsifying Systems

Self-emulsifying or self-micro emulsifying systems are used to form emulsion in situ in the gastrointestinal tract. The mixture of oil, surfactant, co-surfactant, one or more hydrophilic solvents and co-solvent forms a transparent isotropic solution, known as the self-emulsifying drug delivery system (SEDDS). These do not contain the external phase (water) and forms fine o/w emulsions or micro-emulsions spontaneously upon dilution after reaching the aqueous phase in the GIT. It is used to improve the dissolution and absorption of lipophilic drug.

One of the advantages of SEDDS is that

1. The emulsion is formed spontaneously when the components are mildly agitated, and
2. The emulsion formed is thermodynamically stable.

The disadvantages of this system include

1. Chemical instabilities of drugs, and
2. High surfactant concentrations.
3. The large quantity of surfactant (30-60%) in self-emulsifying formulations irritates the GIT.
4. Most self-emulsifying systems are filled to administration in lipid filled soft or hard gelatin capsules due to the liquid nature of the product.
5. Interaction between the capsule shell and the emulsion should be considered so as to prevent the hygroscopic contents from dehydrating or migrating into the capsule shell.

Since SMEDDS contain high concentration of surfactants, they should be limited to oral applications and may not be used for long term treatment diarrhoea.

11. Liquisolid Methods

The drug dissolved in the liquid vehicle is incorporated into a porous carrier material which is composed of closely matted cellulosic fibres in its interior. Both absorption and adsorption take place. That is, initially the liquid is absorbed in the interior of the particles and then is distributed around its internal structure. Once saturation of this process is attained, adsorption of the liquid onto the internal and external surfaces of the porous carrier particles takes place. The coating material with high adsorptive properties and large specific surface area produces the liquisolid system with desirable flow characteristics. This type of solid system (Liquisolid) possesses acceptable flow properties and compressibility compared to powdered forms of liquid medications. The concept of Liquisolid system is that the liquid drugs having low aqueous solubility is dissolved in suitable non-volatile solvents, converted to free flowing and radially compressible powder by simple mixing with selected powdered excipients called as carrier and coating materials. Microcrystalline and amorphous cellulose and silica powders may be used for this purpose as coating materials.

Exercise

A. Multiple Choice Question Carrying 01 Mark

1. Greater drug absorption is expected from
   (a) Tablet (b) Capsule
   (c) Suspensions (d) Solution
2. Liquid dosage forms are suitable for
   (a) Hygroscopic drugs (b) Moisture sensitive drugs
   (c) Non-hygroscopic drugs (d) Non-deliquescent drugs
3. Which of the following is a biphasic liquid dosage form?
   (a) Solution (b) Syrup
   (c) Suspension (d) Elixir
4. Sweetener is used in which type of formulation
   (a) Injectable (b) Liquid oral
   (c) Eye drop (d) Lotion of external application
5. In which preparation preservative is not added
   (a) Ear drop (b) Eye drop
   (c) Large volume parenteral (d) Small volume parenteral
6. Flavour is not added to
   (a) Emulsion for topical application
   (b) Linctus
   (c) Cough syrup
   (d) Eye drop
7. Which water is used for preparing liquid orals
   (a) Water for injection (b) Sterile water for injection
   (c) Purified water (d) Potable water
8. Which type of oil is generally used for making injectable
   (a) Mineral oil (b) Volatile oil
   (c) Vegetable oil (d) None of the above

9. Dimethyl sulphoxide is used as a
   (a) Solubilizer (b) Stabilizer
   (c) Preservative (d) Wetting agent
10. HLB values of antifoaming agent is within
   (a) 3 – 7 (b) 7 – 9
   (c) 7 – 10 (d) 1 – 3
11. HLB values of emulsifying agent is within
   (a) 1 – 3 (b) 7 – 10
   (c) 8 – 17 (d) 3 – 7
12. Microcrystalline cellulose
   (a) Is soluble in water
   (b) Is soluble in alcohol
   (c) Forms dispersion in water
   (d) Shows dilatant flow when dispersed in water
13. Sodium carboxymethyl cellulose
   (a) Is a suspending agent (b) Is insoluble in water
   (c) Is a preservative (d) Is an antioxidant
14. Carbomer is a
   (a) Natural polymer (b) Synthetic polymer
   (c) Semisynthetic polymer (d) Clay
15. Which of the following is not a protective colloid
   (a) Acacia (b) Gelatin
   (c) Carboxymethyl cellulose (d) Albumin
16. To control zeta potential, an electrolyte is used in
   (a) Solution (b) Elixir
   (c) Suspension (d) Ointment
17. Benzyl alcohol is used as
   (a) Humectant (b) Suspending agent
   (c) Emulsifier (d) Preservative
18. Which of the following possesses different activity
   (a) Glycerin (b) Sodium sulphite
   (c) Sodium thiosulphate (d) Gallic acid

19. Which of the following is not a cause of oxidation
    (a) Atmospheric oxygen
    (b) Microbial contamination
    (c) Presence of an oxidant
    (d) Moisture
20. Dielectric constant of water is
    (a) Least
    (b) Low
    (c) High
    (d) Medium

B. Question Carrying 05 Marks

1. Write down the reasons in favour of liquid dosage form
2. What are the limitations of liquid dosage form?
3. Prepare a list of excipients used in oral liquid which is solution; mention the expected purpose of each.
4. Prepare a list of excipients used in oral liquid which is suspension; mention the expected purpose of each.
5. Prepare a list of excipients used in liquid intended for injection intramuscularly; mention the expected purpose of each.
6. Prepare a list of excipients used in liquid which is solution intended for intravenous administration; mention the expected purpose of each.
7. What are methods used to prepare inclusion compound for solubility enhancement.
8. Discuss on the suspending agents used in suspensions.
9. What are different categories of surface-active agents used in liquid formulation?
10. Write note on cosolvents used in liquid formulations.

C. Question Carrying 10 Marks

1. Discuss the benefits and limitations of liquid dosage forms
2. Prepare a list of excipients used in oral solution, suspension and emulsion dosage forms.
3. Make a list of excipients used to prepare small volume and large volume parenteral solutions.
4. What are methods used to enhance the solubility of a drug?

Answers

A. Multiple Choice Questions

1. (d)	2. (a)	3. (c)	4. (b)	5. (c)
6. (d)	7. (c)	8. (c)	9. (a)	10. (d)
11. (d)	12. (c)	13. (a)	14. (b)	15. (c)
16. (c)	17. (d)	18. (a)	19. (d)	20. (c)

Chapter 8

Monophasic Liquids

Definitions and Preparations of Gargles, Mouthwashes, Throat Paint, Ear Drops, Nasal Drops, Enemas, Syrups, Elixirs, Liniments and Lotions.

Introduction

The term Monophasic refers to the system that contains only one phase. The phase may be prepared by mixing two or more than two components. For administration of drug or medication these are the simple preparation. Simple Syrup, gargles, mouthwashes, throat paint, eardrop, nasal drops belong to this category of preparation. These preparations may be classified into two categories:

- Liquids intended for internal administration,
- Liquids intended for external application

Monophasic liquid can be defined as a homogeneous one phase liquid system containing two or more than two components. Generally, in such liquid's solvent is present in large quantity. Exception is simple syrup which contains 66.7% (large quantity of solute) of sucrose and the solvent (water) is only 33.3%.

The liquids intended for external application include the following preparations:

- Gargles
- Mouthwashes
- Throat paint
- Douches
- Enemas
- Ear drops
- Nasal drops and sprays
- Liniments, and
- Lotions

Definition and Preparation of Gargles

Gargles are aqueous solutions used for the treatment of throat infections such as pharynx and nasopharynx part). These preparations are available in concentrated solutions which are diluted before use as per the direction given by the prescriber. Usually these are diluted with warm water at the time of administration.

In the posterior part of the mouth cavity the diluted preparation is agitated (gargled) with exhaled air for one to two minutes. For this reason, these are called gargles. After gargling the solution is thrown out of mouth.

This has already been mentioned that these are solution preparations. These are intended for use as a prophylactic or in the treatment of throat infection. These are used either 'as is' or after dilution with water. They may contain antiseptics, antibiotics with or without an anaesthetic. The preparation is taken in mouth and held in throat, then air from the lung is forced through the solution (gargle). After this the gargle is spitted or expectorated from the mouth. However, very few preparations are swallowed after gargling. The repeated process brings the medicaments of the gargle into intimate contact with the membranous lining of the throat where mild sore is present and a relief to the throat-sore is achieved.

The gargle does not make any protective covering on the throat membrane, hence, no oily substance with or without any suspending agent, or no drug with mucilaginous nature should be used in these preparations.

Gargles are packed in clear, fluted glass or plastic bottles so that these can be distinguished from the preparations intended for internal administration. The container must be airtight and light resistant. Labels on the bottles must mention clearly and boldly that 'For external use only', also the direction for use, and the ratio of dilution with warm water.

If the preparation contains any light sensitive material a coloured bottle should be used.

Advantages of gargles

- These are convenient for use in the treatment of infections in mouth cavity infection of (pharynx and nasopharynx).
- The solution after proper dilution is simply gargled with exhaled air for few minutes.
- On gargling the soreness in mild throat infection is relieved and deodorant effect is provided.
- Smaller size container is required since concentrated solution is supplied

- Gargles can be prepared with various drugs such as antibiotics, antiseptics, local anaesthetics, anti-inflammatory agents, antifungal agents, analgesics, etc.

Disadvantages

Gargles have various advantages; but this category of preparation suffers from some disadvantages.

- These provide temporary effect
- For the patients having respiratory problem these preparations are not suitable.
- If exhaled air is not held constantly during gargling, little amount may be swallowed.

Preparation of Gargles

Apart from active pharmaceutical ingredient following excipients/additives/ adjuvants are used to formulate this type of preparation.

- Vehicle or solvent – Most of the preparations are formulated with purified water as the solvent with or without alcohol.
- Other solvents such as glycerine, sorbitol liquid, propylene glycol, etc. are used as cosolvent; sometimes to improve the solubility of active ingredient.
- Flavouring agents – Most accepted flavouring agents are either volatile oils or volatile substances. In general, cinnamon oil, cardamom oil, menthol, etc. are used as flavouring agent. These flavouring agents also have antiseptic property.
- Colours – In each type of pharmaceutical preparation FDA approved colours must be used.
- Preservatives – Liquid dosage forms must contain suitable preservative system. Because most of the liquid preparations are good medium for microbial growth. There are various sources of contamination such as raw material, processing vessels, equipment, manufacturing environment, personnel, packaging materials, etc. Thus, to arrest or prevent growth of microorganisms suitable preservatives. Only pharmaceutical preparations which are freshly prepared and administered and parenteral preparation administered intravenously do not require any preservative. Ideally preservative should have following characteristics:
  - Preservative used should be broad spectrum and should be effective against wide range of microorganisms.

- Preservative used should be physically, chemically and microbiologically stable to maintain the shelf life of the preparation.
- Preservative should be nontoxic, non-sensitizing, adequately soluble in the vehicle.
- It should be compatible with other ingredients of the formulation
- At the recommended concentration it should have acceptable odour and taste.

Selection of preservative should be done on the basis of intended use of the preparation. Preservatives are classified into four categories –

1. Acidic,
2. Neutral,
3. Mercurials, and
4. Quaternary ammonium compounds.

Examples and their usual concentrations are given in the Table 8.1 below.

Table 8.1 Different types of preservatives and their usual concentrations in pharmaceutical formulations.

Type of preservative	Name of preservative	Usual and effective Concentration (%)
Acidic	Phenol	0.5
	o-phenyl Phenol	0.005 – 0.01
	Chlorocresol	0.05 – 0.1
	Benzoic acid and its salts	0.1 – 0. 5
	Boric acid and its salts	0.05 – 0.2
	Parahydroxy benzoic acid and its salt	0.1 – 0.5
Neutral	Chlorobutanol	0.5
	Benzyl alcohol	1.0
	β-Phenylethyl alcohol	0.2 – 1.0
Mercurials	Thiomersal	0.001 – 0.1
	Phenylmercuric acetate or nitrate	0.002 – 0.005
	Nitromersol	0.001 – 0.1
Quaternary Ammonium compounds	Benzalkonium chloride	0.004 – 0.02
	Cetylpyridinium chloride	0.01 – 0.02

- Antioxidant – These substances stabilize the liquid formulations. During storage for long time (shelf life) the products may undergo degradation. To stop such degradation suitable antioxidants and buffer systems are used. Table 8.2 presents the list of substances commonly used to stabilize the liquid preparations containing both aqueous and oil base.

Table 8.2 Stabilizers commonly used in pharmaceutical liquid preparations.

Antioxidants used in aqueous preparations	Antioxidants used in oil preparations
Ascorbic acid	Ascorbyl palmitate
Cysteine hydrochloride	Butylated hydroxy toluene
Sodium formaldehyde sulphoxylate	Butylated hydroxy anisole
Sodium metabisulphite	Hydroquinone
Sodium bisulphite	Lecithin
Sodium sulphite	Nordihydroguaiaretic acid
Sodium thiosulphate	Phenyl naphthylamine
Thioglycerol	Propyl gallate
Thioglycolic acid	α- tocopherol
Thiosorbitol	
Thiourea	

Method of Preparation

Since most of the substances used to prepare gargles are soluble either in water or in alcohol, these preparations are prepared by solution method. Most common active substances used in gargles are:

- Anti-infective agents – Phenol, Thymol
- Antiseptics and deodorants – volatile oils
- Astringents – Potassium chlorate
- Bactericidal – Potassium permanganate

Formulation 1: Phenol Gargle BPC

Standard for Phenol: It contains not less than 99.0%w/w of phenol, calculated as C_6H_6O.

Standard for Product: Content of Phenol: 0.84 – 1.13%w/v calculated as C_6H_6O.

Composition

It contains Phenol Glycerine BPC 5%v/v in water.

Colour used, Amaranth.

Use: Bactericidal gargle.

Lot size: 100 ml.

Manufacturing Formula:

Phenol Glycerine BPC	5.0 ml
Amaranth solution, 1.0%	1.0 ml
Purified water IP q.s to	100 ml

Manufacturing Method

Preparation of Phenol Glycerine –

Phenol	1.6 g
Glycerine	8.4 g

Transfer accurately weighed amount of phenol into a 25ml clean, dry beaker, add glycerine and stir to dissolve, if required heat the mixture until phenol is completely dissolved.

Note: Handle phenol carefully, it is very caustic and whitens the skin. Use spatula and gloves.

Preparation of Phenol Gargle

- Transfer 1.0 ml of phenol glycerine using a pipette into a 25 ml measuring cylinder,
- Add 0.2 ml of amaranth solution to it, mix,
- Make up the volume with purified water, stopper and shake,
- Filter the solution through cotton wool, fill the solution in a clean, amber bottle, seal and label properly,
- Carry out the test.

Note: The label must mention, *not to be swallowed.*

Formulation 2: Potassium Chlorate and Phenol Gargle BPC

Standard for Potassium chlorate: It should be of reagent grade or pharmaceutical grade as per IP.

for Liquefied Phenol: It contains not less than 88.0%w/w of phenol, calculated as C_6H_6O.

Standard for the product: Content of Phenol, 1.10 – 1.40%w/v, calculated as C_6H_6O.

Content of potassium chlorate, 2.85 – 3.15%w/v, calculated as $KClO_3$

Composition

It contains Phenol IP 1.25%w/v

Potassium chlorate IP 3.0%w/v

Liquefied Phenol IP 1.25%w/v in purified water,

Colour used: Amaranth

Use: Antiseptic (Bactericidal) and mild astringent gargle.

Lot size: 100 ml

Manufacturing Formula

Liquefied Phenol IP	1.5 ml
Potassium chlorate IP	3.0 g
Amaranth solution, 1.0%	1.0 ml
Purified water IP qs to	100 ml

Manufacturing Method

- Take weighed quantity of potassium chlorate in a clean 25 ml stopper cylinder, add about 10 ml of purified water, shake until dissolve,
- Add measured volume of liquefied phenol, mix thoroughly,
- Add measured volume of amaranth solution and make up the volume with purified water, stopper the cylinder and shake,
- Filter the solution through cotton wool and fill in a colour bottle, seal with a pilfer proof cap,
- Carry out the tests and label properly.

Note: The label must mention, *not to be swallowed.*

Definition and Preparation of Mouthwashes

These are aqueous solutions, sometimes concentrated solutions, commonly used for cleansing and deodorizing the buccal cavity. The solution is swished in the oral cavity and then thrown out.

Mouthwashes are formulated and used for-

1. Therapeutic purposes,
2. Diagnostic purposes and
3. Cosmetic use.

The therapeutic mouthwashes are used for the treatment of plaque, gingivitis, dental carries and stomatitis. For example, a mixture of antihistaminic, hydrocortisone, nystatin and tetracycline is used for stomatitis which is a painful side effect of cancer chemotherapy. Pilocarpine is used for dry mouth (xerostoma). Chlorhexidine gluconate is used for plaque. The mouthwash can also be used for diagnostic purpose. Oral cancer or lesions can be diagnosed by using toludine blue mouthwash. The cosmetic mouthwash contains antimicrobial drugs with or without a flavour and is used to reduce the bad breath.

Besides active constituents a mouthwash contain other excipients like alcohol, surface active agents, humectant, colouring agents and flavouring agents.

- Alcohol is used in the range from 10% to 20%. At this concentration it can act as a cosolvent, preservative, solubilizer and enhancer of flavours and taste masking agent for the unpleasant taste of the drug.
- Glycerine or sorbitol is used as humectant to increase the viscosity, sweetness of the mouthwash. It can improve the mouth feel or body to the preparation and preservation of the product.
- A suitable surface-active agent, non-ionic, anionic or cationic is used in the concentration of 0.1% - 0.5% to solubilise the flavour, to remove the debris from the preparation through foaming action.

Containers: Mouthwashes are usually packed in white fluted bottles.

Labelling: Along with necessary information a direction should be given whether the preparation is to be diluted before use and the proportion of dilution. The label must clearly and distinguishably mention that the preparation is not intended for internal administration.

Formulations 1: Sodium Chloride Mouthwash, Compound BPC

Standard for Sodium Chloride: It should contain not less than 99% and not more than 100.5%w/w of NaCl on dried basis.

Standard for Sodium Bicarbonate: It should contain not less than 99% and not more than 101%w/w of $NaHCO_3$.

Standard for product: Content of Sodium Chloride; 1.42 – 1.58%w/v calculated as NaCl.

Content of Sodium Bicarbonate; 0.95 – 1.05%w/v calculated as $NaHCO_3$.

Composition:

It contains

Sodium Chloride IP	1.5%
Sodium Bicarbonate IP	1.0%
Quillaia Extract	0.5%

In flavoured aqueous base.

Use: Cleansing of mouth.

Lot size: 100 ml

Manufacturing Formula:

Sodium Chloride IP	1.5 g
Sodium Bicarbonate IP	1.0 g
Peppermint oil (0.4% solution in alcohol)	2.5 ml
Quillaia Liquid Extract, 0.5%w/v	0.5 ml
Purified water IP qs to	100 ml

Manufacturing Method

- Take 2.5 ml of peppermint oil solution in a clean test tube add 0.5 ml of quillaia extract and mix,
- Dissolve 1.5 g of sodium chloride and 1.0 g of sodium bicarbonate in 50 ml of freshly boiled and cooled purified water, into a clean 100 ml measuring cylinder,
- Add 3.0 ml of peppermint oil and quillaia mixture into bulk solution and mix thoroughly, make up the volume with purified water and mix.
- Carry out the tests, if necessary, filter through cotton wool,
- Fill the solution into a fluted bottle and seal with a cap,
- Label the preparation properly.

Note: This preparation should be diluted with equal volume of warm water before use.

Formulations 2: Zinc Sulphate and Zinc Chloride Mouthwash BPC

Standard for Zinc Sulphate: It should contain not less than 99% and not more than 104%w/w of $ZnSO_4 7H_2O$.

Standard for Zinc Chloride: It should contain not less than 95% and not more than 100.5%w/w of $ZnCl_2$.

Standard for product: Content of Zinc; 0.89 – 0.98%w/v calculated as Zn.

Composition:

It contains Zinc Sulphate	IP	2.0%
Zinc Chloride	IP	1.0%

Use: Prevention of sour and bitter taste in the mouth.

Lot size: 100 ml

Manufacturing Formula

Zinc Sulphate IP	2.0 g
Zinc Chloride IP	1.0 g
Tartrazine solution, 1.0%	1.0 ml
Dil. Hydrochloric Acid	1.0 ml
Purified water IP qs to	100 ml

Manufacturing Method

- Take weighed quantity of Zinc Sulphate and Zinc Chloride in a 100 ml stopper measuring cylinder, dissolve in 50 ml of purified water,
- Add measured volume of dilute hydrochloric acid, mix thoroughly,
- Add tartrazine solution and make up the volume,

- Determine the content of zinc,
- Filter the solution through cotton wool, if necessary, and fill in white fluted bottle, seal with a cap and label.

Note: This preparation should be diluted to 20 times with warm water before use.

Definition and Preparation of Throat Paint

These are viscous liquid preparations. These are used for the treatment of mouth and throat infections. Throat paints are made viscous to retain the drug for longer period of time in contact with mucous membrane in the mouth. As a result, the therapeutic action of the drug can be extended for longer period. Most commonly this type of preparations contains glycerine because glycerine has high viscosity, sweet, and palatability.

These products are packed in air-tight, coloured fluted bottles to differentiate these from the formulations intended for internal administration. The paint is applied over the affected area or part of the mouth. Either a camel brush or cotton plug twisted at the top of a thin wooden stick is used to apply the paint. Paints are not diluted like gargles before application; they are applied as such.

The label must clearly and boldly mention the following information: 'For External Use Only', 'Apply it with a camel brush or cotton plug', 'Keep away from children', and all other necessary information as per the D&C Act.

The throat paints possess certain advantages and some limitations also. For the treatment of sore, injuries, pharyngitis, laryngitis, follicular tonsillitis, etc. such paints are most suitable.

Advantages

- These are convenient to use over the affected area of the mouth
- These are very useful for the treatment of pharyngitis, laryngitis, follicular tonsillitis, and abscesses of the throat.
- They can retain the drug on the area of application for adequate time due to their high viscosity and the drug can elicit its therapeutic action
- The taste of the preparation is acceptable due to the presence of glycerine

Disadvantages

- The usefulness is not well favoured because of problem in application of the preparation over the affected area. Either a camel brush or cotton plug twisted at the end of the thin wooden stick is used for application.

- Use of brush or stick needs careful application of the paint
- The paint after application initiates salivation, as a result frequent spitting is made. This is an inconvenience to the patient.

Generally following types of active ingredients are used to prepare throat paints.

- Antiseptics such as iodine, crystal violet, etc.
- Astringent such as tannic acid, boric acid, etc.
- Anti-infectives such as phenol, ichthammol, etc.

Formulation Considerations

As stated above, throat paint should be adequately viscous so that the drug is not washed out immediately after application. Hence, the vehicle required to make the preparation must be viscous. Usually glycerine is most preferred vehicle, because it is palatable and sweet in taste. Sometimes liquid paraffin is used as a solvent. However, suitable hydrocolloid can be used to increase the viscosity of the preparation.

Besides vehicle other suitable additive such as colouring agent, sweetening agent, flavouring agent which can improve the organoleptic properties of the product are also used to prepare a throat paint. If required, to enhance the stability of drug in the formulation other ingredients such as antioxidant, buffers are also used.

Hydrocolloids are soluble in water. These can make their aqueous solution viscous. These are high molecular weight solid substances. Usually these are used as emulsifying and suspending agent. These are also known as gums. Their principal constituents are polysaccharides and proteins. Some of the hydrocolloids are more soluble in hot water such as gelatin and agar. On cooling either they precipitate or form gel. Some of the hydrocolloids like methylcellulose, hydroxy propyl methyl cellulose are more soluble in cold water.

Based on the source hydrocolloids are classified into three categories:

- **Natural** hydrocolloids are obtained from plants, animals and minerals. Gum acacia, gum tragacanth, and agar are obtained from plants. Gelatin and casein are obtained from animals; while colloidal silica, colloidal alumina, bentonite, and Veegum are from minerals.
- **Semi-synthetic** hydrocolloids are obtained by chemical modification of cellulose of wood and cotton. These are water soluble. Methyl cellulose, sodium carboxymethyl cellulose, hydroxy ethyl cellulose, hydroxy propyl cellulose, etc. belong to this class.

- **Synthetic** hydrocolloids are synthetic products. Most common example of this class is carbopol which is very commonly used in pharmaceutical preparations. Others are not used in pharmacy.

Formulation 1: Mandl's paint

Standard for Iodine: It should contain not less than 99.8% of I.

Standard for product: Content of I; 1.1875 to 1.3125%w/v calculated as I.

Composition:

It contains Iodine IP 1.25%

Use: Antiseptic.

Lot size: 100 ml

Manufacturing Formula:

Iodine IP	1.25 g
Potassium iodide IP	2.5 g
Peppermint oil	0.42 ml
Alcohol (90%)	3.75ml
Purified water IP	2.5 ml
Glycerine qs to	100 ml

Manufacturing Method:

- Take weighed quantity of Iodine and Potassium iodide in a 100 ml stopper measuring cylinder, dissolve in 2.5 ml of purified water, swirl till iodine is completely dissolved
- Add measured volume of alcohol and peppermint oil mix thoroughly in a 10 ml cylinder,
- Add oil solution to iodine solution, mix thoroughly,
- Add sufficient glycerine to make up the volume to 100 ml
- Determine the content of iodine,
- Filter the solution through cotton wool, if necessary, and fill in an amber fluted bottle, seal with a cap and label.

Note: This preparation should be stored in dark place.

Formulation 2: Tannic Acid-Glycerine Paint IP'66

Composition:

It contains Tannic Acid IP 20%w/w

Use: Astringent.

Lot size: 100 g

Manufacturing Formula

Tannic Acid IP	20.0 g
Sodium citrate IP	1.0 g
Dried Sodium sulphite	0.2 g
Glycerine qs to	100 g

Manufacturing Method

- Take weighed quantity of tannic acid, sodium citrate and dried sodium sulphite in a mortar pestle, crush with glycerine to make a paste.
- Add glycerine gradually and mix thoroughly until a smooth paste, transfer the paste into a 150 ml tarred beaker
- Add sufficient glycerine to make up the weight to 100 g
- Heat the mixture over a sand bath at about 120°C with occasional stirring until a clear solution is obtained
- Fill the product in an amber fluted bottle, seal with a cap and label.

Definition and Preparation of Ear Drops

Ear drops may be in the form of solution, emulsion, or suspension. When examined under suitable conditions of visibility solutions must be practically clear and practically free from particles.

Suspensions may sediment at the bottom; but the sediment must disperse readily after mild shaking and the dispersed particles must remain dispersed for sufficient period, so that a correct dose of the drug can be removed from the container and administered.

These preparations may contain certain adjuvants such as tonicity modifier, buffer, stabilizer, dispersing agents, solubilizing agents, and viscosity modifying agents. If buffers are added to the preparations to be used in surgical procedures, the nature and concentration of buffer must be suitable. If the active ingredient is susceptible to oxidation, a suitable antioxidant should be present in the preparation. However, the antioxidant added must be compatible with the other ingredients including active ingredient. Any additive present in the preparation should not adversely affect the intended therapeutic efficacy of the active ingredient and cause local irritation. Certain ear drops are supplied in dry and sterile form. These are constituted in an appropriate sterile liquid immediately before use.

Aqueous preparations supplied in multiple application containers may contain suitable antimicrobial preservatives at appropriate concentration. The preservative used should be compatible with other ingredients of the formulation and should remain effective throughout the shelf-life of the product and during the use of the preparation. If the product itself has adequate antimicrobial property, no antimicrobial preservative is required. The containers used for multiple application of the product should permit the withdrawal of the successive doses of the preparation. Such a container should normally contain no more than 10 ml of the preparation.

During development of a formulation of ear drops if an antimicrobial preservative is recommended, the need for it and its efficacy must be demonstrated by the test for efficacy of the antimicrobial agent. During manufacture, packaging, storage, and distribution of ear drops suitable tests should be conducted to ensure the quality with respect to microbial contamination.

Ear drops intended for use in surgical procedures or application to injured ear must be sterile. Such preparations should not contain antimicrobial preservatives and should be packed in single dose containers. Sterile ear drops should ensure sterility and the processes adopted should not allow contamination with microorganisms and growth of microorganisms.

Ear drops should be packed in well-closed containers. If the preparation is sterile, it should be stored in sterile, tightly closed, tamper-evident containers. Containers should be made of materials that do not cause deterioration of the product due to diffusion into or across the materials of the construction; the container must not produce foreign substances which come into the product. Ear drops should be packed in coloured fluted glass bottles fitted with a plastic screw cap incorporating a glass dropper tube fitted with a rubber teat, or in plastic squeeze bottle fitted with a plastic cap incorporating a dropper device.

The container must bear a label with a mention in bold letter, 'For External Use Only'.

Applications of Ear Drops

The ear drops are used for the following purposes

- Treatment of mild infections
- Softening of wax in the ear
- Cleansing after infections
- Drying weeping surfaces
- For antisepsis and anaesthesia.

Formulations

Product: Hydrocortisone and Neomycin Ear Drop BPC

Standards for product: Content of Hydrocortisone acetate: 90.0 – 110.0% of the stated amount; content of Neomycin sulphate: 90.0 – 115.0% of the stated amount

Composition:

It contains Hydrocortisone Acetate USP 1.5%

Neomycin Sulphate USP 0.5%

Use: Astringent.

Lot size: 100 ml

Manufacturing Formula:

Hydrocortisone Acetate USP	1.5g
Neomycin Sulphate USP	0.5g
Methylcellulose	0.2 g
Purified Water qs to	100 ml

Manufacturing Method:

- Take required quantity of neomycin sulphate; dissolve in 40 ml of freshly boiled and cooled purified water in a clean 100 ml beaker.
- Add weighed amount of methylcellulose to 50 ml freshly boiled and cooled purified water in a clean 250 ml beaker; stir gently till the gum dissolves completely.
- Filter the solutions through G4 sintered glass crucible and transfer the filtrate into clean 250 ml beaker.
- Take the required quantity of hydrocortisone acetate in a clean mortar pestle; make paste with little amount of filtered solution to until required degree of fineness is obtained.
- Transfer the hydrocortisone acetate paste to the beaker and make up the volume with freshly boiled and cooled purified water.
- Stir the suspension for at least 1hr.
- Fill the product in an amber fluted bottle, seal with a cap and label.

Note: The suspension must have fine particles of hydrocortisone acetate as mentioned: 75% of the particles have a maximum diameter less than 10 µm; not less than 99% of the particles have a maximum diameter of 20 µm and no particle has a maximum diameter greater than 500µm.

Definition and Preparation of Nasal Drops

Intranasal drug delivery is recognized to be a useful and reliable alternative to oral and parenteral routes. The nasal route of drug delivery can be used for both local and systemic drug delivery. For instance, localized nasal drug delivery is usually used to treat conditions related to the nasal cavity, such as congestion, rhinitis, sinusitis and related allergic conditions. A diverse range of drugs including corticosteroids, anti-histamines, anti-cholinergic and vasoconstrictors can be administered locally. In recent years, achieving a systemic drug action using the nose as the entry portal into the body has received more attention. Also, the nasal delivery seems to be a favourable way to circumvent the obstacles for blood brain barrier (BBB) allowing the direct drug delivery in the bio-phase of central nervous system (CNS)-active compounds. It has also been considered to the administration of vaccines. Now a day's multiple types of formulation are used to administer drug by nasal route, which includes nasal spray, nasal drop, nasal powder, nasal gels & nasal insert etc. Administration of drugs through the nose in the spray dosage form is a non-invasive method that gives rapid onset of drug action. Because the nasals spray dosage form is cost-effective, easy to use/carry and self-administrable, it has high patient compliance. Therefore, nasal drug delivery has become a popular route of drug administration and has strong growth opportunity.

Nasal preparations may be liquid, semisolid, and solids (powders) containing one or more medicaments. These are prepared for administration/instillation to the nostrils. These may be used either for local or systemic action.

Nasal drops may be solution, suspension, or emulsion preparations intended for instillation or spraying into the nostrils. Emulsions should produce a uniform appearance after shaking and should not show any sign of phase separation. Suspension may show sediment of the dispersed phase; but the dispersed phase must immediately disperse on shaking and produce uniform, stable, and smooth dispersion. In suspensions the size of the dispersed particles should be such that the particles can deposit in the nostril easily.

Nasal drops must comply with the test, Uniformity of content along with other tests as mentioned in the individual monograph.

Advantages of Nasal Drug Delivery System

- Nasal Drug Delivery System is non-invasive, essentially painless, easy to deliver the drug and are adequately tolerable.
- Provides rapid drug absorption.
- Avoids hepatic first – pass metabolism

- Loss of drug due to hepatic metabolism is less
- By use of permeation/ absorption enhancer the bioavailability of larger drug molecules can be improved
- For smaller drug molecules better nasal bioavailability is expected.

Limitations

- Area of application of drug being small, dose size is limited
- Compared to GIT absorption surface area is less.
- Continuous air-movement through nasal cavity limits the time available for drug absorption
- At diseased state, particularly of nose the drug absorption may be hampered.
- Histological toxicity of the absorption enhancers is not yet clearly established; hence safety of using such substance is doubtful.
- The preparation may cause nasal irritation
- Some surfactants used in high concentration as chemical enhancers may disrupt and even dissolve membrane.

Excipients used in Nasal Spray Formulations

Various types of excipients are used in nasal formulations. Excipients those are commonly used are:

- **Buffers:** The pH of the administrated dose of nasal preparation may be altered due to nasal secretions. This can affect the concentration of un-ionized drug available for absorption. Thus, a formulation having adequate buffer capacity may be required to maintain the pH in-situ. The buffers used in nasal spray are sodium phosphate, sodium citrate, citric acid.
- **Solubilizer:** For nasal drug delivery in solution aqueous solubility of drug is always a factor. Conventional solvents or co-solvents such as glycols, small quantities of alcohol, transcutol (diethylene glycol monoethyl ether), medium chain glycerides and labrasol (saturated polyglycolyzed C_8- C_{10} glyceride) can be used to enhance the solubility of drugs. Other compounds can be used like, the use of surfactants or cyclodextrins such as HP–Cyclodextrin that serve as a biocompatible solubilizer and stabilizer in combination with lipophilic absorption enhancers. In these cases, their impact on nasal irritancy should be considered.
- **Preservatives:** Most nasal formulations are aqueous based. Hence, these require preservatives to control or prevent microbial growth. Parabens, phenyl ethyl alcohol, benzalkonium chloride, EDTA and benzoyl alcohol are commonly used preservatives in nasal formulations.

- **Antioxidants:** To prevent oxidation of drug a small quantity of antioxidants are incorporated into the formulation. Antioxidants commonly used are sodium bisulfite, butylated hydroxytoluene, sodium metabisulfite and tocopherol. Usually, antioxidants do not affect drug absorption or cause nasal irritation.
- **Humectants:** Mucous membrane dries out and crust is formed due to allergic and chronic diseases. Some preservatives or antioxidants can cause nasal irritation usually when used in higher quantities. To prevent dehydration required amount of intranasal moisture is essential. Humectants present especially in gel-based nasal products maintain the moisture content. Humectants can also avoid nasal irritation and do not affect drug absorption. Commonly glycerine, sorbitol and mannitol are used as humectant.
- **Surfactants:** Use of surfactant in nasal dosage forms can modify the permeability of nasal membranes. This may help the nasal absorption of drug. It also increases the stability of suspension. Common examples include polysorbet.
- **Bioadhesive polymers:** Bioadhesive polymers are capable of interacting with biological material through interfacial forces and can retain on these materials for prolonged periods of time. If biological material is mucus membrane, these are called as mucoadhesive. The bioadhesive force of a polymer material depends on the nature of the polymer, the pH of the surrounding medium, swelling and some physiological factors such as mucin turnover, disease state. From a safety (nasal irritancy) point of view use of a combination of carriers is often recommended.
- **Penetration enhancer**: Chemical penetration enhancers are widely used in the nasal drug delivery.

General Method of Manufacture

The nasal preparations may be of different types:

- Solutions
- Suspension
- Sprays and
- Inhalation sprays

The general method of manufacture is same as followed for preparation of solution or suspension. All aqueous-based oral inhalation drug products must be manufactured as sterile products, and their sterility should be ensured through the expiration dating period. If micronization is used for the drug substance and/or excipients, the process should be fully validated and the equipment, operating conditions, and process controls should be described in detail. For example, the description of the controls for a milling operation could include the rate of feed, air pressure, air flow rate, particle size being fed, number of times a lot is micronized, re-use of carryovers from previous micronized lots. Potential contamination of the material during the micronization process should be controlled with appropriate tests and acceptance criteria. See the discussion of testing attributes specific for micronized material such as particle size distribution, crystal forms, or amorphous form.

Definition and Preparation of Enemas

There are certain solutions or suspensions intended for rectal or vaginal administration. These may be aqueous or oily solutions or suspensions and are used either for their local effects or for systemic absorption of the medicament. These are called enemas. The enemas may be classified according to their use into two categories,

1. Retention enemas, and
2. Evacuation enemas.

Retention enemas are solutions intended for rectal administration for local effects, for example, hydrocortisone enema, or for systemic absorption, e.g. aminophylline enema. If aminophylline is administered orally the unwanted gastrointestinal problems occur, which can be avoided through rectal administration in the form of its enema. Within half an hour from rectal administration the drug can reach to its effective concentration in the blood. Inflammation of ulcerative colitis is sometimes treated with retention enema of corticosteroids. Example of therapeutic enemas are, chloral hydrate, paraldehyde (sedative); barium sulphate enema for X-ray examination of the lower bowel, etc.

Evacuation enemas are commonly used to evacuate the bowel. Enemas of definite volume are commercially available. For example, solutions of sodium phosphate and sodium biphosphate, light mineral oil, etc. The mechanism of action of this type of enema may be either stimulation of peristalsis or lubrication of impacted faeces. Stimulation of peristalsis is done either by larger volume, from 500 ml to 1Lt or due to osmotic retention of water in the bowel. The later type is of lesser volume, usually 100 ml. 5% solution of soft soap, turpentine enema, are of this type. Olive oil, arachis oil enemas are lubricating enemas.

Large volume enemas should be administered after warming to body temperature. Small volume (100 ml) enemas available in disposable sealed polythene bags fitted with a rectal nozzle are convenient for self-administration. The user needs to insert the nozzle and squeeze the bag.

When oral or nasal feeding are not possible, the drug can also be administered rectally.

Containers: Enemas should be supplied in coloured fluted glass bottles or in single use plastic packs fitted with a rectal nozzle.

Formulations

Product: Paraldehyde Enema

It contains Paraldehyde 0.1%v/v in sodium chloride solution.

Use: Sedative.

Lot size: 500 ml

Manufacturing Formula:

Paraldehyde	USP	0.50 ml
Sodium chloride	IP	40 g
Purified water, freshly boiled and cooled	IP qs	500 ml

Manufacturing Method

- Take sodium chloride in a 500 ml clean beaker,
- Add about 400 ml of purified water and stir to dissolve sodium chloride,
- Transfer the solution into a 500 ml clean measuring cylinder, add measured volume of paraldehyde and stir to dissolve,
- Make up the volume with purified water, mix thoroughly,
- Fill the solution in a suitable bottle, seal and label properly.

Note: It must be freshly prepared.

Dose: 5 ml per kg of body weight, maximum of 300 ml for rectal administration.

Product: Sodium phosphate Enema

Standard for product: Content of sodium acid phosphate: 15.2 – 16.8%w/v calculated as NaH_2PO_4, $2H_2O$.

Content of sodium phosphate: 5.6 – 6.4%w/v calculated as Na_2HPO_4, $12H_2O$.

Use: Evacuation of bowel.

Lot size: 100 ml

Manufacturing Formula

Sodium Acid Phosphate	IP	16 g
Sodium Phosphate	IP	6 g
Purified water, freshly boiled and cooled,	IP qs	100 ml

Manufacturing Method

- Take 90 ml of freshly boiled and cooled purified water in a clean 100 ml of stoppered cylinder,
- Add weighed quantities of sodium acid phosphate and sodium phosphate, stir to dissolve,
- Transfer the solution into a clean 100 ml measuring cylinder, make up the volume with purified water, carry out the tests,
- Filter the solution through 0.2μ membrane filter under aseptic environment,
- Fill in suitable sterile bottle and seal with sterile rubber stopper and aluminium cap.
- If necessary, keep the bottle in boiling water for 50 min or sterilise at a temperature 116°C for 45 minutes, Label the bottle properly.

Note: If not sterilised or filtered through membrane filter, a suitable preservative can be used.

Definition and Preparation of Syrups

Syrups may be medicated or non-medicated. The non-medicated syrups containing 66.67% of sucrose can be used as flavouring agent, sometimes as colouring agent also. These have been used primarily as vehicle to prepare medicated oral liquid preparations which may be solution or suspension depending on the solubility and other physicochemical properties of the drug(s). The drugs which are water soluble and stable in the solution state can only be formulated in this form. The non-medicated syrups are also used as drink after diluting with adequate amount of water.

Usually medicated syrups are prepared commercially by mixing all components of the formulation including sucrose. Mostly such a syrup contains preservatives, buffers, flavours and colours, in addition to sucrose. Some syrups contain stabilizing, thickening, solubilising agents. When flavoured syrup is used as a vehicle, care should be taken for selection. Since, some medicated syrup are acidic, some are neutral or slightly basic. The drug should be stable in the chosen syrup.

The major and common constituent of syrup is sucrose. As syrups can contain up to 85% of sugars (as per BP), they are capable of resisting bacterial growth by virtue of their osmotic effect. They may contain lower concentration of sugars. But, in some cases, other glycogenetic substances (converted to glucose in the body) like sorbitol, glycerine; propylene glycol, etc. are used to replace sucrose partly or fully. Which can maintain a high osmotic gradient? These can also act as cosolvents for maintaining solubility of the ingredients and also for prevention of crystallisations.

Sometimes, neither sucrose nor any glycogenetic material is used, a suitable cellulose derivative, e.g. methyl cellulose or hydroxy ethyl cellulose along with artificial sweetener is used to maintain desired consistency with sweetness. Such syrups are commonly meant for diabetic patients. In fact, these celluloses of required viscosity grade can act as excellent substitute of sucrose.

Artificial sweetening agents are sodium saccharine and aspartame, which are about 300 and 200 times sweeter than sucrose respectively. Sodium saccharine has bitter after-taste and beyond certain concentration it gives bitter taste. The use of saccharine is presently restricted because of its toxic effect.

The **advantages** of syrups are:

- ➢ An unpleasant or disagreeable drug can be administered orally. When a required volume syrup is swallowed, a portion of the dissolved drug can come in contact with taste buds and rest passes down the throat concealing the taste. A simple solution cannot do this.
- ➢ Infants, children, elderly patient and any other who cannot swallow a solid dosage form, can swallow a liquid.
- ➢ Usually syrup contains little or no alcohol, so it can be safely administered to infants.

Additives:

The common additives of a syrup are

- Preservatives to protect the preparation from microbial growth,
- Buffers to stabilise the dissolved drug,
- Colouring and flavouring agents to enhance the organoleptic properties of the product for better acceptability.

The list of preservatives, buffers, colouring and flavouring agents has been presented earlier of this chapter.

Problems encountered and their solutions:

1. **Surface dilution:** It occurs in a closed container as a result of solvent evaporation that condenses on the upper internal surface of the container and then flows back on the surface of the product, thereby produces a diluted layer which provides ideal medium for microbial growth.

   Solution:

   (a) By incorporating a sufficient concentration of preservative, so that a diluted sample of a product resists microorganisms to grow.

   (b) Adding 5 – 10% of alcohol. The vapour pressure of alcohol is greater than that of water and normally vaporises to the surface of the liquid and the cap area. This minimises the potential for microbial growth.

2. **Crystallization:** Crystallization of sugar occurs on storage and during use, within the screw cap used to seal the container.

   Solution

   (a) This can be avoided by adding polyhydric alcohol,

   (b) By using invert syrup (mixture of glucose and fructose) in place of simple syrup.

Formulations

Product: Simple Syrup IP

Composition: It contains 66.67% w/v of sucrose

Use: Vehicle

Lot size: 20ml

Method of preparation:

- Take 13.4g of sucrose, pharmaceutical grade into a 100ml beaker
- Add 6ml of purified water and boil
- Continue boiling till solution is complete
- Cool to about 60°C, make up the volume to 20ml.
- Filter the solution through sintered crucible4
- Fill into a clean, dry bottle, seal with a pilfer-proof cap, and label properly.

Product: Citric Acid Syrup BPC

Composition

Each 100 ml contains

Lemon tincture	1.0 ml
Citric acid, hydrous	1.0 g
In syrup base	

Use: Flavoured vehicle.

Lot size: 100 ml

Manufacturing Formula

Lemon Tincture IP		1.0 ml
Citric Acid, Hydrous IP		1.0 g
Purified water IP		1.0 ml
Simple Syrup IP	qs to	100ml

Manufacturing Method

- Take weighed quantity of citric acid in a clean,100 ml measuring cylinder,
- Add purified water, shake to dissolve.
- Add lemon tincture through a pipette, shake to mix,
- Make up the volume with simple syrup, mix with a glass rod.
- Filter through G_4 sintered glass crucible under vacuum.
- Determine alcohol content, it should not be less than 1%.
- Fill in glass bottle, seal with pilfer proof cap.
- Label properly, store at a temperature below 25°C

Product: Disodium Hydrogen Citrate Syrup

Standard for product: Content of Disodium hydrogen citrate; 97 – 105% of the label claim.

Composition:

Each 5 ml contains

Disodium Hydrogen Citrate IP 1.4 g

In a flavoured syrup base

Use: Systemic alkaliser

Lot size: 100 ml

Manufacturing Formula:

Citric Acid Monohydrate IP	24.92 g
Sodium Bicarbonate IP	19.92 g
Sugar IP	22.8 g
Liquid Glucose	14.0 g
Methylparaben sodium IP	0.1 g
Propylparaben sodium IP	0.01 g
Essence Pineapple	0.1 ml
Tartrazine	0.01 g
Purified water IP qs to	100 ml

Manufacturing Method

- Take 5 ml of hot purified water in a clean 50 ml beaker, add weighed quantity of sodium bicarbonate, stir with a glass rod till it is dissolved, and allow it to cool.
- Dissolve the weighed quantity of sugar and citric acid in 10 ml of purified water,

- Add this solution slowly to the solution of sodium bicarbonate with continuous stirring.
- Add liquid glucose to the bulk solution,
- Dissolve methylparaben sodium and propylparaben sodium in 5 ml of hot purified water,
- Add this solution to the bulk and mix well.
- Make up the volume with purified water, stir well.
- Check the pH, it should be within 4.5 – 4.7 and specific gravity within 1.236 – 1.250;
- Estimate the content of disodium hydrogen citrate.
- Add weighed quantity of colour and flavour, mix well, allow it stand for overnight.
- Filter through G4 sintered glass crucible under vacuum, if the solution is not clear, add 0.5 g of talcum powder, mix thoroughly and filter again.
- Fill the solution in bottle and seal with pilfer proof cap and label properly.

Note:

1. While mixing sodium bicarbonate and citric acid solutions effervescence shall take place, care should be taken so that no material is lost.
2. Instead of preparing, directly disodium hydrogen citrate can be used.

Product: Chloroquine Syrup

Standards: Standard for the Drug: It contains not less than 98.5% and not more than 101% of

$C_{18}H_{26}ClN_3,2H_3PO_4$; calculated on dried basis.

Standard for the Product: Chloroquine syrup contains Chloroquine Phosphate or Chloroquine Sulphate equivalent to Chloroquine, $C_{18}H_{26}ClN_3$, not less than 95% and not more than 105% of the stated amount.

Composition:

Each 5 ml contains

Chloroquine Phosphate 125 mg
(equivalent to chloroquine base 78 mg)
In a flavoured syrupy base
Colour used- sunset yellow.

Use: Anti-malarial,

Lot size: 100 ml.

Manufacturing Formula

Chloroquine Phosphate	IP	2.5g*
Citric Acid	IP	1.25 g
Glycerine	IP	5.0 ml
Saccharine sodium	IP	4.0 mg
Simple Syrup	IP	5.0 ml
Methylparaben sodium salt	IP	100 mg
Propylparaben sodium salt	IP	40 mg
Sorbitol solution (70%)	USP	2.0 ml
Soluble essence of wild cherry		0.2 ml
Sunset Yellow		2.0 mg
Purified water IP	qs to	100 ml

Manufacturing Method

- Take 10 ml of purified water in a 25 ml beaker, heat to about 90°C, add methylparaben,
  - propylparaben and citric acid, stir till dissolve glycerine, saccharine sodium, simple syrup
  - add and sorbitol solution (70%) to it, mix thoroughly (solution 1).
- Weigh accurately the required quantity of chloroquine phosphate and transfer into a 50 ml
- Clean beaker, add about 10 ml of purified water heat to dissolve over a boiling water-bath
- (solution 2).
- Add the solution-1 to the solution-2, mix well.
- Make up the volume with purified water, determine the pH, weight/ml and estimate the drug content as per IP.
- Dissolve the colour in a small quantity of the preparation, add this to the bulk, mix,
- filter the solution through G4 sintered glass crucible under vacuum, add the flavour and
- mix thoroughly.
- Fill the preparation in a clean, dry bottle, seal with pilfer proof cap, label properly.

Note: *Calculate the quantity of supplied chloroquine phosphate on the basis of its assay value.

Product: Acacia Syrup

Composition

Each 100 ml contains

Acacia IP 10 g

In a flavoured base.

Use: Flavoured vehicle.

Lot size: 25 ml.

Manufacturing Formula

Acacia	IP	2.5 g
Sodium Benzoate	IP	0.025 g
Sucrose	IP	20.0 g
Vanilla Tincture	BPC	0.125 ml
(Alcohol content 38-42%)		
Purified water	IP	qs

Manufacturing Method:

- Weigh accurately the required quantity of acacia, sodium benzoate and sucrose, transfer into a 50 ml beaker, add 20 ml of purified water, mix, heat over a boiling water bath stir frequently until these dissolve completely.
- Allow the solution to cool, remove the froth, if any.
- Filter through a clean cloth, add vanilla tincture and mix well.
- Fill in a clean bottle, seal with a pilfer proof cap and label properly.

Product: Orange Syrup

Standard: Alcohol content 2 – 5%

Composition:

Each 100 ml contains

Sweet Orange Peel Tincture 5 ml

In syrup base.

Use: Flavoured vehicle.

Lot size: 100 ml

Manufacturing Formula

Sweet Orange Peel Tincture	5.0 ml
(Alcohol content 62 – 72%)	
Citric Acid IP	0.50 g

Sucrose	IP		0.82 g
Purified water IP	qs to		100 ml

Manufacturing Method

- Weigh accurately citric acid and sucrose, transfer these into a 150 ml clean beaker,
- Add 80 ml of purified water, stir with a glass rod till dissolve.
- Add measured volume of sweet orange peel tincture, stir well; add 1 g of talcum powder and mix thoroughly.
- Filter the solution through G4 sintered glass crucible under vacuum, repeat the filtration till a clear filtrate is obtained.
- Make up the volume with purified water, mix thoroughly.
- Determine the alcohol content, weight per ml.
- Fill in a clean, dry bottle, seal with pilfer proof cap, label properly.

Product: Cough Syrup.

Standard for the Drugs, Chlorpheniramine Maleate - It contains not less than 98% of $C_{16}H_{19}ClN_2$, C4H4O4; calculated on dried basis.

Sodium Citrate - It contains not less than 99% of $C_6H_5Na_3O_7$, calculated on dried basis.

Ammonium Chloride – It contains not less than 99% and not more than 100.5% of NH_4Cl, calculated on dried basis.

Standard for the product – It should contain not less than 90% and not more than 110% of the stated amount of Chlorpheniramine Maleate, calculated as $C_{16}H_{19}ClN_2,C_4H_4O_4$; not less than 90% and not more than 110% of the stated amount of Sodium Citrate, calculated as NH_4Cl and not less than 90% and not more than 110% of the stated amount of Sodium Citrate, calculated as $C_6H_5Na_3O_7$.

Composition

Each 5 ml contains

Chlorpheniramine Maleate	IP	2.5 mg
Sodium Citrate	IP	55.0 mg
Ammonium Chloride	IP	125.0 mg
Menthol	IP	1.15 mg
In a flavoured vehicle		

Colour used- Sunset yellow.

Use: Antitussive and Expectorant.

Lot size: 100 ml.

Manufacturing Formula

Chlorpheniramine Maleate IP	50.0 mg
Sodium Citrate IP	1.1 g
Ammonium Chloride IP	2.5 g
Menthol IP	23.0 mg
Simple Syrup IP	62.0 ml
Methylparaben IP	0.108 g
Propylparaben IP	0.012 g
Saccharine sodium	0.1 g
Disodium Edetate IP	0.092 g
Sunset Yellow FCF	0.044 g
Soluble Essence of Pineapple	0.44 ml
Chloroform IP	6.0 ml
Purified water IP qs to	100 ml

Manufacturing Method

- Weigh accurately sodium citrate, ammonium chloride and sodium edetate, transfer these into a 100 ml clean beaker, add 25 ml of purified water, heat on a boiling water bath with stirring.
- Continue heating till the solids get dissolved. when a clear solution is obtained,
- Add measured volume of syrup to the solution, stir to mix.
- Add weighed quantity of chlorpheniramine maleate, methylparaben, propylparaben and saccharine sodium to the bulk solution, stir well till all these dissolve,
- Take weighed quantity of sunset yellow mix with the bulk solution, allow the solution to cool.
- Dissolve menthol in chloroform, add to the bulk solution and mix thoroughly.
- Filter the solution through G4 sintered glass crucible under vacuum, make up the volume with purified water, mix well again.
- Evaluate the product completely, add the essence of pineapple and mix well.
- Fill the product in a clean, dry bottle and seal with pilfer proof cap.
- Label correctly.

Warning: This Medication may cause drowsiness in an occasional patient. Such patient should not drive vehicle or operate machinery for 4 to 6 hours after taking the last dose.

COUGH SYRUP **100ml**

Each 5ml contains

Chlorpheniramine Maleate	IP	2.5 mg
Sodium Citrate	IP	55.0 mg
Ammonium Chloride	IP	125.0 mg
Menthol	IP	1.15 mg

In a flavoured vechicle
Colours: Sunset yellow.

Caution: It is dangerous to take this preparation except under medical supervision.

Dosage: As directed by the physician
Store in a cool place.
Mfg.Lic.XXX

Manufactured in India by
XYZ Pharmaceutical
Kohka-Kurud road, Bhilai

B.No. 1234
Mfd. MM.YYYY
Exp. MM.YYYY

Definition and Preparation of Elixir

Elixirs are clear liquid preparations of potent or sometimes nauseous drugs in pleasantly flavoured, palatable hydroalcoholic base. The drugs may be antibiotics, anti-histaminics, sedatives, etc. the vehicle usually contains high proportions of glycerine, propylene glycol, syrup, etc. in addition to other adjuvants, e.g. flavouring and colouring agents, preservatives, chemical stabilisers, etc. In fact, there is no sharp distinction between elixirs and syrups on the basis of alcohol content. The alcohol content in elixirs may vary from 3 – 43%.

Elixirs are usually stable preparations when packed in air-tight, light-resistant containers and if these are not diluted or mixed with other preparation. Of course, some elixirs are there such as chloral elixir paediatric which must be recently prepared because of their poor stability and even some are so unstable that these are supplied in the form of granules or powders and at the time of dispensing adequate solvent is added to prepare the elixir. An appropriate warning regarding the limited shelf-life should be given on the label. For example, elixirs of phenethicillin and phenoxy methyl penicillin are available.

Elixirs as such usually do not favour the growth of micro-organisms; but as they contain higher quantity of syrup, glycerol or sorbitol, on dilution may become suitable medium for microbial growth. Therefore, for dispensing a prescribed dose of the drug if an elixir needs to be diluted with a suitable or prescribed vehicle, the diluted elixir must be freshly prepared and should be consumed within two weeks' time unless otherwise mentioned in the individual monograph.

A clear instruction in this regard should be given to the patient.

Some of the elixirs are described in the official monographs, commercially available under the title **syrup**. Sometimes these terms have been used synonymously.

Labelling:

The label of an elixir prepared and supplied by a manufacturer should contains all information as per general requirements for labelling of the product.

If an elixir is to be prepared before issue to the patient, the label on the container of granules or powder should state,

- the name of the preparation in form of Granules or Powder for the Elixir, as mentioned in the individual monograph,
- the name and concentration of the active ingredient in the elixir when prepared as per the directions given by the manufacturer,
- direction for storage,
- the date after which the preparation should not be used.

However, the manufacturer either through the label on the container or through a leaflet, inserted inside the pack, should state,

- The direction for preparing the elixir,
- Storage conditions, and
- Shelf-life of the prepared formulation.

Formulations

Product: Aromatic Elixir

Standards: Alcohol content 21 – 23%v/v.

Composition:

Each 100 ml contains

Compound Orange Spirit USP	1.2 ml
Simple Syrup USP	37.5 ml
Alcohol(95%v/v) USP	23.8 ml
Purified water	qs

Use: As a flavoured vehicle.

Lot size: 50 ml

Manufacturing Formula

Compound Orange Spirit USP	0.6 ml
Simple Syrup USP	18.8 ml
Alcohol (95%v/v) USP	11.9 ml
Purified water	qs

Manufacturing Method

- Transfer simple syrup into a100 ml measuring cylinder through a 20 ml graduated pipette,
- Transfer compound orange spirit through a 2 ml graduated pipette, mix by swirling,
- Add alcohol (95%) to the mixture and mix well,
- Add required amount of purified water gradually with continuous swirling the cylinder to make up the volume 50 ml.
- Mix well, add2 g of talcum powder, mix thoroughly,
- Filter through Whatmann No.1 filter paper, soaked with alcohol, refilter the solution till a clear filtrate is obtained.
- Estimate the alcohol content and fill the product in an amber bottle, seal with pilfer proof cap and label properly.

Note: Talcum has been used as adsorbent to clarify the solution, the solution can be filtered under

vacuum through G4 sintered crucible.

All the glass wares to be used should be clean and dry.

Product: Diphenhydramine Hydrochloride Elixir

Standard for the drug: It should contain not less than 99% and not more than 101% of

$C_{17}H_{21}NO$, HCl, calculated on dried basis.

Standards for the product: It should contain $C_{17}H_{21}NO$, HCl within 94 – 110% of the label claim.

Composition:

Each 5 ml contains:

Diphenhydramine Hydrochloride, IP 12.5 mg

In a flavoured syrup base

Colour used: Amaranth.

Use: Antihistaminic (Histamine H_1-receptor antagonist)

Lot size: 25ml

Manufacturing Formula

Diphenhydramine HCl, USP	62.5 mg
Orange oil	0.006 ml
Cinnamon oil	0.003 ml
Clove oil	0.002 ml
Coriander oil	0.00075 ml
Anethole	0.00075 ml
Colour Amaranth	10.0 mg
Alcohol (85%)	4.2 ml
Simple Syrup USP	9.00 ml
Purified water	qs

Manufacturing Method:

Preparation of solution of flavours

- Take a clean and dry 50 ml stopper measuring cylinder,
- Transfer 34 ml of alcohol (95%) add sufficient purified water to make 40 ml; mix well. The prepared alcohol is of 85%.
- Take three clean, dry test tubes, marked 1, 2, 3. Transfer accurately required volume of flavour and alcohol (85%) into the test tubes, as indicated below, mix.
- Take ml of the diluted flavour from test tube-3 for the preparation.

Test tube-1	Test tube-2	Test tube-3
Flavour + alcohol →	diluted flavour + alcohol →	diluted flavour + alcohol
Orange oil, 0.1 ml + 4.9 ml →	1.0 ml + 1.0 ml →	1.2 ml + 0.8 ml
Cinnamon oil, 0.1 ml + 4.9 ml →	1.0 ml + 1.0 ml →	0.6 ml + 1.4 ml
Coriander oil, 0.15 ml + 1.85 ml →	0.1 ml + 0.9 ml →	0.5 ml + 4.5 ml

- Take a clean, dry 25 ml measuring cylinder, transfer 10 ml of purified water,
- Add weighed amount Diphenhydramine HCl, shake well to dissolve, add weighed quantity of Colour Amaranth and shake again till a clear solution is obtained.
- Add 4.2 ml of the solution of flavours slowly and stir with a glass rod.
- Add slowly the measured volume of simple syrup and stir with glass rod, make up the volume with purified water.
- Take out the glass rod, stopper the cylinder and mix well.
- Check pH of the product, pH should be 4.5 ± 0.2,

- Estimate the drug content,
- Filter the solution through G_4 sintered glass crucible under vacuum, fill in a clean, dry amber bottle, seal with pilfer proof cap.
- Label the bottle properly.

Product: Piperazine Citrate Elixir

Standard for the Drug: It contains not less than 98%w/w of $(C_4H_{10}N_2)_3$-$2C_6H_8O_7$, calculated on dried basis.

Standard for Product: Content of piperazine citrate, 15.1 – 17.8%w/v calculated as $C_{24}H_{46}N_6O_{14}$.

Weight/per ml at 20°C: 1.24 – 1.26 g

Composition

Each 5 ml contains

Piperazine citrate IP 37.5 mg.

In a coloured, flavoured palatable syrupy base

Colour: Green S and Tartrazine.

Use: Anthelmintic.

Lot size: 25 ml.

Manufacturing Formula

Piperazine Citrate		4.6 g
Peppermint Spirit	BPC	0.125 ml
Green S and Tartrazine Solution	BPC	0.375 ml
Glycerine	IP	2.5 ml
Syrup	IP	12.5 ml
Purified Water	IP	qs

Manufacturing Method

- Dissolve the required amount of piperazine citrate in 10 ml of purified water in a 50 ml beaker, marked at 25 ml,
- Add green S and tartrazine solution, glycerine, syrup and peppermint spirit gradually with constant stirring,
- Make up the volume with purified water and mix thoroughly,
- Carry out the tests,
- Transfer the preparation into a 25 ml amber bottle and seal with a pilfer proof cap,
- Label the bottle properly.

Green S and Tartrazine Solution BPC: 0.5% w/v solution of green S and 0.5%w/v of tartrazine in purified water are mixed at a ratio of 1:1.

Peppermint Spirit: A 10%v/v solution of peppermint oil in alcohol (90%).

Product: Chloral Elixir, Paediatric. BPC

Standard for the Drug: It contains not less than 99.5% and not more than 102.5% of chloral hydrate, calculated as $C_2H_3Cl_3O_2$.

Standard for the Product: Content of chloral hydrate, 3.80 – 4.20%w/v calculated as $C_2H_3Cl_3O_2$.

Weight per ml at 20°C, 1.32 – 1.33 g

Composition

Each 5 ml contains Chloral hydrate USP 200 mg

In a flavoured, palatable base

Use: Sedative.

Lot size: 25 ml

Manufacturing Formula

Chloral Hydrate		1.0 g
Black Currant Syrup	BPC	0.5 ml
Purified Water	IP	5.0 ml
Syrup	IP	qs

Manufacturing Method

- Dissolve required quantity of chloral hydrate in 5 ml of purified water in a clean, 50 ml beaker marked at 25 ml,
- Add black currant syrup, mix thoroughly,
- Make up the volume with syrup and mix well.
- Carry out the tests,
- Transfer the product into a clean, dry amber bottle, seal with a pilfer proof cap.
- Label properly.

Product: Ephedrine Hydrochloride Elixir

Standard for the Drug: It should contain not less than 99% and not more than 101%w/w of

$C_{10}H_{15}NO$, HCl calculated on dried basis.

Standard for the product: Content of Ephedrine hydrochloride, 0.27 – 0.33%w/v calculated as $C_{10}H_{15}NO$, HCl.

Weight per ml at 20°C, 1.30 – 1.33 g. Alcohol content, 11 – 13%v/v

Composition

Each 5 ml contains

Ephedrine hydrochloride IP 15 mg
In a coloured, flavoured palatable syrupy base.
Colour: Tartrazine.

Use: Sympathomimetic

Lot size: 25 ml

Manufacturing Formula:

Ephedrine Hydrochloride	IP		75 mg
Lemon Oil, soluble			0.05 ml
Tartrazine			2.0 mg
Glycerine	IP		5.0 ml
Invert syrup			5.0 ml
Purified water	IP		1.5 ml
Alcohol	IP		3.5 ml
Syrup	IP	qs	25 ml

Manufacturing Method

- Transfer required quantity of ephedrine hydrochloride into a 50 ml beaker, marked at 25 ml, add purified water and stir to dissolve,
- Add glycerine and invert syrup with constant stirring,
- Add tartrazine and mix well,
- Add alcohol and lemon oil, mix thoroughly,
- Make up the volume with syrup, stir continuously,
- Carry out the tests,
- Fill the product in a clean, dry amber bottle, seal with a pilfer proof cap,
- Label properly.

Product: Glycyrrhiza Elixir

Standards for the product: Alcohol content 21 – 23%

Composition:

Each 100 ml contains

Glycyrrhiza Fluid Extract	12.5 ml
Aromatic Elixir	87.5 ml

Use: Flavoured vehicle.

Lot size: 50 ml

Manufacturing Formula

Glycyrrhiza Fluid Extract	USP	6.25 ml
(Alcohol content 21 – 24%)		
Aromatic Elixir	USP	43.75 ml
(Alcohol content 21 – 23%)		

Manufacturing Method

- Measure accurately required volumes of Glycyrrhiza Fluid Extract and
- Aromatic Elixir, transfer into a clean, dry 25 ml stopper measuring cylinder, mix these thoroughly.
- Filter the solution through cloth, determine the alcohol content,
- Fill the product in a bottle, seal with pilfer proof cap and label properly.

Product: Low Alcoholic Elixir

Standards for the product: Alcohol content 8 – 10%

Composition

Each 100 ml contains

Compound Orange Spirit	USP	1.0 ml
Glycerine	IP	20.0 ml
In a flavoured syrup base		

Use: Flavoured vehicle.

Lot size: 50 ml

Manufacturing Formula

Compound Orange Spirit	USP	0.5 ml
Glycerine	IP	10.0 ml
Syrup	IP	10.0 ml
Alcohol	IP	5.0 ml
Purified water	IP	qs

Manufacturing Method:

- Measure accurately required volume of compound orange spirit, glycerine and
- alcohol; transfer into a 100ml stopper cylinder, stir with a glass rod, add about
- 20 ml of purified water and stir to mix well.
- Stopper the cylinder and keep it for 24 hrs.

- Filter the solution through G4 sintered glass crucible under vacuum, add syrup and mix well.
- Make up the volume with purified water and mix well.
- Determine the alcohol content, fill in a clean, dry bottle and seal with pilfer proof cap, label properly.

Product: Elixir Terpin Hydrate

Standards for the product: Alcohol content 39 – 40%

Composition

Each 5 ml contains

Terpin Hydrate	85 mg
Benzaldehyde	0.0025 ml

In a coloured palatable base.

Colour: Erythrosine.

Use: Expectorant.

Lot size: 50 ml

Manufacturing Formula

Terpine Hydrate		0.85 g
Orange oil	USP	0.05 ml
Benzaldehyde		0.025 ml
Sorbitol solution (70%)	USP	5.0 ml
Propylene Glycol	USP	20.0 ml
Alcohol	IP	21.5 ml
Erythrosine		0.0025 g
Purified water	IP	qs

Manufacturing Method

- Transfer the measured volumes of propylene glycol and sorbitol solution into a 100 ml clean beaker, heat to about 50°C, add the required quantity of terpine hydrate and stir until dissolve, allow to cool to room temperature.
- Take required volume of alcohol in a 50 ml clean beaker, add measured volumes
- of orange oil and benzaldehyde, mix thoroughly.
- Add this solution to the bulk, stir well.
- Add sufficient purified water to make up the volume, mix thoroughly.

- Determine the alcohol content, pH and weight per ml.
- Filter the solution through G_4 sintered glass crucible under vacuum,
- Fill the solution in a bottle, seal with pilfer proof cap and label it properly.

Definition and Preparation of Liniments

These are either solutions or emulsions of medicinal substances which are applied by rubbing on the skin. Two types of solvents are commonly used to prepare liniments, one is alcoholic and the other is oleaginous. For example, Soap Liniment BPC contains alcohol while, Methyl Salicylate Liniment BPC or Camphor Liniment BP contains oil. The medicinal substances which have analgesic, counterirritant, rubefacient action or which need to penetrate the skin, are prepared in the form of liniment using alcohol or hydroalcohol as vehicle; because, alcohol helps the medicament to penetrate into the skin. The pain from fibrositis, sciatica and similar problems can be masked by alcohol-based liniments by producing warmth sensation on the affected area of the skin. If the liniment is used for massage, oil-based preparation is suitable. The oil-based liniments are less irritating than alcohol-based liniments. They also have better spreadability. Thus, during formulation of a liniment, selection of a proper vehicle is important. The selection of vehicle is based on two criteria- the type of action desired and the solubility of the medicament. Liniment should not be applied to broken or bruised skin, as it may increase the irritation.

For preparation of oleaginous liniments either fixed oils, e.g. sesame oil, peanut oil, cotton seed oil, almond oil, arachis oil, etc. or a mixture of fixed oils and volatile oils, e.g. turpentine oil, wintergreen oil, etc. can be used.

The label of liniments must mention the statements, '*For external use only*', '*Not to be applied to wounds or broken skin*'. If the liniment contains alcohol, that should also mention '*Inflammable*' with a note, '*Keep away from flame*'. The liniment, which is an emulsion or contains some insoluble substances, if any, should bear the label with a statement, '*Shake well before use*'.

The liniments should be packed in tightly closed containers, like coloured, fluted bottles; and should be stored in a cool place.

Containers: Liniments should be filled in coloured fluted bottles.

Labelling: The label should clearly mention, For external use only

Formulations

Product: Methyl Salicylate Liniment

It contains Methyl Salicylate 25%v/v in arachis oil.

Standard for product: Content of Methyl Salicylate: 23 – 26.5%v/v.

Weight / ml at 20°C: 0.973g – 0.989 g

Use: Pharmaceutical aid.

Lot size: 20 ml

Manufacturing Formula

Methyl Salicylate		5.0 ml
Arachis Oil	qs	20.0 ml

Manufacturing Method

- Take the measured volume of methyl salicylate in a clean, dry measuring cylinder,
- Add arachis oil sufficiently to make up the volume,
- Mix thoroughly, carry out the tests and transfer the solution into a amber coloured bottle, seal with a pilfer proof cap,
- Label properly.

Product: Soap Liniment

It contains Camphor 4% in hydroalcoholic flavoured base.

Standard for product: Content of Oleic acid: not less than 3.8%w/v.

Weight/ml at 20°C: 0.880g – 0.900g

pH: 7.4 – 8.0

Use: Local antipruritic.

Lot size: 20 ml

Manufacturing Formula

Camphor		0.8 g
Oleic Acid		0.8 g
Rosemary Oil		0.3 ml
Potassium hydroxide solution, 5%w/v		2.80 ml
Alcohol, 95%	IP	13.3 ml
Purified water, freshly boiled and cooled, IP	q.s	20.0 ml

Manufacturing Method

- Transfer the measured volume of oleic acid into a clean, dry 25 ml beaker, add 7 ml of alcohol and stir with a glass rod to dissolve oleic acid,
- Add measured volume of potassium hydroxide solution with stirring,

- Dissolve weighed quantity of camphor separately in 3 ml of alcohol in a 10 ml beaker and add measured quantity of rosemary oil to this, mix well,
- Add this solution to the bulk and mix well,
- Add sufficient purified water with stirring to make up the volume,
- Transfer the preparation into a clean, dry, amber bottle, seal tightly with a pilfer proof cap, keep it for 7 days, filter through a G4 sintered glass crucible under vacuum,
- Carry out the tests,
- Fill finally into a clean, dry, amber coloured bottle, seal with a pilfer proof cap and label properly.

Product: White liniment

Standard for product: Content of volatile oil: 24.5 – 27.5%v/w,

Refractive index of the oily distillate at 20°C: 1.465 – 1.477

- volume of turpentine oil and mix,
- Add dilute ammonia solution and mix,
- Add 7.6 ml (0.9ml + 1ml + 1ml likewise)

Use: Counterirritant and rubefacient.

Lot size: 20 ml

Manufacturing Formula

Ammonium chloride	0.25 g
Dilute Ammonia solution, 37.5%v/v	0.9 ml
Oleic acid	1.7 ml
Turpentine oil	5.0 ml
Purified water, freshly boiled and cooled,	12.5 ml

Manufacturing Method

- Take measured volume of oleic acid into a clean, dry 50 ml stopper measuring cylinder,
- Add measured volume (7.5 to 7.6ml) of warm (40 – 45°C) purified water and shake, carefully to avoid spouting,
- Dissolve ammonium chloride solution prepared separately in 10 ml of purified water in a 25 ml clean beaker and add to the bulk solution and mix well.
- Rinse the beaker with purified water and add to the bulk solution, make up the volume and shake well,
- Carry out the tests and fill the preparation into a clean, dry, amber coloured bottle, seal with pilfer proof cap and label properly.

Definition and Preparation of Lotions

Lotions are liquid preparations intended for application over the skin. Lotions should be taken on lint or other soft absorbent material and applied without any friction. Most of the lotions are solutions and their main ingredients are simple salts, e.g. copper and zinc sulphates, lead subacetate, etc which are water soluble. For preparing salicylic acid lotion alcohol is used as solvent. Medicaments which can treat the skin conditions or can treat local infection are primarily selected for lotions. For example, copper and zinc sulphate lotion is used for its astringent action, salicylic lotion for treating dandruff, mixture of salicylic acid and mercuric chloride for treating follicular infection. Salicylic acid is also used for its antifungal, keratolytic and bacteriostatic activity. If alcohol is present in a preparation, it accelerates the rate of drying of the lotion and provides a sensation of cooling effect on the skin. When glycerine is incorporated in a preparation, it protects the skin from drying and renders the skin moist for a considerable time. If the alcohol content is high in a lotion, castor oil should be used to counteract the defatting action of alcohol.

Since lotions may contain highly inflammable solvents like acetone, alcohol, caution should be mentioned in the label for their proper storage and the label should mention clearly, *For external use only* and SHAKE WELL BEFORE USE.

Formulations

Product: Copper and Zinc sulphate Lotion

Standards for the product:

Copper sulphate: 0.86 – 0.97%w/v calculated as $CuSO_4,5H_2O$

Zinc sulphate: 1.30 – 1.47%w/v calculated as $ZnSO_4,7H_2O$

Each 100ml contains:

Copper sulphate IP 914 mg

Zinc sulphate IP 1.37 g

Camphor water qs

Use: Astringent.

Lot size: 100ml

Manufacturing Formula

Copper sulphate	914 mg
Zinc sulphate IP	1.37 g
Camphor water qs to	100 ml

Manufacturing Method

- Take 50 mg of camphor accurately weighed in a 250ml stopper conical flask, add 50 ml of purified water, shake until dissolved.
- Take 914 mg of copper sulphate and 137 mg of zinc sulphate accurately weighed in a separate 100 ml stoppered measuring cylinder; stopper tightly, add about 45 ml of camphor water, stopper tightly and shake well till a clear solution is obtained.
- Make up the volume with camphor water, mix thoroughly.
- Transfer into a well-closed container and label it properly.

Product: Calamine Lotion

Standard for calamine: It should contain not less than 98% and not more than 100.5% of ZnO, calculated on dried basis.

Standard for product: Content of Zinc oxide: 14.4 – 17.6%w/v calculated as ZnO.

Each 100ml contains:

Calamine	16 g
Zinc oxide	16 g
In flavoured vehicle	

Use: Topical protectant.

Lot size: 50ml

Manufacturing Formula:

Calamine		86 g
Zinc oxide		8g
Bentonite		0.625g
Glycerine IP		1 ml
Calcium Hydroxide Solution		36.5 ml
Purified water	qs to	50 ml

Manufacturing Method

Preparation of calcium hydroxide solution

Take 100 ml of purified water in a stopper conical flask, cool it. Transfer 0.3 g of calcium hydroxide into the flask and shake occasionally for 1 hr, allow the solution to settle; decant about 60 ml of supernatant liquid carefully.

- Take 50 ml of hot purified water into a 250ml beaker, sprinkle 1.25 g of bentonite in portions, allowing each portion to become thoroughly wetted without stirring. Allow it to stand for overnight; then mix thoroughly with a glass rod until uniform mucilage is obtained.

- Add 12.5 ml of calcium hydroxide solution to the bentonite mucilage and mix thoroughly.
- Triturate 4 g of calamine and 4g of zinc oxide with 1 ml of glycerine in a mortar pestle, add about 5 ml of bentonite mucilage in portions, triturate properly after each addition until a smooth uniform paste is obtained.
- Transfer the paste into a 100 ml beaker marked at 50 ml, attach to a suitable electric stirrer, continue stirring,
- Rinse the mortar pestle with the bentonite mucilage in portions to effect complete transfer of calamine paste. Continue stirring for 1 hour. Stop stirring and uplift the stirrer.
- Make up the volume with calcium hydroxide solution; continue stirring for at least 2 hrs.
- Determine the content of zinc oxide, fill in suitable bottle, seal properly and label.

Product: Oily Calamine Lotion

Standard for calamine: It should contain not less than 98% and not more than 100.5% of ZnO, calculated on dried basis.

Standard for product: Content of Zinc - 2.52 – 3.35 5w/v calculated as Zn.

Composition

Each 100 ml contains:

Calamine 5 g

In an oily flavoured base.

Use: Topical protectant.

Lot size: 50 ml

Manufacturing Formula

Calamine	2.5 g
Wool fat	0.5 g
Oleic acid	0.25 ml
Arachis oil	25 ml

Calcium hydroxide solution qs to 50ml

Manufacturing Method

- Take weighed quantity of wool fat, oleic acid and arachis oil in a 50 ml beaker; heat to melt and stir with a glass rod.

- Take the calamine in a mortar pestle, add the molten mass and triturate properly to make a uniform smooth slurry.
- Transfer the slurry into a 100 ml beaker marked at 50 ml, attach the beaker with a suitable electric stirrer; continue stirring, rinse the mortar pestle with 4 ml of calcium hydroxide solution for 4 to 5 times, add to the slurry and continue stirring for 2 hrs.
- Stop stirring, make up the volume with calcium hydroxide solution and continue stirring for further 2 hrs.
- Fill in the clean and dried bottle, seal and label properly.

**calcium hydroxide solution is to be prepared as per the method described under calamine lotion.*

Product: Phenolated Calamine Lotion

Standard for calamine: It should contain not less than 98% and not more than 100.5% of ZnO, calculated on dried basis.

Standard for product: Content of Zinc oxide: 14.4 – 17.6%w/v calculated as ZnO.

Composition

Each 100 ml contains:

Calamine	8 g
Zinc oxide	8 g
Liquefied Phenol	1 ml

Use: Antiseptic and protectant.

Lot size: 50 ml

Manufacturing Formula:

Calamine		4g
Zinc oxide		4g
Glycerine		1 ml
Avicel		1g
Sodium carboxymethyl cellulose		1 g
Liquefied Phenol		0.5 ml
Calcium hydroxide solution	q s	50 ml

Manufacturing Method

- Prepare the mucilage of sodium carboxymethyl cellulose with 25 ml of calcium hydroxide solution in a 100 ml beaker, add Avicel and mix thoroughly with a glass rod.

- ➢ Take the calamine and zinc oxide in a mortar pestle, ad glycerine and triturate properly to make a smooth, uniform paste. Add sodium CMC mucilage in portions, continue trituration.
- ➢ Transfer the slurry into a 100 ml beaker marked at 50 ml, attach with a suitable electric stirrer, continue stirring, rinse the mortar pestle with 4 ml of calcium hydroxide solution for 4 to 5 times, add to the slurry and continue stirring for 2 hrs.
- ➢ Stop stirring, make up the volume with calcium hydroxide solution and continue stirring for further 2 hrs.
- ➢ Determine the content of zinc oxide.
- ➢ Fill in the clean and dried bottle, seal and label properly.

***Calcium hydroxide solution** is to be prepared as per the method described under calamine lotion.

- ➢ Dissolve 6.855 g of ferric ammonium citrate, accurately weighed, in 40 ml of chloroform water in a 50 ml stopper cylinder.
- ➢ Make up the volume with chloroform water.
- ➢ Determine the content of ferric ammonium citrate and calculate in terms of Fe.
- ➢ Fill in a clean bottle, seal and label properly.

Exercise

A. Multiple Choice Question Carrying 01 Mark

1. Monophasic liquid preparation
   (a) Contains only one phase
   (b) Contains only one component
   (c) Is intended for oral administration
   (d) Is intended for topical application
2. Which of the following preparations is not monophasic
   (a) Throat paint (b) Gargle
   (c) Suspension (d) Ear drop
3. Which of the following statements is correct?
   (a) Gargles are nonaqueous preparations
   (b) Gargles are oral liquid preparations
   (c) Gargles make a protective covering on throat membrane
   (d) Gargles contain antibiotic, antiseptic, etc.

4. Which of the following antioxidants is used in aqueous preparations
   (a) Ascorbyl palmitate (b) Cysteine HCl
   (c) Hydroquinone (d) Lecithin
5. Which of the following preservatives is acidic?
   (a) Chlorobutanol (b) Thiomersal
   (c) Benzalkonium chloride (d) Phenol
6. Which of the following antioxidants is used in non-aqueous preparations
   (a) Propyl gallate (b) sodium metabisulphite
   (c) thioglycerol (d) Thiosorbitol
7. Mouthwashes contain
   (a) Alcohol in range from 40% to 50%
   (b) Alcohol in range from 50% to 60%
   (c) Alcohol in range from 10% to 20%
   (d) Alcohol in range from 70% to 80%
8. Throat paint contains glycerine to
   (a) Make it viscous (b) Impart sweetness
   (c) Improve palatability (d) All of the above
9. Which of the following statements is correct?
   (a) Throat paint is not useful for treatment of pharyngitis.
   (b) Throat paint is not useful for treatment of laryngitis.
   (c) Throat paint is not useful for treatment of follicular tonsillitis
   (d) None of the above.
10. Which of the following statements is correct?
    (a) The throat paint should be applied with finger only
    (b) The throat paint should be applied with an ordinary brush
    (c) The throat paint should be applied with a cotton plug or camel brush
    (d) The throat paint should not be applied with a camel brush
11. Which of the following statements is correct?
    (a) Ear drop must be a solution only
    (b) Ear drop does not contain any tonicity modifier
    (c) Ear drop does not contain any viscosity modifier
    (d) None of the above

12. Which of the following statements is not correct?
    (a) Ear drop is a sterile product
    (b) Ear drop does not contain any preservative
    (c) Usually ear drop contains not more than 10ml.
    (d) All of the above.
13. Which of the following statements is not correct?
    (a) Nasal drop may be a solution
    (b) Nasal drop may be a suspension
    (c) Nasal drop may be an emulsion
    (d) None of the above
14. Which of the following statements is correct?
    (a) Enemas can be prepared for retention and evacuation
    (b) Enemas are used for cleaning purpose only
    (c) Enemas do not contain any drug
    (d) Enemas are intended for rectal administration only
15. Which of the following statements is not correct?
    (a) Syrups may be medicated or non-medicated
    (b) Simple syrup contains 66.7% of sucrose
    (c) Apart from sucrose syrups may contain sorbitol and other adjuvants
    (d) None of the above
16. Lotion is administered through
    (a) Oral route (b) Subcutaneous route
    (c) Transdermal route (d) Peritoneal route
17. Liniments is administered through
    (a) Oral route (b) Intramuscular route
    (c) Intravenous route (d) Transdermal route

B. Question Carrying 05 Mark

1. Explain with examples the monophasic liquid.
2. Define the term gargle. State the advantages and disadvantages of gargles.
3. Define the term mouthwashes. What are their applications? Name the excipients generally used to prepare mouthwashes.
4. What is throat paint? Why these are used and what are the limitations?

5. What are different types of hydrocolloids used to prepare throat paint and why these hydrocolloids are used?
6. What is an ear drop? What are the applications of ear drop?
7. What is a nasal drop? What are the advantages and disadvantages of nasal drop?
8. Define enemas. Explain different types of enemas.
9. What is syrup? What are the additives it contains? Mention the advantages of syrups.
10. Define the term elixir. What are liniments?
11. What is a lotion? Write down their applications.

C. Question Carrying 10 Marks

1. Write the general method of preparation of gargles with reference to one formulation.
2. What are the additives used in mouth wash preparations and why? How can you fill a mouthwash? Mention the labelling requirement.
3. Why throat paint is used? What are the points one should consider during formulation of throat paint?
4. What do you know about ear drop? Write down the method of preparation of an official ear drop.
5. What do you know about nasal drop? How can nasal drop be prepared?
6. Write a note on syrup. Explain the problems one has to face during preparation of syrups.
7. Write down the method of preparation of simple syrup.
8. Write a note on elixir and mention their labelling requirements. Write the names of two official preparations.
9. Write note on liniments and lotions.
10. Write down the method of preparation of throat paint and mention the points to be considered for formulation of throat paint.

Answers

A. Multiple Choice Question Carrying 01 Mark

1. (a)	2. (c)	3. (d)	4. (b)	5. (d)
6. (a)	7. (c)	8. (d)	9. (d)	10. (c)
11. (d)	12. (d)	13. (d)	14. (a)	15. (d)
16. (c)	17. (d)			

Chapter 9

Biphasic Liquids: Suspensions

Definition, Advantages and Disadvantages, Classifications, Preparation of Suspensions; Flocculated and Deflocculated suspension & Stability Problems and Methods to Overcome.

Definition

Suspension can be defined as a coarse dispersion system in which insoluble solid particles (drug) are dispersed (dispersed phase) in a dispersion medium (usually an aqueous or in some cases, organic or oily liquids). Suspension can be used as oral dosage form, applied topically on to the skin or mucous membrane surfaces, or given parenterally by injection.

Depending on the particle size of the dispersed solids it may be classified as,

Table 9.1 Types of Dispersions

Size range of the dispersed particles	*Type of dispersion*
1.0 nm – 0.5μm	Colloidal dispersion
0.5 μm – 10 μm	Fine dispersion
10 μm – 50 μm	Coarse dispersion

It is desired that in any suspension the solid particles should remain uniformly dispersed throughout the dispersion, so that, a correct dose can be dispensed. Since coarse dispersions contain particles of relatively larger size range, sedimentation of particles is also faster. However, it is essential that the suspension, if sedimented, it must be redispersible with minimum agitation and should be easily pourable. Thus, it is customary to mention in the label, "shake well before use". These suspensions are called *ready-to – use*.

There are certain drugs whose suspensions are prepared only before use by adding a suitable vehicle, *reconstituted suspension*. Because of stability and other reasons these formulations are prepared and marketed as dry powders. There are certain problems in formulating and stabilizing suspension dosage forms, even then these are prepared because,

- Some drugs are not stable in solution state, but stable in suspension,
- To some patients like infants and elderly it is convenient to swallow,
- Like other liquid dosage forms, it provides the opportunity to adjust the dose as and when required,
- Suspension dosage form has good patient's acceptability for its elegance, taste and flavour.

For prolonged therapy parenteral suspension are best. When an aqueous or oleaginous suspension of a drug is injected subcutaneously or intramuscularly, at the site of injection a depot or reservoir of drug is formed which slowly release the drug. The rate of release of the drug depends on intrinsic aqueous solubility of the drug and the type of vehicle of the suspension. Most common example is Procaine Penicillin G injection.

Advantages of Suspensions

- An insoluble drug can be formulated as a liquid dosage form with improved organoleptic properties.
- Patient compliance, in terms of palatability, is better.
- Easy to administer to the patients who cannot swallow tablets or capsules.
- Increased surface area of the dispersed drug particles provides better therapeutic action, e.g. antacid.
- Bioavailability of drugs is expected to be better than other solid dosage forms (tablets, capsules), since it contains fine particles of drug, no need of disintegration.
- Compared to solutions the suspension can preserve the drug better, as the drug remains mostly in solid state; hence, the stability of the drug is better than in solution.
- It can be designed conveniently for slow and sustained release of drug.

Disadvantages of Suspensions

- Water soluble drugs are not suitable for making suspensions.
- Reduction of particle size makes the drug thermodynamically unstable and hence, invites some problems in formulation.

- Although the drugs mostly remain insoluble in suspensions, a fraction which gets dissolve in the solvent can lead to physical instability of the preparation.
- There is chance of adsorption of preservative and colour present in the suspension by the fine solid particles; thus, the concentration of preservative needs to be increased, this is not desirable.
- The rate of absorption of drug from suspension is slower than that from a solution.
- The uniformity of dose depends on the redispersibility of the sedimented drug.

Classifications of Suspensions

Suspensions can be classified into various types based on its particle size, density and suspension-character of the dispersed particle, route of administration, etc.

Table 9.2 Types of Suspensions

Criterion	Type of suspension
Size of dispersed particles	colloidal suspension and coarse suspension
Density of dispersed particles	suspension with diffusible solids and suspension with indiffusible solids
Dispersion character	flocculated suspension and deflocculated suspension
Route of administration	suspension for internal use and suspension for external use

Preparation of Suspensions

Suspension, usually, contains dispersed phase and a dispersion medium. The solids may be hydrophilic or hydrophobic. Solids which are wetted with water without any surfactant, are called hydrophilic. Hydrophilic solids can absorb moisture at a relative humidity less than 70%. The hydrophobic solids have higher interfacial tension and cannot be easily wetted by water without using a suitable surfactant. These can be wetted by oils or semi polar liquids and thus, these are also called lipophilic.

The drug substance(s) being used for suspension should be microcrystalline powders of uniform or at least of narrow size range (preferably below 10μm) and there should be no impurities adhered on the surface of the particles.

A well formulated oral suspension may contain the following types of additives according to the requirement:

- wetting agent
- viscosity imparting agent (suspending agent)
- buffer and/or stabilizing agent
- preservatives
- sweetening agent
- colour
- flavouring agent

The parenteral suspension does not contain any sweetening, colouring and flavouring agent, while suspension for external use does not contain any sweetening agent.

Additives used in pharmaceutical suspensions are presented in the Table 4.1 and Table 4.2 below

Table 9.3 Lists of surfactants commonly used as wetting agents

Type & Name	HLB value	Remarks
Anionic		
Sodium Lauryl Sulphate	40	Foaming agent, bitter in taste
Sodium Decussate	> 24	- do -
Non-ionic		
Polysorbate 80	15	Most commonly used, bitter in taste
Polysorbate 65	10.5	Bitter in taste
Polysorbate 60	14.9	- do -
Polysorbate 40	15.6	Toxicity is less, bitter in taste
Polysorbate 20	16.7	Bitter in taste
Octoxynol 9	12.2	- do -
Nonoxynol 10	13.2	- do -
Polyoxamer 188	29	Foaming agent
Poloxamer 235	16	Toxicity is less, taste is good

Table 9.4 List of Suspending agents commonly used in suspensions

Type & Name	Effective at pH	Incompatibilities
Cellulose		
Carboxymethyl cellulose sodium Methyl cellulose, microcrystalline Cellulose.	3 – 10	Higher concentration of salts, tannins, Cationic surfactants.
Hydroxy ethyl cellulose	2 – 10	Insoluble in alcohol above 10%
Hydroxy propyl cellulose	2 – 10	- do -
Hydroxypropyl methylcellulose	2 – 10	- do -
Gums		
Guar gum	3 – 9	Alcohol, borax, glycerine above 10%, Calcium and aluminium ions.
Gum acacia	3 – 9	Insoluble in alcohol above 10%
Pectin	2 – 9	Zinc oxide, alcohol above 10%
Sodium alginate	4 – 10	Calcium ions, alcohol above 10%
Tragacanth	3 – 9	Bismuth salt, alcohol above 40%
Xanthan gum	4 – 10	Borax, cationic surfactants
Agar	4 – 10	Alcohol, borax, glycerine above 10%, Calcium and aluminium ions.
Carrageenan	4 – 10	Alcohol, borax, glycerine above 10%, Calcium and magnesium ions.
Clays		
Bentonite (Colloidal aluminium silicate)	3 – 10	Viscosity is increased by polyvalent cations and calcium ions.
Attapulgite (colloidal magnesium aluminium silicate)	3 – 10	Viscosity is increased by calcium ions.
Miscellaneous		
Polyethylene glycols (3350, 8000)	3 – 10	Phenols
Lecithin	5 – 8	Insoluble in water
Povidone (K30)	3 – 10	Oils and lecithin
Gelatin	5 – 8	Acids, bases and aldehydes.

Stability Problems and Methods to Overcome

There are certain problems usually observed in suspensions and these problems if not resolved may cause instability of the suspension formulation. It is responsibility of the formulation development scientist to make a list of those problems normally encountered and take precautionary measured so that a stable formulation is made.

The problems usually associated with suspension formulation are:

- Proper dispersion of the solid particles
- Coagulation of suspended or dispersed particles is the major problem
- Sedimentation of the coagulates
- Phase separation
- Caking

These are the major problems of a suspension that impair stability of a preparation. The factors responsible for instability are:

- Size or size range of the dispersed particles
- Density of the dispersion medium
- Viscosity of the dispersion medium

Therefore, some key points required to be considered to develop a stable suspension are listed below:

- Size of dispersed particles should be around 30mμ.Larger particles agglomerate or settle quickly. Grinding of particles increases the surface free energy of the particles which help in aggregation.
- Powders to be wetted completely for at least 10 hrs with minimum amount of suspending vehicle without agitation. For this purpose, a suitable wetting agent should be used.
- Selection of the suspending and wetting agent should be proper in terms of their grade and concentration. No extra material should be included in the formula.
- The ionic character should be considered when the suspending agent is selected, because these may have ionic character. Ionic character of the dispersed particles is responsible for aggregation of particles; hence energy barrier is necessary to keep these particles apart. A suitable electrolyte must be added to take care.
- Weak monovalent acids, bases, salts or any electrolyte should be used for adjustment of pH and/or tonicity. No strong acid, base or electrolyte should be used which can change the particle charge abruptly.
- The suspending agent should be dispersed or dissolved in the vehicle and sufficient time to be allowed for complete hydration. The type and concentration of suspending agent should be so adjusted that the viscosity of the suspension is increased. The

viscosity of the suspension should be such that the pourability is not affected and the particles remain dispersed for long period.

- The density of the dispersion medium is increased by adding certain thickening agent.
- The mass of wetted particles is to be added slowly to the dispersion medium with low stirring.
- After complete preparation, the suspension should be milled or homogenized.
- The preparation should be stored carefully and protected from any microbial contamination.

Flocculated and Deflocculated Suspension

Look of flocculated suspension is better than that of deflocculated suspension. Hence, consumer prefers to have a flocculated suspension. However, the major problem of suspension formulations is sedimentation and particularly cake formation. The characteristic properties of these two types of suspensions are given below.

Flocculated Suspension

The term flocculated came from 'flocs'; that is 'loose agglomerates of smaller particles'. In a flocculated suspension the particles come together and form loose agglomerates. The total surface area is not reduced during flocculation process, which happens in case of coalescence. This is because the particles in the agglomerates possess their individual surface identity. Flocculated suspensions can be prepared by various ways:

1. Using a polymeric agent – polymers contain chemical groups. These groups interact with the suspended particles. The polymer is added to the continuous phase (dispersion medium). As a result, the polymer attaches to the individual particles and form polymer-particles complexes. Since one polymer molecule can link to two or more particles, a 'floc' is formed. This process is called polymer-bridging; hence in some cases degree of flocculation depends on the concentration of polymer. When concentration of polymer is increased, the particles become surrounded by the polymer and little 'flocs' are formed.
2. This is based on the electrical charge. Suspended particles carry a charge which may be their inherent or acquired (surface charge) during grinding. Particles carrying similar charge (positive or negative) repel one another. Thus, a resistance to formation of flocs of particles is developed. The surface charge of the suspended particles can be reduced by addition of an appropriate electrolyte (electrolyte

having opposite charge that is either anionic or cationic). Repulsion among the particles does not allow them to come closer. That is, the attractive van der Waals forces do not dominate. Thus, by adding suitable electrolyte the surface charge can be reduced and flocs can be formed.

3. By using two surfactants, flocculation can be achieved. For example, an anionic surfactant and a cationic surfactant can be used for this purpose. These are used for proper wetting of particles. This has been observed that at lower concentrations of the anionic wetting agent the suspensions become deflocculated and dispersed particles coalesce, settle and form sediment which cannot be redispersed. By increasing the concentration of the wetting agent the suspension can be made flocculated.

Deflocculated Suspension

This is an opposite type to flocculated suspension. That is, in this type of suspension the flocs or clusters break down into individual particles. Deflocculation is defined as the dispersion of primary particles and this improves overall wettability. Surfactants present in suspension lower the solid-liquid interfacial tension. In deflocculated suspension the particles do not form structures (flocs). The deflocculated suspension provides elegance better than the flocculated suspension. The rheological behaviour of deflocculated suspension depends on the rheological behaviour of the continuous phase (dispersion medium) and on the distortion of the flow characteristics of the particles. When such suspension is made more concentrated and suspended particles come in contact and the suspension become dilatant. Under this circumstance when the dispersed particles settle from the suspension, they settle relatively at slower rate and the sediment produced is a compact cake. This sediment does not redisperse on mild shaking.

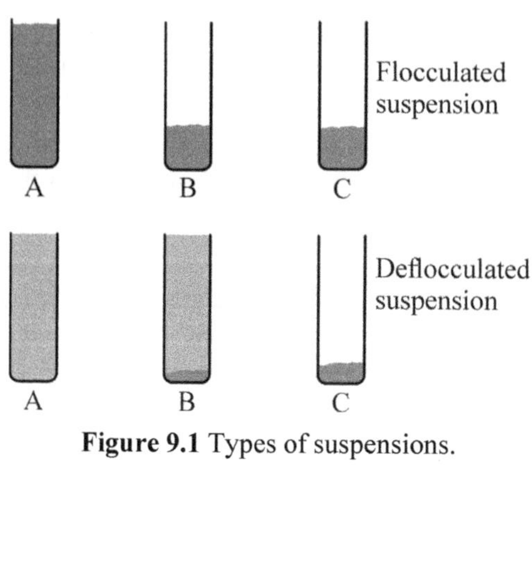

Figure 9.1 Types of suspensions.

The supernatant of this suspension remains cloudy for an appreciable time after shaking, because the settling rate of the smallest particles in the product is very slow. Since the rate of settling is very slow, liquid cannot be entrapped within the sediment, as a result the sediment becomes compacted and non-redispersible or difficult to be redispersed. This phenomenon is also called caking and is the most serious of all the physical stability problems encountered in suspension. The flocculated and deflocculated suspensions are shown in the following figure:

As shown in the figure the flocculated suspension does not look good compared to deflocculated one. (A) There is almost no change in the sediment volume of deflocculated suspension within short period from time of manufacturing, while in flocculated suspension a supernatant liquid is seen. (B) Disperse phase remains dispersed in deflocculated suspension, while in flocculated suspension the sediment volume is further reduced leaving more of supernatant. (C) In flocculated suspension the volume of supernatant increases further with 72 hours, reaches almost ultimate state; but in deflocculated suspension very little change in volume of sediment is noticed even after few days. By increasing the viscosity of continuous phase or dispersion medium the rate of sedimentation can be reduced. At this stage the flow behaviour would seem to be of Newtonian fluid. However, the viscosity cannot be increased beyond certain point because the pourability of the suspension would be affected.

Formulations

Product: Antacid Suspension

Standard for drugs: Dried Aluminium hydroxide gel should contain not less than 47.0% w/w and not more than 60.0%w/w of Al_2O_3.

Magnesium hydroxide should contain not less than 95%w/w and not more than 100.5%w/w of $Mg(OH)_2$.

Dimethicone should contain poly dimethylsiloxane, $[-(CH_3)_2SiO-]_n$ within 90.0%w/w - 99.0%w/w and silicon dioxide, SiO_2, within 4.0 – 7.0%w/w.

Standard for the product: Content of Aluminium hydroxide gel: 90%–110%w/v of the stated amount, calculated as Al_2O_3.

Content of Magnesium hydroxide: 90% – 110%w/v of the stated amount, calculated as $Mg(OH)_2$,

Content of Dimethicone: 85% - 115%w/v of the stated amount.

Composition:

Each 5 ml contains

Dried Aluminium Hydroxide Gel	IP	250 mg
Magnesium Hydroxide	IP	250 mg
Dimethicone activated	IP	50 mg

Use: Antacid.

Lot size: 25 ml

Manufacturing Formula:

Dried Aluminium Hydroxide	USP	1.25 g
Magnesium Hydroxide	IP	1.25g
Dimethicone activated	IP	0.25 g
Sodium CMC, MV		0.125 g
Syrup	IP	18.5 g
Sorbitol Liquid (70%)	USP	1.25 g
Glycerin	IP	1.25 ml
Tween 80		2.5 mg
Methyl Paraben sodium	IP	0.05 g
Propyl Paraben sodium	IP	0.01 g
Sodium Benzoate	IP	0.125 g
Bronopol		2.5 mg
Colour	FCF	0.5 mg
Peppermint oil		0.06 ml
Menthol		0.5 mg
Purified water	IP	qs

Manufacturing Method

- Take required quantity of syrup in a 25 ml clean beaker, heat on a boiling water bath, add weighed quantity of methyl paraben, propyl paraben, sodium benzoate, bronopol.
- Stir with a glass rod until dissolved.
- Add sodium CMC, stir with a glass rod until a mucilage is formed.
- Take aluminium hydroxide, magnesium hydroxide and sodium CMC in a clean mortar pestle, add simethicone and make a smooth paste,
- Transfer the contents of the beaker slowly with continuous trituration.
- Rinse the beaker with 4 ml of purified water and pour into the mortar.
- Add tween 80, glycerine, sorbitol liquid and colour, continue trituration.
- Add menthol and peppermint oil, triturate for at least 30 min.
- Estimate the content of drugs.
- Transfer the suspension into a clean, dry bottle; seal with pilfer proof cap and label.

Product: Ibuprofen Suspension

Standard for drugs: It should contain not less than 98.5% and not more than 101%w/w of $C_{13}H_{18}O_2$, calculated on dried basis.

Standard for the product: It should contain not less than 90% and not more than 110%w/w of the stated amount of ibuprofen, calculated as $C_{13}H_{18}O_2$.

Composition:

Each 5 ml contains

Ibuprofen IP 100 mg.

In a coloured, flavoured base.

Use: Analgesic.

Lot size: 25 ml

Manufacturing Formula:

Ibuprofen	IP	0.50 g
Sorbitol liquid (70%)	USP	11.25 g
Sodium CMC, LV		0.75 g
Syrup	IP	6.8 ml
Sodium benzoate	IP	0.138 g
Methyl paraben sodium	IP	0.026 g
Propyl paraben sodium	IP	0.005 g
Tween 80		0.025 g
Citric Acid	IP	0.067 g
Colour FCF		0.5 mg
Flavour		0.16 ml
Purified water	IP	qs

Manufacturing Method

- Take 5 ml of purified water in a clean 25 ml beaker, add methyl paraben, propyl paraben, heat to dissolve, add sodium benzoate, stir with a glass rod to dissolve.
- Add sodium CMC, stir to make the mucilage.
- Add citric acid and dissolve.
- Take ibuprofen in a clean mortar pestle, triturate with tween 80,
- Add sorbitol solution and triturate,
- Transfer the contents from the beaker gradually with continuous trituration, add syrup.
- Rinse the beaker with 3 ml of purified water and add. Triturate the mixture for at least 30 min.

- Carry out the tests as applicable, add colour and triturate well to mix properly,
- Add the flavour and mix,
- Fill the product in a clean, dry bottle, seal with a pilfer proof cap,
- Label properly.

Product: Ibuprofen and Paracetamol Suspension

Standard for drugs: Ibuprofen: it should contain not less than 98.5% and not more than 101%w/w of $C_{13}H_{18}O_2$, calculated on dried basis.

Paracetamol: It should contain not less than 99% and not more than 101%w/w of $C_8H_9NO_2$, calculated on dried basis.

Standard for suspension: It should contain not less than 95% and not more than 105%w/w of the stated amount of ibuprofen, calculated as $C_{13}H_{18}O_2$ and not less than 90% and not more than 110%w/w of the stated amount of paracetamol, calculated as $C_8H_9NO_2$.

Composition

Each 5 ml contains

Ibuprofen	IP	100 mg
Paracetamol	IP	125 mg

Use: Analgesic and antipyretic.

Lot size: 25 ml

Manufacturing Formula

Ibuprofen	IP	0.5 g
Paracetamol	IP	0.625 g
Aerosil powder		0.02 g
Sorbitol liquid (70%)	IP	11.25 g
Sodium CMC		0.075 g
Syrup	IP	6.8 ml
Sodium Benzoate	IP	0.138 g
Methyl paraben sodium	IP	0.026 g
Propyl paraben sodium	IP	0.005 g
Tween 80		0.025 g
Citric Acid	IP	0.067 g
Colour	FCF	0.5 mg
Flavour		0.16 ml
Purified water	IP	qs

Manufacturing Method

- Take 5 ml of purified water in a clean 25 ml beaker, add methyl paraben, propyl paraben, heat to dissolve, add sodium benzoate, stir with a glass rod to dissolve.
- Add sodium CMC, stir to make the mucilage.
- Add citric acid and dissolve.
- Take ibuprofen and paracetamol in a clean mortar pestle, triturate with tween 80, add sorbitol solution and triturate,
- Transfer the contents from the beaker gradually with continuous trituration, add syrup.
- Rinse the beaker with 3 ml of purified water and add. Triturate the mixture for at least 30 minutes.
- Carry out the tests as applicable, add colour and triturate well to mix properly,
- Add the flavour and mix,
- Fill the product in a clean, dry bottle, seal with a pilfer proof cap.
- Label properly.

Product: Furazolidone, Pectin and Kaolin Suspension

Standard for the drug: Furazolidone contains not less than 97% and not more than 103% of $C_8H_7N_3O_5$ on dried basis.

Standard for the suspension: It should contain not less than 90% and not more than 110% of Furazolidone calculated as $C_8H_7N_3O_5$.

Composition

Each 5 ml contains

Furazolidone	33.3 mg
Pectin	75 mg
Kaolin	1.0 g

Use: Anti-diarrhoeal.

Lot size: 25 ml

Manufacturing Formula

Furazolidone		0.183 g
Pectin		0.375 g
Kaolin, light		5.0 g
Sodium CMC, LV		0.025 g
Guar Gum	IP	0.025 g
Syrup	IP	9.5 ml

Sodium Benzoate	IP	0.125 g
Methyl paraben sodium	IP	0.05 g
Propyl paraben sodium	IP	0.01 g
Tween 80		0.025 g
Citric Acid	IP	0.067 g
Flavour		0.16 ml
Purified water	IP	qs

Manufacturing Method

- Take 10 ml of purified water in a 25 ml clean beaker, add methyl paraben, propyl paraben and heat to dissolve,
- Add sodium benzoate, sodium CMC, guar gum and pectin. Soak for 24 hrs. at room temperature.
- On the next day, take required quantity of furazolidone and kaolin in a clean mortar pestle, triturate with tween80.
- Add the contents from the beaker gradually with constant trituration; add syrup and triturate properly.
- Rinse the beaker with 5 ml of purified water and to the mortar, triturate at least for 30 min.
- Carry out the tests as applicable, add the flavour and mix well.
- Fill the product in a clean, dry bottle and seal with a pilfer proof cap.
- Label the product properly.

Product: Metronidazole Suspension

Standard for drugs: It should contain not less than 98% and not more than 101%w/w of $C_{13}H_{13}N_3O_4$, calculated on dried basis.

Standard for the product: It should contain not less than 90% and not more than 110%w/w of the stated amount of Metronidazole, calculated as $C_6H_9N_3O_3$.

Composition

Each 5 ml contains

Metronidazole Benzoate	IP	
Equivalent to Metronidazole	IP	200 mg

In a flavoured palatable base.

Colour: Tartrazine

Use: Antiamoebic and antiprotozoal

Lot size: 25 ml

Manufacturing Formula

Metronidazole benzoate	IP	1.0 g*
Guar Gum	IP	0.125 g
Sorbitol liquid (70%)	USP	1.25 g
Liquid Glucose		0.625 g
Polysorbate 80		25 mg
Methyl Paraben sodium	IP	25 mg
Propyl paraben sodium	IP	5 mg
Syrup	IP	11.5 ml
Colour	FCF	1.0 mg
Flavour		3.0 mg
Purified water	IP	qs

*Calculate the amount on the basis of assay value of the supplied drug.

Manufacturing Method

- Take 10 ml of purified water in a 25 ml clean beaker, add required quantity of methyl paraben, propyl paraben, place over a boiling water bath, and stir to dissolve.
- Remove from heat.
- Add guar gum and mix well to make mucilage, add syrup, sorbitol liquid and mix thoroughly.
- Take required quantity of metronidazole benzoate into a clean mortar pestle, triturate with polysorbate 80, and add liquid glucose with continuous trituration. Once a smooth paste is made, add gradually the contents from the beaker, continue to triturate.
- Add colour and triturate, rinse the beaker with 4 ml of hot purified water and pour into the mortar.
- Continue trituration for at least 30 min., add flavour and triturate to mix thoroughly.
- Carry out the tests as applicable, fill in a clean, dry bottle and seal with a pilfer proof cap.
- Label properly.

Warning: Metronidazole has been to be carcinogenic in mice and rats. Unnecessary use of the drug should be avoided.

Metronidazole Suspension I.P. 100ml

Each 5ml contains
Metronidazole Benzoate IP
Equivalent to Metronidazole IP 200 mg

In a flavoured palatable base.
Colours: Tartrazine.

SCHEDULE H DRUG
Warning: To be sold by retail on the prescription of a Registered Medical Practitioner only.

Manufactured in India by
XYZ Pharmaceutical
Kohka-Kurud road, Bhilai

B.No. 1234
Mfd. MM.YYYY
Exp. MM.YYYY

Dosage: As directed by the physician
SHAKE WELL BEFORE USE
Storage :Protect from light, keep out of reach of children

Exercise

A. Multiple Choice Question Carrying 01 Mark

1. Which of the following preparations is biphasic liquid?
   (a) Emulsion (b) Elixir
   (c) Tincture (d) None of the above
2. Particle size of the colloidal dispersion is
   (a) Less than 10nm (b) More than 1μm
   (c) More than 1nm (d) More than 40μm
3. Particle size of the coarse dispersion is
   (a) Less than 1nm (b) Less than 20nm
   (c) Less than 30nm (d) Less than 10μm
4. An insoluble drug can be formulated as
   (a) Suspension (b) Solution
   (c) Injection (d) Elixir
5. A soluble drug cannot be formulated as
   (a) Solution (b) Tincture
   (c) Suspension (d) None of the above
6. Which of the following excipients is not used in oral suspension?
   (a) Butylated hydroxy anisole (b) Sucrose
   (c) Sodium benzoate (d) Sodium phosphate

7. Pectin is incompatible with
   (a) Zinc oxide
   (b) Alcohol 5%
   (c) Guar gum
   (d) Sucrose
8. Xanthan gum is incompatible with
   (a) Anionic surfactant
   (b) Phosphate buffer
   (c) Cationic surfactant
   (d) Sucrose
9. Gelatin is compatible with
   (a) Acids
   (b) Bases
   (c) Aldehyde
   (d) Water
10. Common stability problem of suspension is
    (a) Suspending agent
    (b) Solubilization of drug
    (c) Sedimentation
    (d) Maintenance of pH
11. Which one of the following statements is true?
    (a) Sedimentation in deflocculated suspension is slow
    (b) Sedimentation in deflocculated suspension is fast
12. Which one of the following statements is true?
    (a) Sedimentation in flocculated suspension is slow
    (b) Sedimentation in flocculated suspension is fast
13. Which one of the following statements is correct?
    (a) Flocculated suspension is less stable
    (b) Deflocculated suspension is less stable
14. Which one of the following statements is true?
    (a) Smaller particles should be used to prepare suspension
    (b) Coarse particles should be used to prepare suspension
15. Which one of the following statements is correct?
    (a) Polymers in suspension cannot increase the stability of suspension
    (b) Polymers in suspension can increase the stability of suspension
16. Which one of the following statements is true?
    (a) Stability of suspension can be increased by adding electrolyte
    (b) Stability of suspension cannot be increased by adding electrolyte

17. Which one of the following statements is true?
    (a) Viscosity is related to pourability of a suspension
    (b) Viscosity is not related to pourability of a suspension
18. Which one of the following statements is correct?
    (a) Palatability is an important criterion of a suspension
    (b) Palatability is not an important criterion of a suspension
19. Which one of the following statements is correct?
    (a) Wetting of powders is essential for making suspension
    (b) Wetting of powders is not essential for making suspension
20. Which one of the following statements is correct?
    (a) The dose of a drug can be adjusted in suspension dosage form
    (b) Suspension provides fixed dose of a drug.

B. Question Carrying 05 Marks

1. Define the term suspension. Explain the problems associated to suspension.
2. What are the advantages and disadvantages of suspension dosage form?
3. Write down the key points to be considered for development of a stable suspension.
4. Explain why wetting agent is used to prepare a suspension.
5. Explain the use of suspending agent in suspension.
6. Justify the use of surface-active agent in suspension.

C. Question Carrying 10 Marks

1. What is flocculated suspension? Describe the methods used to prepare a flocculated suspension.
2. Write a note on deflocculated suspension.
3. Discuss the stability problems associated with suspension and their solutions.
4. Classify the surface-active agents on the basis of their head groups and explain why they are used in suspension.
5. Describe how a stable suspension can be prepared.
6. Discuss how the particle size and their surface charge can influence the formulation and stability of suspension.

Answers

A. Multiple Choice Question Carrying 01 Mark

1. (a)	2. (b)	3. (d)	4. (a)	5. (c)
6. (a)	7. (a)	8. (c)	9. (d)	10. (c)
11. (a)	12. (b)	13. (b)	14. (a)	15. (a)
16. (a)	17. (a)	18. (a)	19. (a)	20. (a)

Chapter 10

Biphasic Liquids: Emulsions

Definition, Classification, Emulsifying Agent, Test for the Identification of Type of Emulsion, Methods of Preparation & Stability Problems and Methods to Overcome.

Definition

Emulsion is a dispersed system of two immiscible liquids in which one liquid is uniformly dispersed in another. The former liquid is called the dispersed phase or internal phase while the latter- dispersion medium or external phase.

The internal phase remains in the form of fine globules of colloidal dimensions. The size of the globules is very important for stability of emulsions. A third substance called emulsifying agent is added to the system to render the stability of the preparation.

Emulsions are used for oral, parenteral, topical administration including cosmetic purpose and also for diagnostic purposes. The emulsion may be of various types, - macroemulsion (conventional emulsion), microemulsion, multiple emulsion and gel emulsion.

Based on composition, emulsions are generally of two types – oil-in-water (o/w) and water-in-oil(w/o); but, there may be another two types – water-in-water(w/w) and oil-in-oil(o/o). W/w type contains aqueous solutions of immiscible/incompatible substances, like, polysaccharides, synthetic polymers, proteins, etc., while o/o type can be prepared from immiscible organic solvents stabilized by copolymers.

The therapeutic agents and other necessary additives are incorporated in this preparation by dissolving in either of the two phases. The preservatives commonly used in emulsions are chlorocresol, chlorobutanol, mercurial, benzoic acid, sorbic acid, ρ-hydroxybenzoic acids, etc. Since, the surface-active agents (emulsifying agent) used in these preparations have a tendency to bind preservatives and thereby reduce the preservative action; so, the preservative should be carefully selected that can protect both the phases. Alkyl esters of ρ-hydroxybenzoic acids are found to be suitable for these preparations. For external use, choice of the type of emulsion depends on the nature of the drug substance being used, expected emollient effect, the condition of the skin surface, etc.

An emulsion can be diluted with the liquid that constitutes the external phase or is miscible with the external phase. In this process the viscosity of the emulsion will be reduced and in some cases the emulsion type may also be changed.

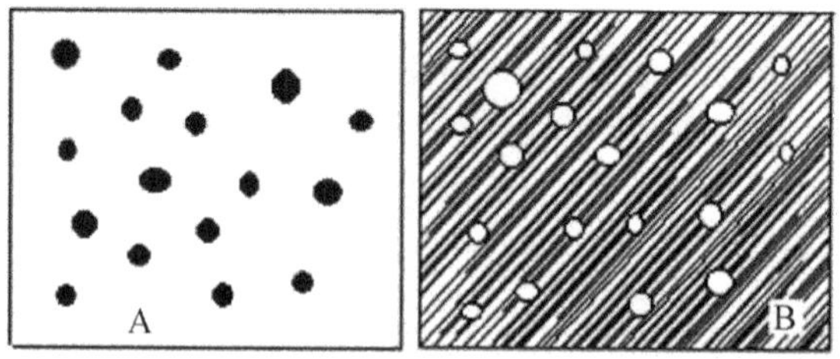

A: Water-in-Oil B: Oil-in-Water

Figure 10.1 Types of emulsion.

Table 10.1 Comparison between suspension and emulsion

Suspension	Emulsion
1. Suspension is a dispersed system in which finely powdered solids (disperse phase) is dispersed in aliquid (dispersion medium).	Emulsion is a dispersed system in which one liquidremains dispersed (disperse phase) in the form of fine globules in an immiscible liquid (dispersion medium).
2. Suspension may be classified on the basis of size of the dispersed particles- colloidal dispersion having particle size ranging from 1nm - 1μm, and coarse dispersion having particle size larger than 1μm.	Emulsion contains dispersed globules with a size range from 0.1 to 100μm.
3. While preparing suspension a high shear is applied along with addition of a surface-active agent to overcome the particle-particle attractive forces.	During emulsification the high shear is applied to break the liquid (disperse phase) into fine globules with addition of a surface-active agent for dispersion of the globules.
4. Suspensions are thermodynamically unstable due to excess surface free energy of the dispersed particles.	Emulsions are also thermo-dynamically unstable due to excess surface free energy of the dispersed globules.
5. Usually suspensions intended for internal use are oil-in-water(o/w) dispersion.	Emulsions may be of two types, oil-in-water(o/w) and water-in-oil (w/o).

Table 10.1 *Contd...*

Suspension	Emulsion
6. Suspension requires a third substance called suspending agent for suspending the particles.	For emulsification, it also requires another substance called emulsifying agent.
7. These are viscous liquid preparations with adequate pourability.	Emulsions are also viscous preparations with adequate pourability.
8. In suspension the distribution of dispersed particles may be fairly uniform.	In emulsions the distribution of dispersed globules is uniform.
9. Suspensions suffer from aggregation, sedimentation and caking.	Emulsions suffer from creaming, cracking and breaking.

Classification of Emulsions

Based on different criteria emulsion can be classified into various types.

Criterion Types of Emulsion

Size of droplets/particles	Macroemulsion – Colloidal and Fine Microemulsion
Orientation of phase	Simple emulsion – water-in-oil(w/o) and oil-in-water(o/w) Multiple emulsions– water-in-oil-in-water (w/o/w) and oil-in-water-in-oil(o/w/o)
Physical state Creams	Liquids
Route of administration	Emulsions for internal use and Emulsions for external use

Emulsifying Agent

For pharmaceutical purposes the ideal emulsifying agent should be stable, inert, non-toxic, odourless, tasteless and colourless. At low concentration it should produce a stable emulsion.

Emulsifying agents are classified into two categories:

1. Primary emulsifying agent: these are true emulsifying agents used to prepare good emulsions.
2. Secondary emulsifiers: these are used to stabilizing the emulsion in presence of primary emulsifying agent.

Emulsifying agents can be broadly classified into four groups – natural, semisynthetic polysaccharides, surfactant and finely divided solids. Synthetic emulsifying agents are of three types.

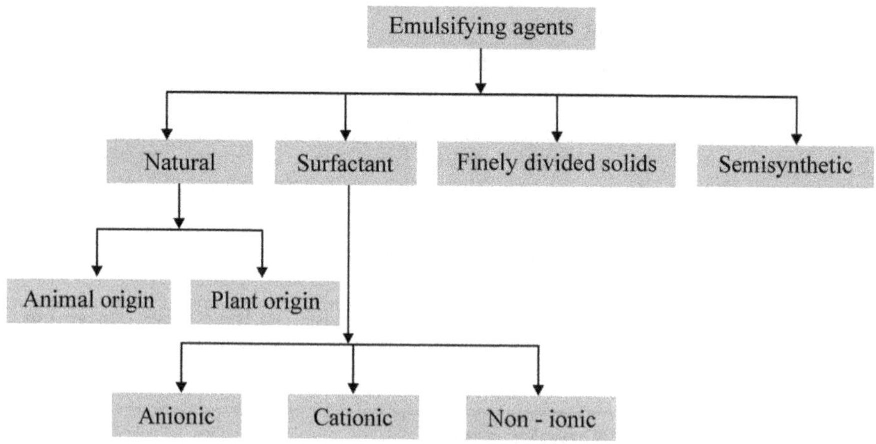

Figure 10.2 Different types of emulsifying agents.

1. **Natural emulsifying agents**

Polysaccharides such as gum, acacia, tragacanth, sodium alginate, pectin, agar, etc. are most commonly used as emulsifying agents. Since these are natural substances, their quality and properties vary. Polysaccharides form multi-molecular layer around the dispersed particles, acts as a barrier between two particles and prevent to coalesce. The polysaccharides usually form oil-in-water(o/w) emulsion.

Among these acacia acts as a primary emulsifier, other polysaccharides are used as secondary emulsifier for stabilizing the emulsion. However, all these materials are susceptible to hydrolysis and microbial contamination. In fact, microorganisms grow easily in these materials because these are polysaccharide, food for microbes. Both hydrolysis and microbial contamination result the loss of emulsifying activity of these polysaccharides. Hence, these require addition of suitable antimicrobial preservative.

Other than acacia, all polysaccharides are prepared by precipitation using alcohol and electrolytes. When these are added, they stabilize the emulsion. Their viscosity depends on the molecular weight; but none of the suspending agent is available with a particular molecular weight. These are available with a range of molecular weight. As per their viscosity these are available as LV (low viscosity) grade, MV (medium viscosity) grade, and HV (high viscosity) grade.

(a) Plant origin

Acacia

For a new oral emulsion acacia is the best emulsifying agent. Even by using a mortar-pestle a good quality and elegant emulsion can be prepared; if acacia is added; a concentrated, viscous and sticky emulsion is prepared by vigorous agitation in a mortar-pestle. As a result, the oil present in emulsion is reduced to fine globules which cannot escape. The viscosity of acacia is low, and emulsion prepared with acacia is of low viscosity. Creaming is a common problem in such emulsions. Hence, a stabilizer such as tragacanth, sodium alginate, etc. can be used. These increase the viscosity of the emulsion. Emulsions containing acacia are palatable and stable at a pH ranging from 2 to 10. Because of their stickiness these are not used for external application.

Tragacanth

It has good emulsifying capability because its mucilage has high viscosity. Emulsions prepared with tragacanth are coarse; hence, it is used as a stabilizer. It should be used with acacia. Generally, one part of tragacanth is used with 10 parts of acacia.

Sodium alginate

Similar to tragacanth the solution of sodium alginate has high viscosity for which it works as a good emulsifying agent. It is commonly used it works satisfactorily as emulsifying agent in emulsions of vegetable oil and animal oil such as fish liver oil; but it is not used in mineral oil emulsions. It can produce good emulsion when a particular volume of oil is shaken with equal volume of 1% mucilage of sodium alginate, and the product is passed through a homogenizer.

In emulsion of mineral oil, it is used with acacia and it is used as the emulsion stabilizer.

Pectin

It is obtained from citrus fruit, soluble in about 20 parts of water. The solution is viscous, opalescent and acidic in pH. It works as a good emulsifying agent when the pH of the emulsion is acidic. If the pH is increased it degrades. It can be used individually or with acacia at a concentration of 10% of acacia. Pectin is used as emulsifying agent or stabilizing agent in pharmaceutical products, food products and cosmetic lotions, creams. If water is added to pectin directly, pectin may form clumps. Hence, it must be properly wetted with alcohol, glycerine or syrup of tragacanth and then used.

Emulsion containing pectin is incompatible with alkalis, strong alcohol, salicylic acid, tannic acid and heavy metals.

Agar

Agar is an extract of some dried seaweeds. The extract is dried to produce powder agar. This is available as white to greyish white shreds, strips or powders. It is soluble in boiling water and the solution has high viscosity. On cooling even 0.5% solution sets as thin gel. Formerly it was used to stabilize liquid paraffin emulsion prepared with acacia. Thus, it works satisfactorily at lower concentration.

(b) Animal origin

Beeswax

Beeswax primarily contains two substances – (1) small amount of ester of cholesterol which is a sterol and can form w/o emulsion, (2) free cerotic acid ($C_{25}H_{51}COOH$) which reacts with borax and forms soap. These are the reasons for which beeswax can be used as emulsifying agent in cold creams (w/o emulsions).

However, it is not an excellent emulsifying agent, but it is used in w/o emulsions (creams) as stabilizing agent. It helps in incorporation of water into the cream. It is available as white to yellow discs or slabs. Its use is restricted due to its deep color. On bleaching it becomes white and can be used in white colour products.

Wool Fat

It is pale yellow, greasy, very sticky material. It melts within 36° – 42°C. It is a type of wax containing mainly fatty acid esters of cholesterol and other sterols along with general fatty alcohols. It is also similar to human sebum.

It is poorly absorbed by the skin; but creams containing wool fat and vegetable oil or soft paraffin can penetrate the skin and such preparation facilitates absorption of drug through the skin. Wool fat can absorb 50% of water; but a mixture of wool fat and other fatty substances can absorb aqueous or hydroalcoholic liquids up to several times of the weight of wool fat in the preparation. Such mixture may be a stable emulsion. Usually wool fat forms water-in-oil emulsion (w/o).

As such it is so sticky that it cannot be used alone. Eye ointments and Simple ointment are prepared by using a mixture of wool fat and hydrocarbon. These mixtures can absorb good amount of water or aqueous solution.

Many people do not like its characteristic odour. On dilution the odour is reduced appreciably. Some people are sensitive to it also. Although it does not rancidify, but its colour may darken even when present in an emulsion. The surface of the mixture darkens. Hence, this requires a suitable antioxidant. Usually wool fat may contain no more than 200 ppm of BHA or not more than 680 ppm of BHT. It is used in creams and ointments as emulsion stabilizer.

Wool Alcohol

On crude fractionation wool alcohol is obtained. It is a golden-brown colour solid with slight odour. It melts at a temperature not less than 58°C.It contains about 30% of cholesterol along with other alcohols. It is sensitive to oxidation and a slowly soluble surface film with poor emulsifying ability is produced. For this reason, it contains 500 – 1000p.p.m of BHA or BHT as antioxidant. Hence, it should be stored as large pieces and protected from light in an air-tight container and in a cool place.

Like wool fat wool alcohol is a good emulsifying agent for w/o emulsions and is used with hydrocarbon to produce hydrophilic bases such as Wool Alcohol Ointment BPC. This is not an emulsion but is used for preparing creams.

Small amounts (within 2.5%) are used to stabilize o/w emulsions and to provide emollient effect. At high concentration it causes phase inversion. At higher temperature wool alcohol emulsions do not produce unpleasant odour or their surfaces darkening do not occur. Cetostearyl alcohol can stabilize the emulsion, if included. Both viscosity and emollients can be improved by this. These are stable to organic acids.

2. **Semi-synthetic emulsifying agents**

Methylcellulose and sodium carboxymethyl cellulose are under this category. These are used in o/w emulsions either as emulsifying agent or as emulsion stabilizer. The emulsions are usually used for external application.

Methylcellulose

This is available in different viscosity grades. Methylcellulose of low viscosity grades are suitable as emulsifying agent and emulsion stabilizer. These are suitable for vegetable and mineral oil, but less suitable for cod-liver oil. To prepare Liquid Paraffin Emulsion BPC 2% mucilage of Methylcellulose 20 has been recommended. Emulsion is prepared by mixing methylcellulose mucilage with the oil followed by stirring with a mechanical stirrer. In laboratory scale the mucilage is taken in a mortar and the oil is added in portions with continuous trituration with the pestle. When addition of oil is completed, aqueous phase gradually added with continuous trituration.

Methylcellulose emulsions are not affected by change of pH and by alcohol. Coagulation takes place when higher concentration of electrolyteis added.

Sodium carboxymethylcellulose

At a concentration of 0.5 to 1% solution of medium viscosity grade of sodium carboxymethylcellulose is suitable for stabilizing the emulsions.

3. **Surface Active Agents**

Based on ionic character surfactants are classified into three categories – anionic, cationic and non-ionic.

Anionic surfactants ionize into a large in their aqueous solution. These are responsible for their emulsifying ability. Their solutions contain small cations.

Alkali metal and ammonium soaps – these are sodium, potassium, and ammonium salts of long chain fatty acids such as stearic acid, oleic acid, and ricinolic acid. These produce o/w emulsions. These emulsions can be prepared by;

1. Using a preformed soap such as soft soap. For example, Terpentine Liniment B.P. is prepared using soft soap.

   Soft soap is prepared by heating a suitable vegetable oil or oils, or their fatty acids, with potassium hydroxide or sodium hydroxide.

2. Using a soap which is formed during preparation of the emulsion. For example, ammonium soap is made from oleic acid with ammonia. Ammonium soap is used to prepare White Liniment B.P.C.

   Fixed oils and fats contain little amount of free fatty acids. Soaps are formed if alkali hydroxide or ammonia is added to these oils or fats. The amount of soap produced would be sufficient to emulsify the oil or fat. There are some oils such as turpentine oil, liquid paraffin which do not have any free fatty acid. Hence, these oils cannot be emulsified by this method.

   Stability of alkali soaps:

   - These soaps are stable at pH more than 10; but these are very sensitive to acid, even to weak organic acid.
   - Acid precipitates free fatty acids and the emulsion breaks down.
   - These soaps are incompatible with polyvalent cations such as Ca^{2+}, Mg^{2+} and Zn^{2+}. The polyvalent cations cause phase reversal. Trivalent cations do it very effectively.

   However, o/w emulsions are suitable for external application, not for internal. The reasons for reversal of phase are:

   - These emulsions are not palatable because of their alkaline pH
   - In contact with acid fatty acids present in these emulsions are precipitated. This happens in stomach.

Applications of these emulsions:

- These emulsions should not be applied over broken skin, since these are alkaline.
- The emulsions are resistant to microbial attack.

Soaps of Di- and Trivalent metals

Generally, calcium soaps are used as emulsifying agent in w/o emulsions. Other divalent cationic soaps such as magnesium-soaps and zinc-soaps can also emulsify.

Calcium-soaps are prepared during preparation of emulsions by adding Calcium Hydroxide Solution B.P.C to the fatty acids or oils containing free fatty acids. However solid calcium hydroxide can be used. For example, for preparing Calamine Lotion, Oily B.P.C, arachis oil is emulsified with calcium oleate. Calcium oleate is prepared by emulsifying oleic acid with lime water. Zinc Cream B.P.C is prepared using calcium hydroxide powder instead of lime water. Wool fat is used in both the emulsions to stabilize emulsion. These emulsions are externally used, not orally.

Amine soap

There are various amines which form soaps with fatty acids. The most commonly used amine is triethanolamine, $N(CH_2.CH_2OH)_3$. Like glycerine this is viscous and miscible with water. Generally it contains 11% of diethanolamine, $NH(CH_2.CH_2OH)_2$ and 2% of monoethanol-amine, $NH_2(CH_2.CH_2OH)$. All these amines have similar emulsifying ability. These combine with fatty acids and form soaps. The most commonly used fatty acids are oleic acid and stearic acid. Amine soaps can be satisfactorily prepared by mixing triethanolamine with fatty acids at a ratio of 1:5. These soaps produce o/w emulsions of almost neutral pH (pH 7.5 – 8.0). These emulsions contain fine particles or globules.

These emulsions can be applied over broken skin but cannot be taken orally. These are highly resistant to polyvalent cations, but susceptible to acids and high concentration of electrolytes. These emulsions darken on storage, particularly if prepared with triethanolamine and oleic acid.

Thus, these emulsions should be stored in dark place, not in contact with metals. Usually triethanolamines are used to prepare cosmetic emulsions.

Alkyl sulphates

Alkyl sulphates are esters of fatty alcohols and sulphuric acid. The most common and important are sodium lauryl sulphate and sodium cetostearyl sulphate. Alkyl sulphates produce o/w emulsions. Such emulsions are less stable. The mixture of alkyl sulphate and fatty alcohols produce the emulsions with excellent stability and quality. Creams of high quality possess the following properties:

- Softness,
- Good spreading capacity, and
- Emolience.

For example, mixture of sodium cetostearyl sulphate (10%), and 90% of cetyl alcohol and stearyl alcohol can produce cream of excellent quality. Emulsifying wax B.P is a mixture of Sodium lauryl sulphate or sodium salt of sulphated higher primary aliphatic alcohols (10%) and 90% of cetostearyl alcohol.

Soap is an example of this group. Soap is produced from long chain fatty acids, sulphated alcohol and sulphonates. On dissociation, the long chain anion renders the surface activity, while cation remainsinactive. Soaps and similar anionic agents for their unpleasant taste and irritant act the intestinal mucosa, are not suitable for oral emulsion. With alkali soaps good o/w emulsion can be prepared; but these are unstable at pH below 10 and are incompatible with acids, polyvalent inorganic and long-chainorganic cations.

Calcium, magnesium, zinc and aluminium soaps are water insoluble and result w/o emulsions. Amine soaps produced from amine, e.g. triethanolamine, iso-propanolamine and fatty acids are less alkaline, stable and more resistant to Ca^{++} and to change of pH.

Cationic Emulsifying Agent

Quaternary ammonium compounds belong to this class of surface-active agents. These have very good disinfectant and preservative actions, and these are frequently used for this purpose. Simultaneously these can emulsify o/w emulsions also.

When this is used alone, a poor emulsifying activity is found. But, when used in combination with a fatty alcohol, excellent stability is attained. The classical example is cetrimide. It is a good disinfectant but poor surfactant, but in combination (1:9) with cetostearyl alcohol is an excellent surface-active agent. Cetrimide cream BPC is a stable o/w cream which contains 50% of liquid paraffin, 44.5% of water and 5.5% of a mixture of cetrimide and cetostearyl alcohol (1:11).

These surfactants are quite stable within the pH range from 3 to 7; these are compatible with other cationic compounds and with calcium and magnesium ions. These are very much incompatible with anionic surfactant and soap which even at minimum concentration can cause instability of the emulsion and can spoil the preservative action of the cationic surfactant. Because of their bactericidal activity no preservative is necessary if they are present in a formulation.

Non-ionic Emulsifying Agent

These surfactants have both hydrophobic and hydrophilic groups. Hydrophobic (lipophilic) group contains a long hydrocarbon chain which has very little affinity for water. A hydrophilic(lipophobic) group contains a functional group like carboxy, hydroxyl, amino, etc. which has affinity for water.

Such a surface active agent when added to an emulsion the molecules of the surfactant are adsorbed at the oil-water interface, the lipophilic groups direct towards oil phase and the hydrophilic groups direct towards water phase resulting formation of a film at the o/w interface. Depending on the dominating groups the surfactant may be hydrophilic, suitable for o/w emulsion or lipophilic, suitable for w/o emulsion.

If the surfactant is a derivative of an alcohol and/or ethylene oxide, the hydrophilic groups will be dominating, and the surfactant will be water soluble. If it is derived from fatty acids of $C_{12} - C_{18}$ chain, the dominating character will be lipophilic, and the surfactant will be water insoluble. However, by varying the number and type of group in the molecule the hydrophilic-lipophilic character can be modified. Esters of polyethylene or polyoxyethylene, oleic acid, lauric, palmitic or stearic acids, etc. belong to this class.

Non-ionic surfactants are classified into following types:

- Glycol and glycerol esters
- Sorbitan esters
- Macrogol esters (polyethylene, polyethylene glycol esters)
- Macrogol ethers such as Cetomacrogol 1000
- Polysorbates
- Poloxalkols
- Polyvinyl alcohols, and
- Higher fatty alcohols

4. **Finely divided solids**

These have balanced hydrophilic and hydrophobic properties. These are adsorbed at oil-water interface and form a coherent film. The film prevents coalescence of the dispersed globules. These can be used to prepare both o/w and w/o emulsions. If the solid particles are properly wetted by oil w/o emulsion would be formed. If the solid particles are properly wetted by water o/w emulsion would be formed. The stability of the foam produced by poorly wetted fine powder can be assessed by shaking powder with water. This indicates the effectiveness of interfacial film of fine powders to stabilize a disperse system. To produce o/w emulsions the substances used are bentonite, aluminium magnesium silicate, and hectorite. These are important and belong to the category of montmorillonite minerals. Apart from these aluminium and magnesium hydroxide and colloidal silicon dioxides are also used. Since these substances have high affinity towards water, hydrated dispersions are formed. The dispersions become viscous. As a result, the stability of these emulsions is improved.

Selection of an emulsifying agent

The selection of an emulsifying agent (emulgent) is based on the following factors,

- Type of emulsion, w/o or o/w and the ultimate use, external or internal.
- Ability to reduce the interfacial tension between the two immiscible liquids,
- Physico-chemical stability of the emulsifying agent,
- Compatibility with all ingredients of the formulation, inertness towards the organoleptic properties, like, colour, taste and odour should not be affected,
- Ability to form coherent film around the globules of the dispersed phase,
- Ability to prevent coalescence of the droplets of the dispersed phase,
- Ability to produce and maintain the required viscosity of the preparation.

Identification of Type of Emulsion

The type of an emulsion can be determined by various methods. The methods used for this purpose are briefly mentioned below.

Methods of identification of emulsion type

- Examining the miscibility of the continuous phase when diluted, either by shaking or by stirring, with oil or water should be taken for phase reversal(*Miscibility Test*).
- Measuring electrical conductance. Aqueous continuous phase will transmit electric current, while oily continuous phase will not transmit or will transmit less electric current(*Conductivity Test*).
- Solution of Scarlet red (Dye) when added to an emulsion, oil is co*loured and become* visible to naked eye (*Dye test*).
- If a drop of emulsion exposed to ultraviolet radiation continuous fluorescence will be observed under microscope, if it is w/o type (*Fluorescence Test /Colour Test*).

- The filter paper treated with cobalt chloride solution is dried. *The dry paper when dipped into* the emulsion. If the colour changes from blue to pink-red, t*he emulsion is oil-in-water* type(*Cobalt paper Test*).

Methods of Preparation

There are various methods used *to prepare emulsion. Broadl*y ther*e are three type*s of methods. Depending on the type and volume of emulsion to be prepared any one of these methods is used:

- Aqueous liquid and oil are shaken in a bottle. Other necessary additives are either dissolved or dispersed in water or oil depend on the type of emulsion is to be prepared. Suitable emulsifying agent is also mixed either with water or with oil depending on the type of emulsion.
- In a mortar the aqueous phase is taken and triturated with oil added gradually in portions. The emulsifying agent is mixed or dissolved in aqueous phase. This produces o/w emulsions. In some cases, if bentonite is added to oil phase, a w/o emulsion is produced.
- The oil phase is mechanically mixed with aqueous phase to prepare emulsion.

The step wise method of preparation of emulsion is given below.

General method of preparation

- ➢ The container and its cap to be used to pack the product should be thoroughly cleaned and dried.
- ➢ Each ingredient to be used in the formulation should be finely powdered.
- ➢ Take the ingredient which is smallest in quantity (weight);dilute it with other ingredients in increasing order of weights, the amount of other ingredients taken should be almost equal to the quantity already present in the mortar, mix all the insoluble excipients thoroughly.
- ➢ Add some amount of vehicle and rub with the pestle to make a smooth paste
- ➢ Dissolve the non-volatile solid in a part of the vehicle, add the solution to the mortar and rub well.
- ➢ Dilute the paste/slurry with adequate amount of vehicle to make the mixture pourable
- ➢ Inspect the suspension carefully; if it contains foreign particles, strain the emulsion through muslin either into a tared bottle or into measuring cylinder.

- The bottle filled with emulsion is properly sealed with pilfer proof cap and labeled.

Usually one of the following methods is used to manufacture an emulsion on laboratory scale.

- Continental or Dry Gum method,
- English or Wet Gum method,
- Bottle or Forbes Bottle method

Continental or Dry Gum Method

In this method for every 4 parts (in volume) of oil 2 parts (in volume) of water and 1 part of gum are added to prepare primary emulsion. That is for emulsification of 50 ml of oil, 25 ml of water and 12.5 g of gum are mixed initially. If any other formulation ingredients or additional water are to be mixed, these are mixed with primary emulsion. Hence, this method is alternatively called as 4:2:1 method.

Generally, acacia or other o/w emulsifier is triturated with oil in a mortar until uniformly mixed. The inner surface of the mortar should have slight roughness for proper grinding and reduction of globule size. Once the gum and oil are thoroughly mixed, water (2 parts) is added at a time and the mixture is triturated immediately and rapidly until creamy white slurry is produced and a crackling sound with the movement of pestle is heard. Usually to prepare the primary emulsion mixing time would be about 3 minutes. Other ingredients miscible or soluble with external phase may be mixed with the primary emulsion. Solid water-soluble ingredients like preservative, stabilizer, color, etc. can be dissolved in minimum amount of water, if water is the external phase (i.e. o/w emulsion) and be added to the primary emulsion. However, no ingredient which can interfere with the stability of the emulsion should be added at this time. For example, alcohol precipitates the gum. If alcohol or alcoholic solution is to be added, it should be added carefully at the time of making up the volume.

The dispersion of gum in oil is the indicator of stability of the emulsion. If the gum is satisfactorily dispersed in oil, the emulsion would be of desired quality.

However, in some cases the amount of gum is required to be increased or decreased to achieve better stability of emulsion. For example, to prepare emulsion of mineral oil, volatile oil, linseed oil, the proportion of oil, water and gum is modified to 3:2:1 or even 2:2:1.

Wet Gum Method

This method is more flexible than the Dry gum method. In this method the same proportion of oil, water and gum are used; but the order of mixing is not same. During preparation the proportion of ingredients can be changed, if required.

Usually the mucilage of gum is prepared by triturating the gum in a mortar with water at a ratio of 1:2. The oil is added gradually with continuous trituration until the oil is completely emulsified. During trituration if the mixture becomes very thick additional amount of water can be added and mixed thoroughly before adding next portion of oil. When entire amount of oil, trituration should be continued till uniform mixture is obtained. The rest of the method is similar to the previous one.

Forbes Bottle Method

For extemporaneous preparation of emulsion of volatile oil or oleaginous less viscous substances this method is suitable. In a dry bottle required amount of powdered gum is taken, two parts of oil are added, and the bottle is stoppered and shaken well. Then water of approximately equal volume of oil is added in portions to the mixture. After addition of each portion of water, the bottle is stoppered and shaken thoroughly. When entire amount of water is added, the bottle is shaken till uniform mixture is obtained. Once the primary emulsion is prepared, it can be diluted with water or aqueous solution of other formulation ingredients.

As the agitation is mild, this method is not suitable for viscous oils. The emulsion prepared by any of these methods if passed through a homogenizer, the quality of the emulsion will be improved. The size of the dispersed globules would be reduced to 5 µm or even less.

Stability Problems and Methods to Overcome

The characteristics of a stable emulsion are:

- There shall be no change in initial size and size distribution of globules during storage.
- The globules, the dispersed phase should remain uniformly distributed throughout the continuous phase during storage.

However, the most common problems associated with emulsion are:

- Cracking,
- Creaming, and
- Phase reversion or inversion.

Cracking

When an emulsion cracks it is not possible to redisperse the globules in the dispersion medium (continuous phase) by shaking. *Separation of dispersed phase as a separate layer due to coalescence of the dispersed globules is called cracking*. Thus, the benefits of the emulsion are lost. The uniform and accurate dosing cannot be possible.

Usually the reasons for which cracking takes place are:

- Addition of improper (opposite type) emulsifying agent
- Decomposition or precipitation of the emulsifying agent
- Addition of excess disperse phase
- Solvent, and
- Microbial action.
- *Addition of improper (opposite type) emulsifying agent*

  Anionic and cationic emulsifying agents are incompatible to each other.

  To produce oil in water (o/w) emulsion, soaps of monovalent metals are suitable and to produce water in oil (w/o) emulsion, soaps of divalent metals are suitable. If soaps of monovalent metals are used in o/w emulsion or if soaps of divalent metals are used in w/o emulsion, cracking may occur, and the emulsion becomes unstable.
- *Decomposition or precipitation of the emulsifying agent*
  1. Acids react with alkali soaps and liberate fatty acids and alkali salts. Neither the fatty acid nor the alkali salt can emulsify; hence addition of acid to a soap based emulsion (e.g. Turpentine Liniment B.P) can cause cracking.
  2. If sufficient amount of sodium chloride is added to a sodium soap emulsion, the emulsifying agent will precipitate out and the emulsion will crack. Similar phenomenon is observed in case of potassium soap emulsions also. This is due to salting out of sodium or potassium soap from the emulsion. Hence, some electrolytes including sodium chloride can salt out sodium soap.
  3. Emulsifying agent having large cations and cationic emulsifying agent are not compatible with anionic emulsifying agent and emulsifying agent containing large anions. Phenol is not compatible with non-ionic emulsifying agent.
  4. If a water miscible solvent in which emulgent is insoluble is added to an emulsion, the emulgent precipitates and the emulsion cracks. For example, gums and proteins (e.g. gelatin, casein, etc.) are insoluble in alcohol and alcohol is miscible with water. If alcohol is added to an emulsion containing gum or protein, the emulsifying agent will precipitate out resulting cracking of the emulsion.
- *Addition of excess of disperse phase*

  When the concentration of disperse phase in an emulsion exceeds 74%, the emulsion tends to crack. Spherical particles of uniform diameter can fill only 74% of the volume of a space; the size of the particles may be any. Thus, if the globules of the emulsion are perfectly spherical not more than 74% of the total volume of the emulsion can be occupied. In practice, the shape of the dispersed globules is not perfectly spherical, and they vary in size also. By hand it is difficult to make emulsion with disperse phase more than 74%.

- *Addition of a common solvent*

  A solvent which is miscible, or which can dissolve both disperse phase and continuous phase, can convert the two-phase system into one if added to the emulsion. For example, alcohol is miscible with water and can dissolve soft soap, castor oil. When alcohol is added to an emulsion made with these substances, the emulsion becomes a solution.

- *Microbial contamination*

  Preservative is sometimes added to an emulsion to protect it from the growth of moulds and bacteria and thus, to prolong its shelf-life. Preservatives in general interact with emulsifying agent and the concentration of the preservative decreases with time. Hence, if the concentration of the preservative is not adequate, its activity is reduced, and growth of microbes occurs. As a result, the emulsion may crack.

Creaming

Milk is a natural emulsion. When it is boiled and cooled, a layer containing fat and other substances (mostly of disperse phase) floats on the surface. This layer is called cream. Thus, creaming may be *defined as the separation and formation of layer of oil, generally in form of globuleseither on the top or at the bottom of an emulsion.* Usually due to the effect of the gravitational force the disperse globules may accumulate at the bottom of the emulsion. If the density of dispersed globules is lesser than that of continuous medium, the globules concentrate in the upper layer of the dilute emulsion. This is found mostly in o/w emulsions.

If the density of dispersed globules is more than that of continuous medium, the globules concentrate in the lower layer of the dilute emulsion. This is found mostly in w/o emulsions. In creaming the globules just concentrate, not coalesce. When they coalesce emulsion breaks. Thus, creaming is not a serious problem because the globules redisperse on mild shaking. However, creaming does not look elegant; hence it is necessary either to prevent or delay creaming in emulsion. In general, by increasing the consistency of the emulsion creaming can be avoided.

The factors responsible for creaming are similar to those responsible for sedimentation in coarse dispersions. The most important factors that can reduce the rate of creaming in emulsions are;

- *Globule size.* If the size of the globules is reduced, the rate of creaming will decrease.
- *Viscosity of the continuous phase.* If the viscosity is increased, the rate of creaming will decrease.
- *Storage temperature.* Storing of emulsion at very low temperature such as refrigeration temperature may cause breaking of an emulsion.

In emulsions the size of the globulesmay vary from 1μm (may be less) to 50 μm or more. The size range can be reduced to 1 - 3μm by an effective homogenization. For a good emulsion the frequency distribution of globule size range is not an important parameter. The degree of emulsification is important. Hence, it is necessary to determine the amount of oil (in terms of volume) present in an emulsion in the form of small globules out of total amount of oil added. If the proportion is high, the emulsion is considered a good one. The volume of oil present in form of small globules can be determined as follows:

Let us assume that the globules are spherical in shape and out of 100 globules in randomly drawn sample the frequency distribution of size ranges are:

No. of globules	Size range (μm)	Av. Size of globules (μm)	Volume Occupied ($n\pi d^3/6$ μm^3)
80	1 - 5	3	1130
15	5 - 15	10	7850
5	15 - 30	23	31837
Total volume occupied by 100 globules = 40817 μm^3			

80% of the globules are small.

Out of 40817 μm^3, the volume occupied by 80% of globules $= \dfrac{1130}{40817} =$ 0.0276

Hence, the volume of the oil present in small globules = 2.76%

When in an emulsion 50% of the volume of oil remains present in the form of globules of size less than 5μm, the emulsion is considered as good or satisfactory.

Phase Inversion

It has been mentioned earlier that the o/w emulsions are prepared by using monovalent metal soaps and ammonium soap, and w/o emulsions are prepared by using divalent metal soaps. The type of emulsion can be known by knowing the solubility of the emulsifying agent used. If the emulsifying agent is more soluble in water than in oil, water is used as continuous phase. That is oil in water emulsion would be formed. Hence, addition of a substance that alters the solubility of the emulsifying agent can reverse the phase. For example,

- If sufficient amount of calcium chloride is added to an o/w emulsion emulsified by sodium soap, calcium chloride reacts with sodium soap and forms calcium soap. As a result, o/w emulsion shall be reversed to w/o type stabilized by calcium soap formed.
- If calcium chloride is added to an o/w emulsion emulsified by triethanolamine phase inversion will take place.
- Beeswax produces w/o emulsion. If soap is added to this emulsion phase inversion will take place; that is, o/w emulsion will be formed.
- Usually stable emulsions can be made when the concentration of dispersed phase remains within 30 – 60%. If the concentration is increased phase inversion may take place.

Exercise

A. Multiple Choice Question carrying 01 mark

1. Which of the following statements is correct?
   (a) In o/w emulsion water is continuous phase
   (b) In o/w emulsion oil is continuous phase
   (c) In o/w emulsion water is dispersed phase
   (d) In o/w emulsion oil is dispersion medium
2. In w/o emulsion aqueous solution is present in
   (a) Continuous phase (b) External phases
   (c) Dispersed phase (d) None of the above
3. The globule size of the dispersed phase of an emulsion should be
   (a) Less than 0.1μm (b) More than 100μm
   (c) Less than 100μm (d) More than 200μm
4. In an emulsion the dispersed phase is
   (a) A liquid or solution (b) A liquid only
   (c) A solution only (d) A solid only

5. An emulsion is a
   (a) Monophasic preparation
   (b) Biphasic preparation
   (c) Monophasic heterogeneous preparation
   (d) All
6. In o/w emulsion aqueous solution is present in
   (a) Continuous phase (b) Dispersed phase
   (c) External phases (d) None of the above
7. To prepare an emulsion
   (a) Low shear is applied (b) High shear is applied
   (c) Medium shear is applied (d) No shear is applied
8. Thermodynamic instability of emulsion is due to
   (a) Surface free energy of the external phase
   (b) Surface free energy of the internal phase
   (c) Surface free energy of the both the phases
   (d) None
9. For making any emulsion at least a third substance is required which is called
   (a) Suspending agent (b) Buffer
   (c) Emulgent (d) Complexing agent
10. Which one of the following is used to stabilize an emulsion?
    (a) Secondary emulsifier (b) Primary emulsifier
    (c) Chelating agent (d) Buffering agent
11. Primary emulsifier is used to
    (a) Stabilize an emulsion (b) Prepare an emulsion
    (c) Prepare o/w emulsion only (d) Prepare w/o emulsion only
12. Secondary emulsifier is used to
    (a) Prepare an emulsion (b) Prepare o/w emulsion only
    (c) Prepare w/o emulsion only (d) Stabilize an emulsion
13. Colloidal emulsion is a type of
    (a) Microemulsion (b) Macroemulsion
14. Emulsions are classified as micro-and macroemulsion, based on
    (a) Particle size (b) Physical state
    (c) Orientation of phase (d) None

15. Emulsions are classified as o/w and w/o, based on
    (a) Physical state (b) Particle size
    (c) Orientation of phase (d) All
16. Emulsions are classified as liquid and cream, based on
    (a) Orientation of phase (b) Physical state
    (c) Particle size (d) All
17. The ideal emulsifying agent should be
    (a) Stable, inert, non-toxic, odourless, tasteless and colourless.
    (b) All
18. Which of the following is a natural emulsifying agent?
    (a) Methylcellulose (b) Cetomacrogol 1000
    (c) Acacia (d) All
19. Which of the following is a semisynthetic emulsifying agent?
    (a) Sodium carboxymethylcellulose
    (b) Tragacanth
    (c) Oleic acid
    (d) Tween 80
20. Polysaccharides are
    (a) Semisynthetic emulsifying agent
    (b) Natural emulsifying agent
    (c) Cationic emulsifying agent
    (d) Anionic emulsifying agent
21. Pectin is an emulsifier of
    (a) Plant origin
    (b) Animal origin
    (c) Synthetic origin
    (d) None
22. Soaps usually produce
    (a) w/o emulsion
    (b) o/w emulsion
23. Wool fat is an emulsifier of
    (a) Plant origin (b) Semisynthetic type
    (c) Animal origin (d) Synthetic origin

24. Aqueous solution of anionic surfactant contains
    (a) Small amount of cations in solution
    (b) Small amount of anions in solution
    (c) Large amount of cations in solution
    (d) None
25. Emulsions prepared with alkali metal soaps are
    (a) Stable in alkaline pH
    (b) Stable in acidic pH
26. Ammonium soaps can usually prepare
    (a) Emulsion of w/o type
    (b) Emulsion of o/w type
27. Emulsions prepared with ammonium soaps can be used
    (a) Over broken skin
    (b) Internally
    (c) Externally over intact skin
    (d) All
28. Emulsions prepared with ammonium soaps
    (a) Are susceptible to microbial attack
    (b) Are resistant to microbial attack
29. Which of the following is nonionic emulsifier
    (a) Methylcellulose (b) Cetostearyl alcohol
    (c) Polysorbates (d) All
30. Which of the following is categorized under finely divided solids
    (a) Colloidal silicon dioxide (b) Poloxalkols
    (c) Polyvinyl alcohols (d) None
31. In which method scarlet red is used for identification of type of emulsion?
    (a) Dilution test (b) Dye test
    (c) Fluorescence Test (d) Conductivity test
32. Usually in dry gum method the ratio of oil, water and gum is
    (a) 1:2:4 (b) 1:3:4
    (c) 4:2:1 (d) 3:2:1

33. Which of the following is used in Cobalt-paper test to identify the type of emulsion
    (a) Cobalt chloride
    (b) Cobalt nitrate
    (c) Cobalt chloride and cobalt nitrate
    (d) All
34. Creaming in emulsion can be avoided by
    (a) Decreasing the consistency of the emulsion
    (b) Increasing the consistency of the emulsion
35. Reason for cracking in emulsion is
    (a) Globule size
    (b) Storage temperature
    (c) Addition of a common solvent
    (d) Viscosity of the continuous phase
36. Reason for cracking in emulsion is
    (a) Storage temperature
    (b) Addition of a common solvent
    (c) Decomposition or precipitation of the emulsifying agent
    (d) Addition of excess of disperse phase
37. Phase inversion may take place due to
    (a) Viscosity of the continuous phase
    (b) Change in solubility of emulsifying agent
    (c) Microbial contamination
    (d) Change of globule size.

B. Question Carrying 05 Marks

1. Define emulsion and compare it with suspension.
2. What are different types of emulsions and classify emulsion
3. Classify emulsifying agents with relevant example
4. Explain various types of surface-active agents
5. What are various methods used to identify the type of an emulsion
6. What is phase inversion and how does it occur?
7. What is creaming? Explain the reasons for its occurrence.
8. Explain briefly instability problems of emulsion.

9. How can an emulsion be made stable?
10. Write note on phase inversion.

C. Question Carrying 10 Marks

1. Explain different types of emulsifying agents.
2. Explain characteristic features of surfactants.
3. Discuss the natural emulsifying agents used in pharmaceutical emulsions.
4. Describe the method of preparation of an emulsion.
5. Explain the factors responsible for cracking of emulsions.
6. Explain the problems responsible for instability of emulsion.

Answers

A. Multiple Choice Question Carrying 01 Mark

1. (a)	2. (c)	3. (c)	4. (a)	5. (b)
6. (a)	7. (b)	8. (b)	9. (c)	10. (a)
11. (b)	12. (d)	13. (b)	14. (a)	15. (c)
16. (b)	17. (b)	18. (c)	19. (a)	20. (b)
21. (a)	22. (b)	23. (c)	24. (a)	25. (a)
26. (b)	27. (a)	28. (b)	29. (c)	30. (a)
31. (b)	32. (c)	33. (a)	34. (b)	35. (c)
36. (a)	37. (b)			

Chapter 11

Suppositories

Definition, Types, Advantages and Disadvantages, Types of Bases, Methods of Preparations, Displacement Value & Its Calculations, Evaluation of Suppositories.

Definition

During ancient era drugs which induce unconsciousness, haemorrhoidal, vermicidel and purgative actions had been inserted though rectal route in the form of suppository. In fact, in recent times many drugs are formulated as suppositories for rectal delivery and have been gaining the demand also. These are capable to provide therapeutic blood concentration of the medicine and thereby enhancing the bioavailability. By inserting the drug through rectal route, the pre-systemic effect in hepatic region and in GIT can be prohibited. The shape of suppositories can be oval or cone. These are very useful especially for patients unable to take drugs orally due to nausea and vomiting, advanced disease, or neurological deficit or for any reason. As per the World Health Organization suppositories can be defined as: *Suppositories are solid single-dose preparations intended for rectal application. They are prepared by moulding or compression. The shape, volume and consistency of suppositories are suitable for rectal application.*

Types of Suppositories

The suppositories can be classified into five types based on their intended use.

- **Rectal suppositories:** these are usually intended for adults, weighed about 2g and have torpedo shape. Suppositories intended for children weigh about 1g.
- **Vaginal suppositories:** these are also called as pessaries. These are molded suppositories, weigh about 3 – 5g and have globular or oviform in shape. These may be compressed into a conical shape on a suitable tablet press.

- **Urethral suppositories:** these are also called bougies, have pencil shape. Suppositories intended for males weigh about 4g and 100 – 150 mm in length. Suppositories intended for female weigh about 2g and 60 – 75 mm in length.
- **Nasal suppositories:** also called nasal bougies or buginaria, prepared for introduction into nasal cavity. Usually prepared with glycero-gelatin base, weigh about 1g and their length varies from 9 – 10mm.
- **Ear cones:** these are rarely used, also called as aurinaria and intended for introduction into ear. Usually prepared with theobroma oil as base. These are prepared in urethral bougies and cut according to the size.

Advantages

1. Improved enzymatic drug stability: Many proteolytic and other enzymes in the GIT Gastrointestinal Tract) cause drug degradation following oral administration. Such degradation of drug can be prevented, and effective absorption can be provided by administering suppository.
2. Partial avoidance of hepatic first pass: Blood from the various rectal arteries is being supplied to the rectum and it is drained by at least three veins. Drug is absorbed through the venous network. Hence, drug absorbed in the rectum reach to the systemic circulation partly through liver and partly direct.
3. Higher drug load: Depending on the amounts of other excipients required to make the formulation, suppositories can accommodate two to three times drug loads higher than that of its normal dose.
4. Lymphatic delivery: In many cases this has been found that some of the drugs enter into the lymphatic system after rectal administration; thus, bypassing the first pass effect.
5. Constant and static environment: Compared to the oral route of administration, the rectal route provides a much more constant environment for absorption of drug.
6. Patients with swallowing difficulty: Children, elderly people who usually cannot swallow or face problems in swallowing are most suitable candidates for rectal administration.
7. Avoidance of overdosing: Certain drugs, viz., sedative oral administration may raise a concern with respect to the possibility of severe accidental or intentional overdosing. This danger is particularly eliminated by rectal administration.
8. Avoidance of gastric irritation: Some drugs cause irritation in the GIT if taken orally. Such drugs in form of suppository can easily be administered through rectum.

9. Local effect on rectal mucosa: For local effect or for action on rectal mucosa drugs can be administered in form of suppository.
10. Used to help evacuation of bowel: Suppositories can be used to evacuate the bowel.

Disadvantages

1. Patient acceptance and compliance: In many cultures such as in India, people do not wish to take drug in form of suppositories.
2. Potential for non-specific drug loss: Under certain circumstances such as (1) premature loss from rectum, (2) interaction between faecal matter and the drug,(3) reduction in absorption due to some excipients may reduce effectiveness, etc. drug may be lost in the rectum.
3. Limited fluid in rectum: The volume of rectal fluid is small; around 3 ml. As a result, adequate dissolution of drug with low aqueous solubility may be found.
4. Formulation: Melting, liquefaction, solubility, particle size, etc. can lead to formulation difficulties.
5. Economy: These can be more expensive as compared to tablets.
6. Not suitable for all patients: Patients suffering from diarrhea cannot take suppository.
7. Incomplete absorption: This may take place because suppository usually helps evacuation of bowel.

Suppository Base

The basic functions of a suppository base are,

- To act as the body of the product, so that the desired physicochemical properties of the dosage form is properly maintained and can be suitably fabricated or manufactured.
- To act as the carrier of the drug, so that the drug is released completely at desired site at right time for absorption.

As the base is the bulk constituent of the product, it plays various important roles from manufacture, transportation, storage to till the drug is released. Hence, the base should have some desired characteristics.

Desired characteristics of suppository base

- On cooling the base should contract slightly for easy removal of product from the mould.
- The base should not solidify very quickly or very slowly. In earlier case, pouring problem will take place and in latter case the productivity will suffer.

- Should not react with the drug under any circumstance.
- Should be sufficiently viscous to hold the dispersed components uniformly during manufacture.
- Should not contain any substance (as impurity) including water to any extent which can encourage microbial growth in the formulation.
- Should not be so soft that the product may soften or melt during its transportation or storage.
- Stability of the base should not be affected on exposure to light, air and humidity.
- Should be capable of releasing the drug at desired site and at desired time.
- Should not be toxic.
- Should not irritate the rectal mucosa.

Types of Bases

Bases used as suppositories base can be classified on the basis of their solubility and source. Based on the water solubility the bases are classified into three types:

1. Fatty base (water insoluble) such as Theobroma oil
2. Water soluble/miscible base such as PEGs, and
3. Emulsifying base such as Witepsol (triglyceride of fatty acids).

Based on composition and source there are three types of bases; however, some consider hydrogel as one type of base. Accordingly, the bases used for making suppositories can be classified into four categories:

1. Natural,
2. Synthetic,
3. Semisynthetic, and
4. Hydrogel

1. Natural bases

Most of the naturally derived suppository bases being used today are derived from cocoa butter. Cocoa butter is obtained from roasted seeds of *Theobroma Cacao* Linn. The cocoa butter contains a mixture of saturated and unsaturated fatty acids (C_{16} – C_{18}) triglycerides.[12] About 97% of the fatty acids are unsaturated. More than 50% acids are oleopalmitostearic acid, 25% are oleodistearic acid. Iodine value being about 35 indicates that cocoa butter is partially unsaturated.

It exhibits marked polymorphism (the ability to exist in different crystalline forms, namely α, β, β' and γ with melting points of 22, 34, 28 and 18°C respectively). For suppositories the most stable β form is preferred. Various crystalline forms are formed due to the storage conditions, and degree of heating and cooling. Heating at temperature more than 36°C for long period causes the formation of the unstable crystal with lower melting points. The conversion to the stable β form takes 1 to 14 days, depending on the storage temperature – the higher the temperature, the faster the change. Thus, minimal use of heat in the process of melting the fat is recommended.

It is probably the first base used for manufacture of suppositories and other semisolid preparations. Advantages of cocoa butter are:

- It is truly non-irritating,
- Well tolerated base,
- Capable of releasing drug rapidly by melting.

There are limitations also.

- It melts at body temperature,
- Any material which can change the melting point of the suppository cannot be incorporated,
- It has insufficient contractibility on solidification,
- Poor chemical stability and
- Poor water absorptive capacity.
- It is not economical also.

There are other natural materials such as gelatin, agar, and waxes which can be used as suppository base. Because of their typical problems these are avoided.

2. **Synthetic bases**

These are produced from petrochemical products, fractionated fatty alcohols. Compared to natural bases these have better characteristics and advantages. In this group the polyethylene glycols are most important. These have melting temperature more than body temperature. These are formulated by chemical reaction (addition polymerization) between ethylene oxide and water. The general formula of polyethylene glycols (PEGs) is $H(OCH_2CH_2)_nOH$, where n is the average number of oxyethylene groups. In body cavity these bases dissolve, not melt and release the drug. Being hydrophilic in nature these can promote absorption of many drugs, e.g. Gentamycin, insulin, heparin, [13] etc. Least problem during manufacture, shipping and storage occur with these bases. As these bases have higher melting point, heat sensitive materials can degrade during suppository manufacture. The melting points of PEGs depend on their molecular weight. Another drawback of this base is drug retention that is they delay in drug release. Higher is the molecular weight more is the drug retention. Since these bases first dissolve and then release the drug, the rectal fluid becomes insufficient for their complete dissolution. More water is drawn from inner layer of the rectal membrane through osmosis. For this local pain is experienced in the rectum.[14] This can be partly solved if the suppository, made of synthetic base, is immersed in water just before insertion.

Further, synthetic bases are susceptible to oxidative degradation and thus, antibiotics like penicillin, chloramphenicol, etc. may lose their potency. The products of these bases should not be stored in humid condition, as the base can absorb moisture.

3. **Semisynthetic bases**

These are prepared by chemical modification of vegetable fats and oils. It is, therefore, possible to prepare the materials of desired characteristics. Their solubility, melting point, stability and chemical inertness can be controlled through chemical reactions, e.g. hydrogenation, trans-esterification. As they are derived from short to medium chain fatty acids, their softness is more also. The products prepared with these bases are not hard and brittle. Hence, patients' compliance is better. These are less irritating also.

The limitation of these bases is that they melt and release the drug as is found with cocoa butter. Hence, a base with fairly low melting point with the strength to resist damage during shipping, storage should be used. Apart from these limitations, like all other fatty materials these bases crystallize on aging which may affect the stability of the product.

4. **Hydrogels**

This is an alternative potential vehicle for rectal drug delivery. Although this has not been commercially used many experiments have been conducted. These have macromolecular networks[15] which do not dissolve, only swell in water. A drug incorporated into the hydrogel matrix loses its mobility after drying of the product. Once the product is inserted into the rectum, the hydrogel starts swelling in rectal fluid and the drug diffuses out from the network for absorption. These hydrogels are prepared with polyvinyl alcohol, hydroxyethyl methacrylate, polyacrylic acid and polyoxyethylene. The rate and extent of diffusion of drug from the network depends on the rate and extent of swelling of the matrix that is on the rate of migration of water into the matrix. Thus, their bioadhession and drug retention properties can be utilized to prepare control drug delivery system for rectal administration.

Methods of Preparations

For commercial production of suppositories one of the three methods is used.

- Fusion or Melting
- Compression
- Injection molding

Fusion Method

This is the most common method and the steps of manufacturing are shown diagrammatically below.

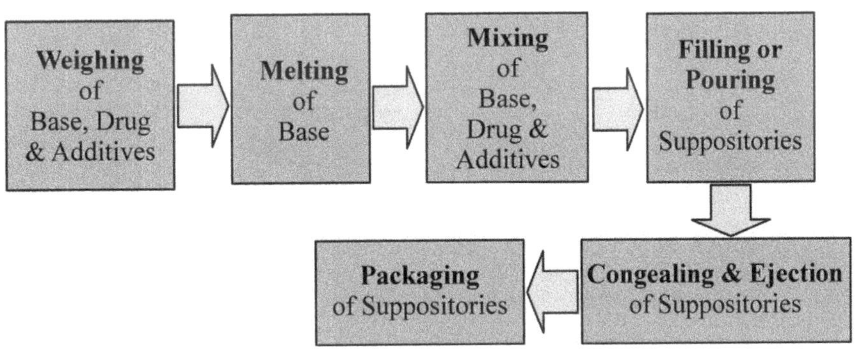

Figure 11.1 Steps of Manufacturing.

- The weighed quantity of base is transferred into a thermostatically controlled melting tank, usually maintained at 45° – 50°C. The tank should be fitted with a suitable stirrer. The base is allowed to be melted completely.
- The additives and drug of desired size range are added to the molten base with continuous stirring. Stirring is continued till mixing is uniform.
- The moulds should be properly lubricated on the basis of type of base being used.
- The homogenized mixture is then poured into the moulds (Fig 1a and b).
- Allowed to solidify by chilling.
- Solidified suppositories are removed from the moulds and packed.

The temperature should be maintained at lower range at each step of manufacturing to retain maximum amount of base at its stable β- form, to protect the physical structure of the product and to reduce thermal exposure (destructive condition) to the drug. The range of temperature and viscosity of the molten mix are fixed on the basis of the physicochemical properties of drug and excipients. Higher temperature may result the formation of granulated suppositories.

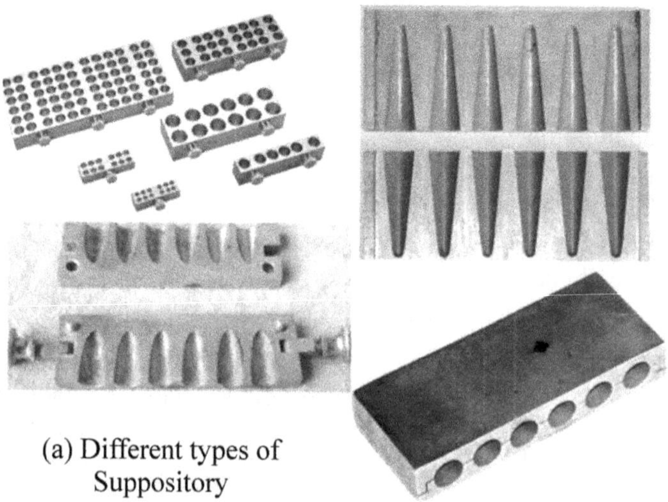

(a) Different types of Suppository

There are pre-shaped, readymade packs, made of aluminium, plastic or other materials, which can directly receive, solidify and pack the products. These are intended for quick shipment and sale.

Now-a-days automated machineries are available with multiple functions. They need to be fed with the required quantity of materials only. The rest operations are automatically performed by the machine and finally the finished packed products will come out.

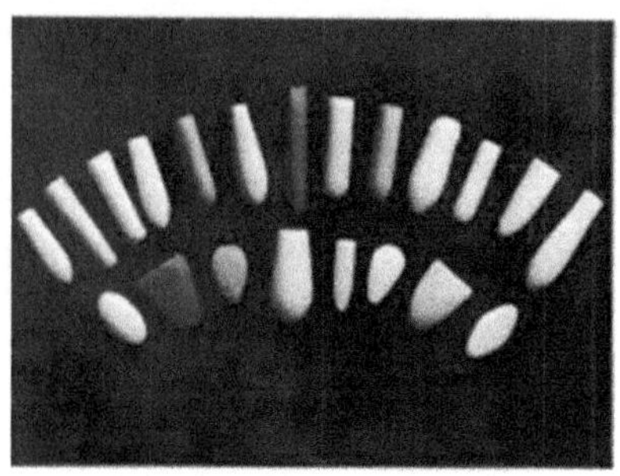

(b) Suppository mold

Compression Method

This method is rarely used as the method is only recommended for thermolabile drugs. The method is similar to tablet manufacturing. In this method the drug and other materials, including bases are finely powdered and mixed uniformly. The mixture is then compressed into tablets of suitable size and shape. The advantages of this method are;

- No separate machineries are required; tablet preparation machines can be used.
- During filling no sedimentation problem occurs, which can take place in fusion method.
- Incompatibility problems are very less.
- No maintenance of temperature is required during manufacturing, which is very essential in case of fusion method.
- There is no temperature-related stability problem, which may be found in fusion method.
- No packaging problem.

However, there are limitations of this method also:

- Handling of fine particles is a problem.
- No scope for adjustment during processing.
- Lubricant used for compression may affect dissolution of the suppository in the rectal fluid. This may affect the rate and extent of absorption of the drug.

Injection Moulding

This is a recently developed technique commonly used in plastic manufacturing industry. The method is similar to melting/fusion method. When all the ingredients are properly mixed with melted base, the mix is injected into the precision – machined multicavity moulds. After solidification the suppositories are ejected from the mould cavities.
The advantages of this method are:

- Higher productivity
- Suppositories of wide size range and different shapes can be manufactured
- Accuracy that is weight variation is not significant.

Calibration of Moulds

The volume of a mould used for casting suppository is fixed, but the weight of the casted product may vary. The nominal capacity of a mould is measured with respect to the base material, e.g. theobroma oil. The composition of a suppository is designed, and the product is prepared on weight basis. A powder drug usually is of higher density. When it is mixed with the base to make a formulation, the density of the formulation differs from that of the base. Thus, before casting the nominal capacity of the mould is required to be calibrated in terms of weight with respect to the particular product.

Displacement Value & Its Calculations

Displacement value of a powder is defined as *the number of unit weight of a powder that can displace one unit of base.* This is illustrated with the help of an example:

Illustration 1:

Say, weight of 10 suppositories of base = a g

Weight of 10 suppositories containing base and drug = b g

If the amount of drug present in 10 suppositories = d g,

Then the amount of base displaced by d g of drug = (b – d)g

So, the displacement value of the drug $= \dfrac{d}{a-(b-d)}$

Illustration 2:

The weight of 6 suppositories containing only base material (a) = 12g

The weight of 6 suppositories containing base material + powder drug (b) = 15g

The drug in the suppositories is 30%w/w,

Then, the amount of drug in the suppositories (d) = 30% of 15g $= 15g \times \dfrac{30}{100}$ = 4.5g, and

The amount of base in the suppositories (b – d) = c =15g – 4.5g = 10.5g

Or, 70% of 15g $= 15g \times \dfrac{70}{100} = 10.5g$

The amount of base displaced by 4.5g of drug [a – (b – d)] = 12g – 10.5g = 1.5g

Therefore, the displacement value of the drug $= \dfrac{d}{a-(b-d)} = \dfrac{d}{a-c} = \dfrac{4.5g}{1.5g}$

= 3.0

= = That is, *1mg of base (usually, theobroma oil) is displaced by 3mg of the drug.*

However, the method is not error free, because air entrapped into the mass during stirring is not removed completely and becomes responsible for error.

Application of Displacement Value

The displacement value of a powdered drug depends on the density of the base and of its own; since the density of a powder is fixed, displacement value of the powder would be base specific. It can be used to make a suppository formulation as shown below:

Example 1: The displacement value of the drug is 3, capacity of each suppository is 2g, the number of suppositories to be prepared is 10 and drug content is 30% w/w. Find out the average weight of the suppositories.

Solution: Applying the formula given above; the displacement value of the drug $= \frac{d}{a-c}$

Say, the weight of drug + base per suppository = b g

Given that, the amount of drug/suppository, d = 30% of b = 0.3b g

Weight of unmedicated suppository = a = 2g, and

Displacement value = 3

So, the value of c = 70% of b = 0.7b g

As per the formula, the displacement value of the drug $= \frac{d}{a-c}$

Or, $3 = \frac{0.3b}{2-0.7b}$

or, $3(2 - 0.7b) = 0.3b$

or, $6 - 2.1b = 0.3b$

or, $2.4b = 6$

so, $b = \frac{6}{2.4} = 2.5g$

Hence the average weight of the suppository **2.5g**

Example 2: The weight of 10 unmedicated suppositories is 20.0g and the weight 10 suppositories containing 20% of drug is 21.542g. Calculate the displacement value of the drug.

Solution: Given that the weight of 10 suppositories containing only base = 20.0g, and

The weight of 10 suppositories containing base and drug = 21.542g

Amount of drug content in 10 suppositories $= \frac{20}{100} \times 21.542\text{g} = 4.31\text{g}$ and

The amount of base present in suppositories $= \frac{80 \times 21.542}{100} = 17.23\text{g}$

So, the base displaced by 4.31g of drug = (20.0 – 17.23)g = 2.77g

Thus, the displacement value of the drug $= \frac{4.31}{2.77} = \mathbf{1.55}$

Evaluation of Suppositories

Evaluation of the product quality is not limited to a single batch; it is necessary to assess the variation from batch to batch. To maintain consistent quality among the batches the specifications for all the input materials, their processing and processing parameters are critically prepared and validated. Accordingly, the processes are strictly monitored, and the in-process quality control is regularly done. As a part of total quality control system, the finished products are subjected to final tests.

The tests fall into three categories – physical, chemical and micro-biological.

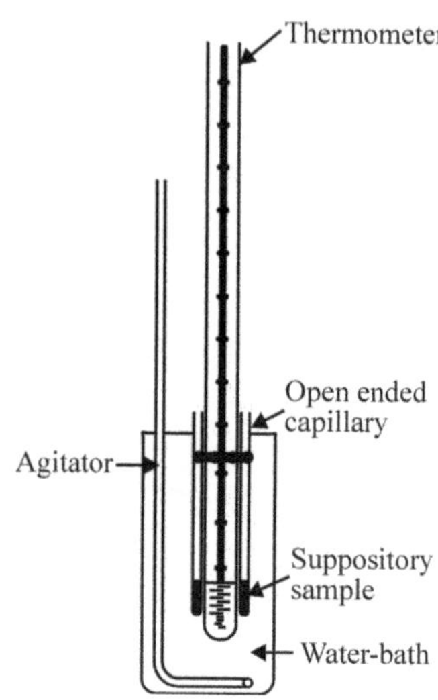

Figure 11.2 Open-ended capillary tube for determination of melting temperature.

Physical Tests

1. **Physical Appearance**

   Description includes colour, odour, surface smoothness, and other surface characteristics, like fissuring, pitting, fat blooming, and exudation, if any.

   Examination for homogeneity is another physical test. This may be done by taking a longitudinal section of the suppository and examining the pattern of distribution of the dispersed particles.

2. **Melting Point**

   Should not be more than 37°C. As the release characteristics of the product depends on its melting point, it is very much necessary to determine the melting point of the suppository.

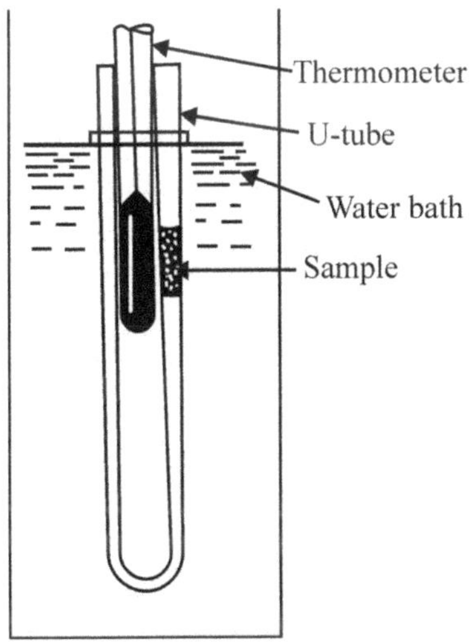

Figure 11.3 U-tube for determination of melting temperature.

The test should be carried out by a non-destructive method. That is the suppository is not melted before the measurement. The base can transform into its metastable form on melting. The test can be performed by any one of the three methods - Open capillary method, U-tube method and Drop point method. The principle of all three methods is same, only some variation in their methods is there.

Open-ended capillary method: This is very simple method. Two open-ended (both sides are open) capillary tubes about 7 cm long are taken. Sample of 1 cm length is introduced in each of the tubes. Both the tubes are tied with thread on two sides of a thermometer. The bulb of the thermometer is kept at the sample level as shown in the Fig 2. Then the assembly is dipped in a water bath fitted with a stirrer for maintaining uniform temperature without any turbulence. The dipping height of the tubes would be 4 cm from the water surface. The temperature of the bath is gradually raised at a rate of 1°C per minute. The temperature at which the sample starts moving up is noted. Average of at least three determinations should be considered.

U-tube method: The apparatus consists of a 8cm long U-tube whose one arm is linear and other arm is gradually tapered towards bending, as shown in the Fig 3. The sample, about 1.5 – 2 cm, height is introduced into the tapered side and pushed at least 3.5 – 4cm below the mouth. Care should be taken that the sample is not melted during its introduction. A thermometer is placed in between the arms, keeping the bulb of the thermometer closed to the sample.

The whole assembly is then placed in a water bath attached to a stirrer for maintaining uniformity of temperature without any turbulence. The temperature is increased slowly at a rate of 1°C per minute. The temperature at which the sample starts melting should be noted and till melting is completed. Average of at least three determinations should be taken into consideration.

3. **Solidification or congealing point**

Determination of solidification point is little critical as it may be influenced by crystallization of base, particularly when the base contains mono- and diglycerides. During formation of glycerides (glycerolysis) free hydroxyl moieties are also formed. These free hydroxyl moieties delay the process of crystallization. Thus, for rapid solidification, base with low hydroxyl index is preferred.

For determination of solidification point or temperature, the most commonly used method is Shukoff's method. According to this method the melted mass is introduced into an evacuated flask and is cooled very slowly. At each temperature the melt is shaken to observe the clarity. The temperature at which the melt becomes turbid is the solidification temperature or solidification point. At this point a transit rise in temperature occurs during cooling.

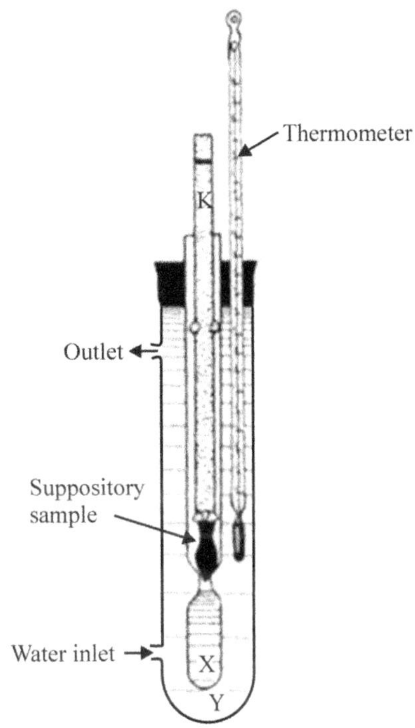

Figure 11.4 Krowczynski's apparatus for determination of liquefaction time.

4. **Liquefaction time**

   Time limit is not more than 30 minutes. The test is done to assess the physical behaviour of a suppository when it is kept at maximum functional temperature (37°C) and under a pressure. Krowczynski's apparatus is the most accepted for this test. A tube with bulb X is filled with distilled water up to the point of constriction; it is then introduced into a water bath Y maintained at a temperature 37 ± 0.1°C. The sample (suppository) is inserted from the top of the tube, X carefully down towards constriction as shown in the Fig 4. A glass rod K of specified weight (say, 30gm) is introduced into the tube X and allows to rest on the top of the suppository sample. The time taken by the glass rod to reach to the point of constriction, due to liquefaction of the suppository, is noted. The method needs to be repeated at least thrice and average should be taken into consideration.

5. **Mechanical strength**

   This is the force required to break a suppository. It indicates the character of the suppository- brittle or elastic. The Erweka method is generally used for this test. The mechanical strength of suppository should not be less than 1.8 – 2.0kg.

The apparatus (Erweka), as shown in the Fig 11.4, consists of a chamber fitted with a stand. With the help of a thermostat the temperature of the chamber can be controlled. The sample suppository is placed inside the chamber. On the top of the suppository a hanging rod is placed by means of a cap that rests on the upper surface of the suppository. Weights are suspended from the hanging rod and the weight is gradually increased till the suppository breaks. The total weight required to break the suppository is expressed as its mechanical strength.

Chemical Tests

Under the chemical tests following tests are essentially to be performed,

- Identification
- Assay
- Content uniformity
- Dissolution

1. **Identification tests**

   The tests are ingredient specific. It provides not only the product identity but, some information about degradation of ingredient during processing, if any. Under this head along with chemical tests chromatographic tests are performed. Chromatographic analysis can be better source of information regarding stability of the drug and other ingredients.

2. **Assay**

   Depending on the active ingredient present in the formulation, the method of analysis will vary. However, before conducting of a particular test for assay it is necessary to make the sample ready for the test. For this purpose, following activities are to be performed,

   - Preparation of representative sample,
   - Extraction of drug from the sample,
   - Separation of other ingredients, and
   - Final analysis of ingredients-active and other ingredients.

   There are certain inactive ingredients such as preservatives, which should be quantitatively analyzed to assess the preservative activity.

   To prepare a representative sample, a definite number of suppositories are randomly drawn from the pooled sample and weighed accurately to determine the average weight.

   These are taken in a beaker and melted completely on a water bath.

   The melted mass is mixed properly by stirring with a stirrer for 5 minutes to obtain a homogeneous mass. The melted mass is then placed in an ice bath for quick solidification.

The beaker is covered properly with a butter paper and placed in a refrigerator for about 20 – 30 minutes at a temperature below 5°C to ensure complete solidification.

Now the sample is ready for further processing.

A required amount of sample is cut, weighed accurately and extracted with a suitable solvent for separation of ingredients or proceed as per the method specified in the individual monograph of the Pharmacopoeia or in an accepted protocol of analysis.

3. **Content Uniformity**

Assay of a composite sample is done to determine the average content of the drug in a batch. To determine the content uniformity in the batch a definite number of the product is to beanalyzed individually. The exact number should be specified in the testing protocol. When the assay result speaks about batch to batch variation, the content uniformity speaks about dose to dose variation in a particular batch. The results of this test can inform about uniformity of mixing during manufacturing. Hence, the test for content uniformity is equally important like assay.

4. **Dissolution test**

This is one of the most important quality control tools for in-vitro evaluation of a product's efficacy. It also provides information about polymorphic transformation between drug and base. When there are established methods for dissolution of other solid oral dosage forms, for suppository it is still lacking. Following difficulties are found when the methods used for tablets or capsules, is used for suppository.

- The filtering disc or membrane or paper fails to filter the solution to be drawn from dissolution medium for analysis. Hence, actual rate of release of drug is difficult to be determined.
- Correct correlation between *in-vitro – in-vivo* is not possible.
- When the vehicle containing drug is insoluble in the dissolution medium, the drug may be partitioned between the two liquids instead of complete dissolution.

Keeping all these problems in view attempts have been made to find out suitable method for dissolution of suppository.

Basket method: In this method USP Method I dissolution apparatus is used. The problem in this method is clogging of wire mesh of the basket with fatty base. Palmier modified the method by using basket with slots in place of mesh and found satisfactory dissolution of aspirin suppository.

Paddle method: This is USP Method II commonly used for tablets and capsules. In this method the suppository is kept sinking at the bottom of the apparatus with the help of a steel spiral. The release of the drug depends on the speed of the paddle.

Membrane diffusion method: The apparatus consists of glass cylinder fitted with a wire mesh at its bottom to hold suppository, a metallic rotating shaft and a magnetic stirring bar. The sample chamber is separated from the dissolution medium by a membrane. The apparatus is attached to a thermostat to control temperature of dissolution fluid. In certain cases, this method works satisfactorily.

Dialysis method: In this method the suppository is introduced into an empty dialysis bag. The bag is tightly fixed at the centre of a beaker either with a heavy clamp or weight and the medium is stirred with a stirrer attached to the beaker. The dissolution fluid is put into the beaker. When the suppository melts, it spreads in the form of a thin film inside the bag and the drug starts diffusing into the dissolution medium. This method fairly mimics the in-vivo process. The USP method II (Paddle type) is a modification of this method.

Continuous flow method: According to this method the suppository is melted and placed on either a wire mesh or glass beads. After congealing the dissolution medium is allowed to flow through the mesh or beads. Use of glass beads is found to be better as it provides larger surface area for spreading of the melted base and greater dissolution can take place.

The dissolution fluid dissolves the drug by washing the suppository and the content of drug in washings can be estimated and rate of dissolution can be calculated.

Exercise

A. Multiple Choice Question Carrying 01 Mark

1. According to the definition of the WHO, Suppository is a
   (a) Liquid dosage form (b) Semisolid dosage form
   (c) Solid dosage form (d) All
2. Buginaria are
   (a) Rectal suppositories (b) Nasal suppositories
   (c) Vaginal suppositories (d) Ear cones
3. Vaginal suppositories are alternatively called
   (a) Bougies (b) Buginaria
   (c) Pessaries (d) None

4. Which of the following is the limitation of suppository?
   (a) Potential for non-specific drug loss
   (b) Avoidance of gastric irritation
   (c) Local effect on rectal mucosa
   (d) Improved enzymatic drug stability
5. Which of the following is the limitation of suppository?
   (a) Lymphatic delivery (b) Higher drug load
   (c) Avoidance of overdosing (d) Formulation
6. Which of the following is the advantage of suppository?
   (a) Partial avoidance of hepatic first pass
   (b) Limited fluid in rectum
   (c) Potential for non-specific drug loss
   (d) Not suitable for all patients
7. The basic functions of a suppository base are to
   (a) Act as the body of the product
   (b) Act as the carrier of the drug
   (c) All of the above
   (d) None
8. Suppository base may be
   (a) Natural, (b) Synthetic
   (c) All of the above (d) None
9. Suppository base may be
   (a) Water soluble/miscible base (b) Fatty base
   (c) All of the above (d) None
10. Which compound is used as suppository base
   (a) Polyvinyl alcohol (b) Propanoic acid
   (c) Polyvinyl pyrrolidone (d) None
11. Suppositories can be prepared by
   (a) Melting (b) Moulding
   (c) All of the above (d) None
12. For commercial production of suppositories by fusion method the tank used should be
   (a) Ordinary type (b) Thermostatically controlled
   (c) Connected with heater (d) None

13. For commercial production of suppositories by compression method which of the following should be used?
    (a) General tablet compression machine
    (b) Moulding machine
    (c) Special compression machine
    (d) None
14. Which of the following method is used to study the dissolution rate test
    (a) Basket method (b) Paddle method
    (c) Dialysis method (d) All of the above
15. Which of the following statements is correct?
    (a) Actual rate of release of drug is difficult to be determined.
    (b) Correct correlation between in-vitro – in-vivo is not possible.
    (c) When the vehicle containing drug is insoluble in the dissolution medium, the drug may be partitioned between the two liquids instead of complete dissolution.
    (d) All of the above

B. Question Carrying 05 Marks

1. Define suppository and briefly mention the uses of different types of suppositories.
2. What are the advantages and disadvantages of suppositories?
3. Write down the fusion method of manufacture of suppositories.
4. Enumerate the features of natural bases used to manufacture of suppositories.
5. Explain the features of synthetic and semisynthetic bases used to manufacture of suppositories.
6. Write down how can the suppositories be manufactured by molding method.
7. Describe how the suppositories can be manufactured by compression method.
8. What is displacement value and how this is applied?
9. Write down the method of determination of drug content of a suppository.
10. How the melting point of a suppository be determined?

C. Question Carrying 10 Marks

1. Explain the features of various types of suppository bases.
2. Explain the various methods used to manufacture suppositories.
3. Explain the application of displacement value with suitable example.
4. Explain briefly the physical tests to be conducted for evaluation of suppositories.
5. Describe the various methods used to find out the rate of dissolution of drug from the suppositories.
6. Briefly write down the chemical tests to be conducted for evaluation of a suppository.

Answers

A. Multiple Choice Question Carrying 01 Mark

1. (c)	**2. (b)**	**3. (c)**	**4. (a)**	**5. (d)**
6. (a)	**7. (c)**	**8. (c)**	**9. (c)**	**10. (a)**
11. (c)	**12. (b)**	**13. (a)**	**14. (d)**	**15. (d)**

Chapter 12

Pharmaceutical Incompatibilities

Definition, Classification, Physical, Chemical and Therapeutic Incompatibilities with Examples

Introduction

Many of the official as well as proprietary preparations contain single drug in their formulations; hence, are administered alone. Some are given in combination. There are few drugs which should never be given in combination with other drugs. The selection of drugs and their preparations to be used in combination with each other's should be done carefully to avoid unwanted changes or action. The drugs which can cause unwanted reactions when mixed or produce unwanted action when administered with other drugs are called antagonistic to one another; and 7 hence, these substances/ drugs are incompatible to each other.

Definition

Incompatibility can be defined as; when two or more substances antagonistic to one another are mixed, an undesirable product may be formed which can affect safety, efficacy, purpose and appearance of the product. Such mixing may be done as per the prescription or manufacturing formula. Incompatibility of one substance with another is an intrinsic property of the particular substance. Incompatibility may occur between two drugs, two excipients, or between a drug with an excipient and it may be observed in two situations – prescription and formulation.

Classification

Incompatibility may be classified into three categories:

- Physical
- Chemical, and
- Therapeutic

Incompatibility in Formulation

Physical Incompatibility

Preformulation is the first step informulation development. The physical and chemical properties of the drug substance alone and in combination with excipients are evaluated. This is called compatibility test. For the following reasons the drug substance is commonly mixed with different excipients:

- To improve manufacturing of the formulation,
- To improve the stability of the product
- To administer correct dose of the drug
- To ease administration
- To release of the active component at desired site at desired rate, and sometimes,
- To stabilize the formulation against degradation from the environment.

Most of the excipients do not have direct pharmacological action but, they can modify useful properties of the formulation. However, they can be responsible for degradation of the drug also. Such problem occurs unintentionally.

Physical and chemical interactions between drugs and excipients can affect the chemical nature, the stability and bioavailability of drug products, and consequently, their therapeutic efficacy and safety. There are several approaches for screening drug-excipient chemical compatibility. The most useful and time saving approach is computational, which can predict drug-excipient chemical compatibility. This requires a complete database of reactive functional groups of drug and excipients, their potential impurities, and in-depth knowledge about the excipients. However, use of this computational approach only as the sole source of information is not sufficient.

Binary mixture compatibility testing is another approach which is commonly used. In this approach, binary (1:1 or customized) mixtures of the drug and excipient are prepared with or without water. Sometimes the mixture is compacted or prepared in the form of slurry. These are then stored under stressed conditions (also known as isothermal stress testing, IST) and analyzed using a stability-indicating method, e.g. high-performance liquid chromatography (HPLC). When the slurry is prepared the pH of the drug-excipient blend and the role of moisture are also investigated. Alternatively, the binary mixtures can be screened using other thermal methods, such as differential scanning calorimetry (DSC). DSC is currently the leading technique for this purpose.

There are several examples of formulation in stability due to solid–solid interactions. Certain classes of compounds are known to be incompatible with particular excipients. Therefore, knowledge of the chemistry of the drug substance and excipients can often minimize formulation incompatibilities.

- Heat and water are primarily responsible (catalysts) for drug excipient interactions. They play a critical role in the degradation of a drug substance. The majority of instability reactions of 'small molecule' API occur through hydrolysis, oxidation and Maillard reaction.
- The moisture content of the drug and excipients plays a critical role in their incompatibility. Heat and moisture accelerate most reactions; moisture brings molecules closer together, and heat increases the reaction rate. Excipients such as starch and povidone may possess a high-water content (the equilibrium moisture content of povidone is about 28% at 75% relative humidity), which can increase drug degradation. The moisture level will affect the stability depending on how strongly it is bound and whether it can come into contact with the drug. It is generally recognized that aspirin is incompatible with magnesium salts. Higher moisture contents and humidity accelerate the degradation even further.
- Many excipients are hygroscopic and absorb water during manufacturing, for example during wet granulation. Depending on the degree of hydrolytic susceptibility, different approaches to tablet granulation can be used to minimize hydrolysis. For example, acetylsalicylic acid readily hydrolyzes; hence, direct compression or dry granulation is recommended.

Therapeutic Incompatibility

Chemical interaction between the drug and excipients may lead to increased decomposition. The degradation may be due to hydrolysis, oxidation, aldehyde amine addition etc. For example,

- *Hydrolysis:* salts of stearic acid (e.g. magnesium stearate, sodium stearate) are avoided as tablet lubricants if the drug is hydrolysable via ion-catalyzed degradation. Excipients generally contain more free moisture than the drug substance. Therefore, formulation can potentially expose the drug substance to higher levels of moisture than normal and the possibility of degradation of even stable compounds increases. In selecting excipients, it is probably best to avoid hygroscopic excipients when formulating hydrolysable compounds. However, the drug can be formulated with over-dried hygroscopic excipients (e.g. Starch 1500) to prevent the drug from coming into contact with water.

- *Humidity* is another major factor that can affect stability in solid dosage forms. Increase of relative humidity usually decreases the stability, particularly for drugs that are highly sensitive to hydrolysis. For example, nitrazepam in the solid state can degrade by interaction with excipients. Molecular mobility is also responsible for solid-solid reactions. Systems with enhanced mobility have more reactivity. Mechanical stress is also expected to accelerate such reactions by creating a larger surface area, increasing the number of defects, and increasing the amount of amorphous material.
- *Oxidation reactions* are complex, and it can be difficult to understand the reaction mechanism. The best approach is to avoid excipients containing oxidative reactants such as peroxides and fumed metal oxides like fumed silica and fumed titanium dioxide. Excipients such as povidone and polyethylene glycols (PEGs) may contain organic peroxides as synthetic by-products which are typically more reactive than hydrogen peroxide. Although most compendial excipients have limits on metals, free ethylene oxide or other oxidizing agents via the peroxide or iodine value there are still some instances of oxidative degradation of drug due to presence of reactive peroxides in excipients such as povidone. For example, oxidative degradation of Raloxifene H.L. occurs via peroxide impurities in povidone. Thus, it is important to understand the purity and composition of the excipient prior to formulation.
- *Aldehyde-amine addition* is another important type of reaction, which is responsible for incompatibility between excipients comprising reducing sugars (e.g. lactose, dextrose) and amine-containing drugs. Aldehyde-amine addition leads to the formation of a Schiff base, which further cyclizes to form a glucosamine followed by an Amadori rearrangement. This sequence of reactions is called the Maillard reaction and is responsible for a large number of incompatibilities between APIs and excipients.

Common solid-state incompatibilities are shown in Table 12.1.

Table 12.1 List of common solid-state incompatibilities

Functional Group of the drug	Incompatible with	Type of Reaction
Primary amine (e.g. Acyclovir)	Mono and disaccharides (e.g. lactose)	Maillard reaction
Esters (e.g. Moexipril)	Basic components (e.g.magnesium hydroxide)	Ester hydrolysis
Lactone (e.g. Irinotecan HCl)	Basic components (e.g.magnesium hydroxide)	Ring opening (hydrolysis)

Table 12.1 *Contd...*

Functional Group of the drug	Incompatible with	Type of Reaction
Carboxyl	Bases	Salt formation
Alcohol (e.g. Morphine)	Oxygen	Oxidation to aldehydes and ketones
Sulfhydryl (e.g. Captopril)	Oxygen	Dimerization
Phenol	Metals, Polyplasdone	Complexation
Gelatin	Cationic surfactants	Denaturation

Some of the common excipients or groups of excipients which have been found to be incompatible with drugs are given below.

- *Polysaccharides:* Lactose is a reducing disaccharide and reactions between it and drugs containing amino groups have been reported. Lactose is one of the most common excipients in pharmaceutical oral dosage forms (tablets) and, is available in crystalline and amorphous forms. Spray dried lactose has been found to interact with dextroamphetamine sulfate.

  In fact, there are a number of reports of the incompatibility between lactose and amine-containing drugs such as aminophylline, ranitidine HCl, thiamine HCl, aceclofenac, etc.

- *Stearates:* Magnesium stearate is widely used as a lubricant in the manufacture of pharmaceutical solid dosage forms. There are numerous reports of the incompatibility between stearates and drugs, such as aspirin, captopril, metformin, amlodipine, etc.Binary mixtures of metformin with starch and lactose showed interaction upon heating, changing the melting point of metformin. Captopril is a pyrrolidine carboxylic acid derivative used in the treatment of hypertension. It shows surface interactions with metallic stearates during grinding.

- *Povidone (Polyvinyl pyrrolidone, PVP):* In tablet formulation PVP is commonly used as a binder, as a film forming agent, and also for forming amorphous dispersions of drugs. It has been found to be incompatible with a wide range of drugs, such as sulphathiazole, oxprenolol, atenolol, haloperidol, indomethacin, ketoprofen, clenbuterol, temazepam, etc.

- *Dicalcium phosphate dihydrate (DCP):* It is commonly used as filler in tablet formulation and as a dental polishing agent in toothpaste. It has been found to be incompatible with various acidic drugs and sodium salt of poorly water-soluble drugs due to its alkaline nature. For example, temazepam is acidic in nature with pKa of 1.61 interacts with DCP. Other drugs which are incompatible with DCP are oxprenolol hydrochloride, ceronapril, β-lapachone, famotidine, nalidixic acid, quinapril, and metronidazole.

- *Eudragit* polymers: These are copolymers obtained from esters of acrylic and methacrylic acid. These are available in different physical forms and widely used for making targeted and controlled release drug delivery systems. Certain drugs have been found incompatible with some Eudragit polymers. For example, ibuprofen, diflunisal, flurbiprofen, piroxicam are incompatible with Eudragit RS100 and RL100.A mild interaction between ranitidine and Eudragit E100, omeprazole and Eudragit L100 has been reported.
- *Celluloses:* In various oral and topical formulations methylcellulose is used. It is extensively used in cosmetics and food products also. MCC is used as filler in tablets and as thickener and stabilizer in processed foods. Based on the grade, HPMC is used in tablets, capsules, and in controlled release products for different purposes. MCC and several other cellulosic products such as starch, sodium starch glycolate, crospovidone, and croscarmillose sodium have been found to accelerate degradation of enalapril maleate. Isosorbide mononitrate interacts with cellulose acetate and MCC. Trichlormethiazide is stable in a solid state under humid conditions, but its tablet containing HPMC is not stable under the same conditions. Trichlormethiazide degrades faster in presence of hydroxypropylcellulose (HPC).
- *Polyethylene glycol (PEG):* As a lubricant, cosolvent, dispersing agent PEG has been widely used in different pharmaceutical formulations. But it also been found to cause degradation some drugs. In degradation of drugs its purity plays an important role. PEG of high purity hardly causes degradation. Ibuprofen degrades in tablets made with PEG. Similarly, aspirin undergoes pseudo-first order decomposition in presence of various grades of PEG.

  When suppository of indomethacin is prepared using PEG, indomethacin decomposes. Other drugs such as ketoprofen, calcium phosphomycin, etc. have been reported to interact with PEG and decompose.
- *Polysorbate 80:* It is commercially known as Tween 80. It is a nonionic surfactant and widely used as emulsifier in pharmaceutical and food preparations. At higher temperature in the presence of air it can affect the stability of oxidation prone drugs such as ibuprofen.
- *Sodium Lauryl Sulphate (SLS):* In tablet it is used to enhance the solubility of poorly soluble drugs. It acts as a surfactant or wetting agent. It is incompatible with certain drugs such as chlopropamide, chlordiazepoxide, clopidogrel besylate, etc.

- *Chitosan:* In a study of developing controlled release tablet of diclofenac sodium chitosan has been found to inhibit the release of diclofenac sodium from the matrix at low pH, may be due to formation of an ionic complex.
- *Magnesium oxide:* It is used as an active ingredient in antacid and sometimes, used to modify pH. For example, in Levothyroxine sodium pentahydrate tablets it is used as pH modifier. But it interacts with ibuprofen at higher temperature (≈ 55°C).
- *Silicon dioxide (Silica):* It has various applications in pharmaceutical industry. In tablets it is used as glidant, in suspensions sometimes colloidal silica is used to facilitate dispersion, etc. However, it causes the thermal decomposition of enalapril maleate.
- *Carbonates:* Many drugs are incompatible with carbonate. For example, stability of adefovir dipivoxil in solid state is affected in presence of sodium carbonate. However, insoluble carbonates, such as calcium carbonate and magnesium carbonate, enhance the stability of adefovir dipivoxil.

Table 12.2 The incompatibilities of various drugs with excipients

Excipient	Drug	Therapeutic category
Lactose	Acyclovir Aceclofenac, Ketoprofen Metformin,Glipizide Amlodipine, Ceronapril, Lisinopril, Oxprenolol Fluconazole Primaquine Promethazine Fluoxetine and Seproxetine Maleate Picotamide Etamsylate Aminophylline and Clenbuterol Baclofen Ranitidine Doxylamine Thiamine HCL Pefloxacin	Antiviral Anti-inflammatory Antidiabetic Antihypertensive Antifungal Antimalarial Antiemetic Antidepressant Anticoagulant Antihemorrhagic Bronchodilator CNS Drug; GI Agent Antihistaminic Vitamin Antibiotic
Mannitol, Pearlitol (80% Mannitol +20% Maize Starch)	Quinapril Primaquine Omeprazole Promethazine	Antihypertensive Antimalarial GI Agent Antiemetic
Starch	Seproxetine Maleate Clenbuterol	Antidepressant Bronchodilator

Table 12.2 *Contd...*

Excipient	Drug	Therapeutic category
Sodium Starch Glycolate	Clenbuterol	Bronchodilator
Dextrose	Pefloxacin	Antibiotic
Stearates Magnesium Stearate	Acyclovir Aspirin, Ibuproxam, Indomethacin, Ketoprofen Glipizide, Chlorpropamide, Glimepiride and Glibenclamide Captopril, Fosinopril, Moexipril, Oxprenolol and Quinapril Cephalexin, Erythromycin, Nalidixic Acid, Oxacillin, Penicillin G Primaquine Promethazine Albendazole β-lapachone Clopidogrel Doxylamine Temazepam	Antiviral Anti-inflammatory Antidiabetic Antihypertensive Antibiotic Antimalarial Antiemetic Antiamoebic Anticancer Anticoagulant Antihistaminic Hypnotic
Stearic Acid	Doxylamine	Antihistaminic
Polyvinyl pyrrolidone (PVP)	Indomethacin, Ketoprofen Atenolol and Oxprenolol Sulfathiazole Haloperidol Ranitidine Doxylamine Temazepam Clenbuterol	Anti-inflammatory Antihypertensive Antibiotic Antipsychotic GI Agent Antihistaminic Hypnotic Bronchodilator
Dicalcium Phosphate Dihydrate (DCPD)	Ceronapril, Oxprenolol and Quinapril Metronidazole β-lapachone,Parthenolide Famotidine Temazepam	Antihypertensive Antiamoebic Anticancer GI Agent Hypnotic
Eudragit RS l00	Diflunisal, Flurbiprofen, Piroxicam	Anti-inflammatory
Eudragit RL100	Ibuprofen	Anti-inflammatory
Eudragit E100	Ranitidine	GI Agent
Microcrystalline Cellulose (MCC), Avicel PH 101	Enalapril Isosorbide Mononitrate Clenbuterol	Antihypertensive Antiangina Bronchodilator

Table 12.2 *Contd...*

Excipient	Drug	Therapeutic category
Cellulose Acetate	Isosorbide Mononitrate	Antiangina
Hydroxypropyl Cellulose	Trichlormethiazide	Diuretic
PEG	Ibuprofen, Ketoprofen Phosphomycin Clopidogrel	Anti-inflammatory Antibiotic Anticoagulant
Polysorbate 80	Ibuprofen	Anti-inflammatory
Sodium Lauryl Sulfate	Chlopropamide Clopidogrel Chlordiazepoxide	Antidiabetic Anticoagulant Hypnotic
Chitosan	Diclofenac, Piroxicam	Anti-inflammatory
Magnesium Oxide	Ibuprofen	Anti-inflammatory
Silicon Dioxide	Enalapril	Antihypertensive
Sodium Carbonate	Adefovir Dipivoxil	Antiviral
Sodium Bicarbonate	Ibuprofen	Anti-inflammatory
Miscellaneous		
Plasdone	Glimepiride	Antidiabetic
Ascorbic acid	Atenolol	Antihypertensive
Citric acid	Atenolol	Antihypertensive
Butylated hydroxyanisole	Atenolol	Antihypertensive
Succinic acid	Phosphomycin	Antibiotic
Na dioctylsulfocuccinate	Phosphomycin	Antibiotic
Ca and Mg salts	Tetracycline	Antibiotic
Talc	Seproxetine maleate	Antidepressant

Chemical Incompatibility

The incompatibility due to chemical changes occurred between preparations dispensed together is known as Chemical Incompatibility. Due to such incompatibility, toxic, non-toxic, inactive product may be formed. Chemical incompatibility may be identified or characterized by decomposition, precipitation, effervescence, change of colour, and explosion. The changes may be of several types and may be classified as follows:

1. Chemical change without any visible change, such as
   - The neutralization of acids by bases.
   - The glucosides break down into acids.
   - The action of acids on the activity of pancreatic ferments and of alkali on gastric ferments.

2. Precipitation of newly formed chemical substances as a result of the interaction between two chemical substances in solution.

   Salts of the alkaline earths react with alkali hydroxides and carbonates, phosphates, borates, oxalates. The corresponding insoluble salts of the alkaline earths formed are precipitated. The corresponding free acids formed are also incompatible.

   - Salts of the metals in solution are incompatible with hydrates, carbonates, phosphates, oxalates and the corresponding acids; in many cases these are incompatible with proteins, tannins, acacia, and sometimes with alkaloids and phenozone. Salts of silver, mercurous, lead, and bismuth are also incompatible with bromides and iodides. Similarly, the metals such as calcium, barium and strontium are incompatible with sulphates and sulphuric acid.
   - Hydrates or carbonates of the alkalis such as sodium, potassium, and ammonia are incompatible with salts of metals and alkaline earths, and with alkaloids and with some glucosides.
   - Alkaloids form insoluble salts with other organic acids such as acetic acid, citric acid, etc.; the free alkaloid is very less soluble than their salts. It is precipitated by alkali hydrates and carbonates and by borax. Ammonium carbonate and bicarbonates do not cause precipitation so readily. Iodides, bromides, salicylates, benzoates, usually cause a precipitation of tannic acid, and iodine in a solution of mercuric iodide; precipitation may be prevented in many of these cases using 15-50% alcohol. Alkaloids may cause precipitation with many metallic salts especially of mercury.
   - Proteins are precipitated by alkaloids, many metal salts, tannin and alcohol.

3. Change of colour due to the formation of some soluble but undesired substance.

   - An objectionable appearance of preparations containing tannic acid, gallic acids and iron salts; ammonia and carbolic acid; gallic acid and thymol; ferric chloride and salicylates, carbolic acid, creosote, guaiacol, salol, acetanilide, phenazone, phenacetin, oils of wintergreen, cloves, pimenta, and thyme, podophyllin, aloin, gamboge, asafetida, storax, myrrh, balsam of Peru, balsam of Tolu, morphine and apomorphine.
   - The change in colour is the indication of a chemical change. Such changes occur in mixture of salicylates, phenozone, and acetanilide with the free nitrous acid in Spirits of Nitrous Ether (isonitroso-compounds are formed).

4. Chemical splitting of one of the substances and the formation of an undesired substance. This may result the following:
   - Release of a volatile component, in part or entirely, depending upon the amount formed in the solution. For example, hydrochloric acid reacts with nitric acid and releases nitrous oxides; strong acids when reacts with alcohol releases ethers; chloral and butyl chloral react with alkalies and chloroform is released.
   - Dextrose or other sugar is formed when glucosides react with acids and alkalies.
   - Sudden liberation of gas which may be sufficient to cause an explosion. For example, reaction between chromic acid, concentrated nitric acid, nitrates, permanganates, chlorates, with substances like sulphur and sulphides, sulphites, iodides, phosphorus, hypophosphite, reduced iron, and many organic substances such as sugar, tannin, etc. These reactions occur only when the dry substances are triturated together or in some cases when mixed in very concentrated solutions.
5. In some cases when two solids are triturated together a soft sticky or a damp mass, or a liquid is formed; probablythe chemical reaction takes place. Such substances are camphor, carbolic acid, thymol, phenozone, phenacetin, chloral, sodium phosphate, lead acetate.

Incompatibility in Prescriptions

Now-a-days, official or proprietary formulations of drug are being prescribed. Hardly the physicians write the names and quantities of ingredients in the prescription and indicate the form in which these are to be mixed and dispensed. However, incompatibilities may occur due to dilution or mixing of these products. This may be due to physicochemical with or without therapeutic interactions.

Physical Incompatibility

Usually, physical incompatibility occurs due to immiscibility or insolubility. It can cause invisible, non-uniform products from which removal of an accurate dose is very difficult.

Classification:

- Immiscibility
- Insolubility
- Liquefaction

- Immiscibility
  - ➢ Oils are immiscible with water and hence, combination of oily drugs with water produces a product possessing two separate layers.

    Remedy: This problem can be overcome by emulsification or solubilization.
  - ➢ Care must be taken when concentrated hydroalcoholic solutions of volatile oils such as spirits and concentrated waters, are used as adjuncts (e.g. as flavoring agents) in aqueous preparations. Large globules of oils may be separated.

    Remedy: To prevent the formation of large globules, the hydroalcoholic solution should either be gradually diluted with the vehicle before admixture with the remaining ingredients or poured into the vehicle with constant stirring.
  - ➢ Addition of high concentrations of electrolytes to a saturated aqueous solution of a volatile oil causes separation of the oil whichdeposits as a surface layer.

    Example: This happens in Potassium Citrate Mixture B.P.C. in which large quantity of soluble solids salts out the lemon oil.

    Remedy: To disperse the droplets evenly, quillaia tincture is to beadded as wetting agent.
- Insolubility
  - ➢ Liquid preparations containing indiffusible solids such as chalk, aromatic chalk powder, succinyl sulfathiazole and sulphadimidine (in mixtures); calamine and zinc oxide (in lotions).

    Remedy: A thickening agent is necessary to obtain uniform product from which uniform doses can be removed.
  - ➢ Some insoluble powders such as sulphur and certain corticosteroids (hydrocortisone acetate) and antibiotics are difficult to wet with water.

    Remedy: Wetting agents such as saponins for lotions containing sulphur; polysorbates in parenteral suspensions of corticosteroids and antibiotics are used to distribute the powder and to prevent formation of slow dispersing, solid stabilized foam on shaking.
  - ➢ When a resinous tincture is added to water, the water insoluble resin agglomerates and forms indiffusible clots.

    Remedy: This is prevented by adding the undiluted dispersion of protective colloid (Tragacanth mucilage) slowly.

Example: Lobelia & Stramonium tincture which should be mixed with tragacanth mucilage and stirred constantly. This will produce a stable preparation.

- High concentrations of electrolytes cause cracking of soap emulsions (ionic) by salting out the emulsifiers.

- Liquefaction

When certain low melting solids are powdered together, a liquid or soft mass is produced due to lowering of the melting point of the mixture to below room temperature. A eutectic mixture is formed.

Any two of the following exhibits this type of behaviour, camphor, menthol, phenol, thymol and chloral hydrate, and sodium salicylate with phenazone.

Example:

Rx

Thymol	250 mg
Camphor	2 mg
Menthol	2 mg

Make powder.

Comments: If these ingredients are triturated together, they form a eutectic mixture.

Method I:

All the ingredients are triturated. A eutectic mixture (liquid) is formed. Then the liquid is triturated with enough absorbent powder e.g. light kaolin or light magnesium carbonate. This produces a free-flowing powder.

Method II:

Each ingredient is triturated separately with small amount of adsorbent or diluent and then these powders are lightly mixed (by tumbling action) and packed.

The diluent largely prevents contact between the ingredients and adsorbs any liquid that may be produced.

Example:

Rx

Chloral hydrate	250 mg
Prepare capsules. Supply	10 capsules.

Label: Take the capsules at night-time.

Comment: Chloral hydrate is hygroscopic in nature. It will absorb moisture and soften the hard gelatin capsule shells and the shape of the capsule may change physically.

Remedy: An equal quantity of light magnesium oxide should be mixed with chloral hydrate. Other adsorbents such as kaolin, talc, starch etc. may be used.

Example:

Rx

Aminopyrine	0.3 g
Acetyl salicylic acid	0.2 g
Codeine sulphate	0.015 g
Belladonna extracts	0.010 g

Prepare capsules.

Comment: In this prescription aminopyrine and acetyl salicylic acid form eutectic mixture and wetting of belladonna extract give green colour.

Remedy: Light magnesium oxide (approximately 65 mg) may be added. The half quantity of magnesium oxide is mixed with aminopyrine and the other half is mixed with acetyl salicylic acid separately. The two are then mixed gently and thereafter other ingredients are added and mixed gently.

Therapeutic Incompatibility

Usually this type of incompatibility occurs when one or more drugs produces response or intensity different from that intended in the patients. This may happen due to the following reasons:

- Overdoses
- Under doses
- Improper consumption by the patient
- Contraindicated drugs

Overdoses: This may be divided into two groups.

- *Excessive single dose:* Sometimes a single dose may become overdose depending on the health of the patient. The dose of a drug is based on the body weight of a normal adult person which is considered as 70 kg. The dose may become overdose if the weight of the patient is very less than the normal. However, the number of doses should not be more 2 to 3.

Example 1

Rx

Atropine sulphate	6 mg
Phenobarbital	360 mg

Make capsules.

Label: One capsule to be taken thrice a day.

Comments: The doses of both atropine and phenobarbital are for 12 doses and it was intended for 12 capsules. Hence, the prescription is either mistakenly prepared or incomplete one. The Pharmacist must consult the Physician before dispensing.

The correct prescription would be

Rx

Atropine sulphate	6 mg
Phenobarbital	360 mg

Make 12 capsules.

Label: One capsule to be taken thrice a day.

Example 2

Rx

Strychnine sulphate	20 mg
Iron and Ammonium citrate	500 mg

Prepare and supply 12 capsules

Label: One capsule to be taken three times a day after meals.

Comment: Dose of strychnine hydrochloride is10 times of the normal dose. In this case the daily dose of drug is exceeded. The pharmacist should consult the physician and obtain the permission to change the dose.

The corrected prescription would be

Rx

Strychnine sulphate	2 mg
Iron and ammonium citrate	500 mg

Prepare andsupply 12 capsules.

Label: One capsule to be taken thrice a day after meals.

Example 3

Rx

Codeine phosphate	15 mg
Ammonium chloride	500 mg

Prepare capsules and supply 24 capsules.

Label: Two capsules to be taken every hour for cough.

Comment: The U.S.P. recommends that the prescribed dose should be taken after every four hours and not every hour. Hence the physician should be consulted.

- *Additive and synergistic combinations:*

There are certain drugs possessing similar pharmacological activity. If these drugs are combined together, they may produce additive or synergistic action. In such case advice of the physician is necessary.

Example 1:

Rx

Amphetamine sulphate	20 mg
Ephedrine sulphate	50 mg

Syrup qs100 ml

A mixture to be made

Label: Take 25 ml every four hourly.

Comment: Both of the drugs are sympathetic and stimulants; they are prescribed in their full dose. The formulation will produce additive overdose effect. Hence, the dose of individual drug should be reduced.

Under dose: In this type of incompatibility, the effect of one drug is lesserthan another one or is antagonized by the presence of another drug. This can be exemplified by combination of following types of drugs:

Stimulants like nuxvomica, strychnine sulphate, caffeine etc. with sedatives like barbiturates, paraldehyde etc.

Sympathomimetic or adrenergic like ephedrine, nor-adrenaline with sympatholytic drugs like ergotamine.

Sympathetic stimulants like methamphetamine with parasympathetic stimulants like pilocarpine.

Purgatives like castor oil, liquid paraffin etc., with antidiarrheal agents like bismuth carbonates.

Acidifiers like dilute hydrochloric acid and alkalisers like sodium bicarbonate, magnesium carbonate.

Example,

Rx

Aspirin	300 mg
Probenecid	500 mg

Prepare capsules.

Label: One capsule a day for gout.

Comment: Aspirin is an NSAID given to reduce the pain and swelling in case of gout attack. Probenecid blocks the active re-absorption of uric acid from the lumen of nephron, but salicylates (aspirin) blocks this action of probenecid. Hence, both of the drugs are antagonistic to each other, so its combination is therapeutically useless.

- *Improper consumption by the patient:*

  In certain prescription some special directions should be written. If the patients are nor advised the drugs may not produce the desired action due to low bioavailability.

  Example

  Rx

Tetracycline hydrochloride	250 mg
Prepare capsules. Supply	10 capsules.

  Label: Take one capsule every six hourly.

  Comments: Calcium present in milk inactivates the tetracycline, hence a patient may not get any therapeutic effect if he/she takes the capsule with milk.

  Remedy: The pharmacist should advise the patient to take the capsule with water and not with milk. The patient should not take antacid containing calcium salts.

- *Contra-indicated drugs*

  Certain drugs should not be given in particular disease condition. Some examples are given below;

  (i) Corticosteroids are contraindicated in patients with peptic ulcer.

  (ii) Vasoconstrictors are contraindicated in hypertensive patients

  (iii) Some drugs should not be given in asthmatic patients e.g. barbiturates, morphine etc.

  (iv) If a person is allergic to a drug (e.g. penicillin injection) then it should not be given to the patient.

  (v) Certain combination of drugs contraindicates.

  Example:

  Rx

Sulphadiazine	0.25 g
Sulphamerazine	0.25 g
Ammonium chloride	0.50 g

  Prepare capsules

  Label: Take two capsules six hourly for cough.

Comment: In this prescription ammonium chloride is a urinary acidifier and it could cause deposition of sulphonamide crystals in the kidney.

Exercise

A. Multiple Choice Question Carrying 01 Mark

1. Which one of the following statements is correct?
   (a) When two drugs antagonistic to each other are given together, incompatibility occurs.
   (b) When two drugs antagonistic to each other are given together, synergistic action results.
   (c) When two drugs antagonistic to each other are given together, additive action results.
   (d) None of the above.
2. Which one of the following statements is correct?
   (a) To avoid incompatibility, physicochemical properties of drug substance are determined.
   (b) To avoid incompatibility, physicochemical properties of drug substance and of the selected excipient are determined.
   (c) To avoid incompatibility, physicochemical properties of drug product are determined.
   (d) None of the above.
3. Drug is mixed with different excipients
   (a) To improve manufacture of the formulation
   (b) To improve the stability of the formulation
   (c) To administer correct dose of the drug
   (d) All of the above
4. Which one of the following statements is correct?
   (a) Drug is mixed with different excipients to ease administration
   (b) Drug is mixed with different excipients not to ease administration
   (c) Drug is mixed with different excipients to destabilize the drug product
   (d) Drug is mixed with different excipients to administer correct dosage form.

5. For drug excipient interaction
   (a) Oxygen in air is primarily responsible
   (b) Heat is also primarily responsible
   (c) Temperature is primarily responsible
   (d) Heat and moisture are primarily responsible
6. Which one of the following statements is correct?
   (a) Hygroscopic excipients do not release moisture
   (b) Hygroscopic excipients release moisture
   (c) Hygroscopic excipients absorb moisture
   (d) Hygroscopic excipients do not absorb moisture
7. Which one of the following statements is correct?
   (a) Moisture content of the drug and excipient may help degradation of drug
   (b) Moisture content of the drug and excipient are not responsible for degradation of drug
   (c) Moisture content of the drug and excipient are responsible for release of drug
   (d) None of the above
8. Which one of the following statements is correct?
   (a) Moisture content of only the drug plays an role in incompatibility
   (b) Moisture content of only the drug does not play an role in incompatibility
   (c) Moisture content of only the excipients plays an role in incompatibility
   (d) Moisture content of the drug and excipient plays an role in incompatibility
9. Primary amine such as Acyclovir is incompatible with
   (a) Lactose (b) Glucose
   (c) Fructose (d) All of the above
10. Alcohol is incompatible with
    (a) Sucrose (b) Oxygen
    (c) Moisture (d) None of the above
11. Gelatin is not compatible with
    (a) Cationic surfactant (b) Anionic surfactant
    (c) Nonionic surfactant (d) All of the above

12. Magnesium oxide interacts with
    (a) Ibuprofen at lower temperature
    (b) Ibuprofen at higher temperature
    (c) Ibuprofen at normal temperature
    (d) None of the above
13. Magnesium stearate is not compatible with
    (a) Thiamine HCl (b) Thiamine nitrate
    (c) Aspirin (d) Promethazine
14. Physical incompatibility includes
    (a) Immiscibility (b) Insolubility
    (c) Liquefaction (d) All of the above
15. Therapeutic incompatibility may result from
    (a) Overdoses
    (b) Under doses
    (c) Use of contraindicated drugs
    (d) All of the above
16. Alkaloids should be taken with
    (a) Citric acid (b) Sodium citrate
    (c) Sucrose (d) None of the above
17. Which of the following statements is correct?
    (a) Chemical splitting of one of the components of a drug product indicates chemical incompatibility
    (b) Chemical splitting of one of the components of a drug product and formation of an undesired substance indicates chemical incompatibility
18. Incompatibility results when
    (a) Two substances are triturated together
    (b) More than two substances are triturated together
    (c) Two substances are triturated together, and the mass becomes soft sticky or a liquid
    (d) All of the above

B. Question Carrying 05 Marks

1. Define pharmaceutical incompatibility with relevant examples.
2. During formulation development the drug is mixed various excipients and tested – explain why it is done.

3. Classify pharmaceutical incompatibilities with relevant example.
4. Mention the various reasons for which physical incompatibilities take place.
5. Define chemical incompatibility and mention the visible signs to predict chemical incompatibility.
6. What is meant by 'incompatibility in prescription', mention at least two examples.
7. Explain with example how insolubility and liquefaction cause incompatibility in prescription.

C. Question Carrying 10 Marks

1. Explain under what circumstances physical incompatibilities occur.
2. Explain under what circumstances physical incompatibilities occur in prescription.
3. Explain how therapeutic incompatibilities occur due to some chemical interactions.
4. Discuss the various reasons for chemical incompatibility with relevant example.
5. Enumerate therapeutic incompatibility with relevant examples.
6. Explain how incompatibilities occur in prescription, justify with appropriate examples.

Answers

A. Multiple Choice Question Carrying 01 Mark

1. (a)	2. (b)	3. (a)	4. (a)	5. (d)
6. (c)	7. (a)	8. (d)	9. (d)	10. (b)
11. (a)	12. (b)	13. (c)	14. (d)	15. (d)
16. (a)	17. (b)	18. (c)		

Chapter 13

Semisolid Dosage Forms

Definitions, Classification, Mechanisms, and Factors Influencing Dermal Penetration of Drugs Preparation of Ointments, Pastes, Creams and Gels. Excipients used in Semi Solid Dosage Forms. Evaluation of Semi Solid Dosages Forms.

Definitions

Creams, ointments, pastes and gels are considered as semisolid dosage form. *Semi-solid preparations usually contain single drug substance or a mixture of drug substances either in dissolved state (solution) or in the form of dispersion in a suitable basis intended for application over the skin.* The basis is usually non-aqueous. Commonly an ointment is used for,

- To provide emollient effect on the skin,
- For protection of the skin, and
- To provide local medication.

Emollient and protective ointments may contain vegetable oils, synthetic esters of fatty acids or wool fat along with an inert base, e.g. soft paraffin.

Classification of Ointment Bases

Primarily there are four types of ointment bases. Each of these has different composition and applications.

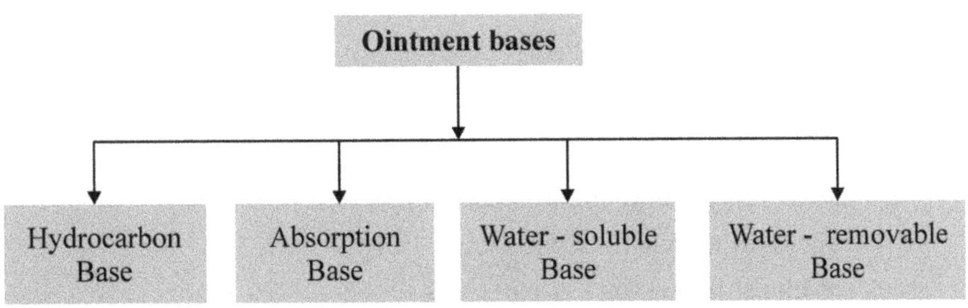

Figure 13.1 Types of ointment bases.

1. *Hydrocarbon Bases* are alternatively called 'oleaginous ointment base'. These are sticky, inert, and usually immiscible with water. These are not commonly absorbed by the skin. Hence, ointments prepared with this type of base act as a barrier to heat and moisture and can keep the skin soft. This type of base is represented by white petrolatum and white ointment. The major limitation of this base is small amount of aqueous component can be incorporated into this. The ointment prepared with hydrocarbon base can keep the medicament in prolonged contact with the skin and act as occlusive dressings. For example, petrolatum, hard paraffin, liquid paraffin is used as hydrocarbon base.
2. *Absorption Base* can be divided into two basic types – One can considerably be mixed with aqueous solution and form water-in-oil (w/o) emulsion containing hydrophilic petrolatum and lanolin. The second type containing only lanolin can accommodate more of aqueous solution and form water-in-oil (w/o) emulsion.These ointments also can provide emollient action.

   Lanolin is a hydrous wool-fat; hence, it can accommodate more of water. The USP provides a monograph of hydrophilic petrolatum containing cholesterol 3%, stearyl alcohol 3%, white wax 8%, and white petrolatum 86%.
3. *Water-soluble Bases* are alternatively called "greaseless ointment base". It is prepared with water soluble ingredients such as polyethylene glycols (macrogols). The most common example of this type is Polyethylene Glycol Ointment. According to the mol. wt. of the polyethylene glycols, their physical state vary from liquid to solid, and these are known by the number respective to their molecular weight. For example, Polyethylene glycol(PEG) 200, 300, 400 are viscous liquids, while PEG 1500 is semisolid and PEG 1540, 3000, 4000, and 6000 are waxy solid. These have waxy texture. Depending on the molecular weight their solidification temperature varies from 40° to 60°C. The liquid PEGs are more hygroscopic than solid PEGs. These can be sterilised by heat, solids by dry heat and liquids by moist heat. These are non-toxic and non-irritating to the skin. This type of bases is absorbed by the skin, fairly compatible with most drugs and stable during storage (ageing effect).
4. *Water-removable Bases* are alternatively called "water-washable bases". These are hydrophilic in nature and can form oil-in-water (o/w) emulsion. These are very suitable for making o/w cream or ointment. The general composition of this type of base is –

   Emulsifying wax – 3 parts,

   White soft paraffin – 5 parts, and

   Liquid paraffin – 2 parts.

Depending on the type emulsifying agent used, the base may be anionic, cationic and non-ionic. This type of ointment base is fairly inert, miscible with secretions from lesions and possesses good cosmetic appearance. Due to the presence of a surfactant (emulsifying agent) its skin adherence is also good.

But, this type of base has certain **limitations**:

- Limited miscibility with water. By incorporating higher fatty alcohols, e.g. cetostearyl alcohol, water miscibility capacity can be increased, and the texture of the base can also be improved.
- Reduces antibacterial activity of certain substances, e.g. quaternary ammonium compounds, phenol, p-hydroxybenzoates, etc. Even some antibacterial agents become inactivated, e.g. penicillin.
- Because of hygroscopic nature these are less bland than paraffins.
- Macrogol ointments should not be packed in containers made of polythene, Bakelite due to their solvent action.

Mechanism of Drug Penetration

Absorption through the skin involves passive diffusion of substances. The mechanism of permeation or percutaneous absorption involves passage of drug through the epidermis itself or diffusion through shunts, particularly present and distributed relatively every where within hair follicles and eccrine glands. However, it is now believed that the trans-epidermal pathway is primarily responsible for diffusion through the skin. Skin works as a barrier system to the body and any material just cannot pass through it. The main resistance offered by the outer most layer of the skin, stratum corneum. The stratum corneumis also called "horny layer". It contains principally proteins (75-85%) and lipids. Thus, to understand the protective nature of the skin, one should first understand the structure and function of the stratum corneum. Stratum corneum present in the skin of most parts of the body is composed of 15 – 25 layers of "acutely flattened and metabolically inactive cells". In soft tissues it is densely present. Depending on the actual location the thickness of individual cell layer varies from 0.2μm to 0.5μm. The platelets building blocks of the stratum corneum look like polygons. The longest side of these polygons measure approximately 30 – 40μm.

The drug substance can permeate the skin primarily by two ways: (1) the transepidermal route, and (2) through pores. The transepidermal route comprises the transcellular and the intercellular route. The more direct route is the transcellular. In this case, the drug has to cross the skin by directly passing through both the lipid structures of the stratum corneum and the cytoplasm of the dead keratinocytes. This is the shortest route. But the drug substance has to face significant resistance to its permeation because it has to cross both lipophilic and hydrophilic structures. Thus, intercellular route is the more common route for drugs to permeate the skin.

Factors Influencing Penetration of Drug through Skin

There are various factors that influence the penetration of drug through skin. The factors are;

- *Permeability of the skin:* Skin is selectively permeable. It allows only certain substances to enter into the pores. The stratum corneum is the first layer of the epidermis. It is a dense layer made up of dead, flattened cells that are filled with keratin (an insoluble protein). This layer of dead cells resists substances that are water-soluble or fat-soluble.
- The skin has an oily secretion. The medication applied over the skin surface is absorbed best when the medication is suspended or dissolved in oily media. Drugs combined with inorganic substances such as petroleum are not absorbed.
- *Particle size of the drug:* The size of the drug particles in the ointment is an important factor in skin absorption. If the size of the drug particles in the ointment preparation are large and insoluble very little absorption will take place; for example, little amount of zinc oxide is absorbed from zinc oxide ointment. On the other hand, a greater amount of absorption takes place when an ointment containing a solution of wintergreen in olive oil or in a lanolin base is rubbed on the skin.
- *Degree of Skin Hydration:* Medication is absorbed by the wet skin better. That is, if the cornified layer (the top layer of the epidermis) is moist. Ointments soften the skin by wetting it, allows the medication in the ointment to be absorbed into the skin easily.
- Alternatively, to get moisture into the skin is to use an occlusive dressing over the skin lesion. An occlusive dressing is a dressing that prevents the loss of moisture from the skin's surface. Moisture is kept in the skin allowing the medicine to be absorbed into the skin. If a corticosteroid medication has been used, this medication will reduce skin inflammation faster.
- *Contact Time:* Absorption of drug through the skin is increased by keeping it in contact with the skin for longer periods of time. Since all disease organisms are not killed at the same time, there is a gradual decrease in the number of organisms. The longer the medication is on the skin lesions, the more organisms will be killed.

- *Degree of Friction:* Skin medication can be absorbed better by increasing the degree of friction; that is by rubbing for a longer time.
- *Skin Temperature:* If the temperature of the skin increases, the medication is absorbed faster through the skin. Also, in many cases heat alone is enough to kill disease organisms.
- *Epidermal Damage:* The epidermal layer of the skin is the protective layer. If the medication is applied to an area in which this layer has been damaged greater amount of medication would be absorbed quickly. Because, there is nothing to keep the medication out.

Factors Involved in Preparation of Semisolids

There are some factors that are to be considered during developing a semisolid preparation like cream, ointment, gel, and paste. These are:

- The intended application of the preparation, such as protective, emollient or therapeutic.
- The characteristics of the skin surface over which the preparation shall be applied.
- In case of a medicated preparation, the stability of the drug in the base.
- Effect of the base on the permeability and release characteristics of the drug.
- Intended therapeutic action, such as (1) completely localised surface action or (2) systemic action.
- Selection of the appropriate base and optimization.

Most of the drugs, topically applied, cannot permeate the skin due to presence of the epidermal barrier. When a drug needs to penetrate the diseased cells in the skin, some amount of drug reaches the blood stream. In such case, the drug and its metabolites are to be eliminated from the body through general pathway. Otherwise on repeated administration the drug and its metabolites will accumulate causing serious side effects. Drugs usually penetrate the epidermis either through keratinized cells of the horny layer or through hair follicles.

Ointments

General Method of Preparation of Ointment

Ointments are defined as *semisolids intended for external application to the skin or mucous membranes. They usually contain less than 20% water and volatiles and more than 50% hydrocarbons, waxes, or polyols as the vehicle.*

Depending on the nature of the ingredients there are two general methods,

1. Fusion, and
2. Incorporation.

1. **Fusion:** In this method the ingredients, except thermo labile(heat sensitive) and volatile substances, are first melted together with constant stirring till the mass is congealed. This method is called *melting method.* When the temperature of the mass comes down to about 40°C the volatile and thermo labile substances are added and mixed thoroughly. If these contain any solid material, it should be finely powdered before mixing.

   If the ointment contains ingredients to be emulsified or an emulsion base, both melting, and emulsification are done to prepare the product. The oil soluble heat stable components are melted with oil and waxes over boiling water bath or in a steam bath to about 70 – 75°C. Similarly, water soluble, heat stable materials are mixed required quantity of water and heated to 70 – 75°C. Then, the hot aqueous solution is gradually mixed with the melted mixture with constant stirring. The temperature during stirring is initially maintained at about 70 – 75°C for 5 – 10 minutes. Thereafter, the mixture is cooled slowly and stirring is continued till the product is congealed.

2. **Incorporation:** In this method the ointment base is prepared separately, cooled to room temperature and the active component is gradually incorporated into ointment base by trituration. Hence, this method can be alternatively called *trituration method.* Other solid ingredients of the formulation are finely powdered in a mortar pestle for extemporaneous compounding. The required amount of base is taken and other ingredients in the form of powder mixture or liquid mixture or solution are incorporated into the base in portions. After each addition or incorporation, it is mixed using a spatula to make the mixture smooth and uniform. The process of incorporation is continued until entire powders are completely mixed with the base. It is always better to incorporate powders using a levigating agent like glycerine when water is the external phase or mineral oil when oilis the external phase. By this uniform mixing become possible.

Preparations

Product: Methyl Salicylate Ointment

Standard for drug: It contains not less than 98%w/w of Methyl Salicylate, calculated as $C_8H_8O_3$

Standard for product: Content of methyl salicylate: 45.0 – 52.5%w/w, calculated as $C_8H_8O_3$

Composition

Each g contains

Methyl Salicylate 500mg

In a suitable flavoured base.

Use: Local analgesic

Lot size: 10 g

Manufacturing Formula

Methyl Salicylate	5.0 g
White Beeswax	2.5 g
Hydrous Wool Fat	2.5 g

Method of Preparation

- Take weighed quantity of white beeswax and wool fat in a shallow porcelain dish, place over a boiling water bath to melt,
- When the base is completely melted, remove the dish from the heat, add gradually the weighed quantity of methyl salicylate with continuous stirring till the ointment becomes cold,
- Carry out the tests,
- Fill in a suitable collapsible tube and seal properly.
- Label the preparation.

Product: Bacitracin Ointment

Standard for drug: Bacitracin should have minimum of 40 U.S.P Units per mg.

Standard for product: Content of Bacitracin: 450 – 575 Units per g.

Composition:

Each g contains

Bacitracin 1.25%w/w in a suitable non-aqueous ointment base

Use: Antibacterial.

Lot size: 5 g

Manufacturing Formula

Bacitracin	USP	75 mg
Liquid paraffin, heavy	IP	125 mg
Soft paraffin, white	IP	4.8 g

Method of Preparation

- Weigh accurately the required amount of bacitracin and transfer into a mortar pestle,
- Add liquid paraffin to the drug and levigate properly to make a smooth paste, add gradually the soft paraffin with continuous levigation until a uniform paste is obtained,
- Carry out the test, fill in a suitable collapsible tube or in a wide mouth glass bottle, seal properly and label.

Product: Paraffin Ointment

Use: Ointment base.

Lot size: 10 g

Manufacturing Formula

Hard Paraffin	0.3 g
Soft paraffin, white	9.0 g
White Beeswax	0.2 g
Cetostearyl Alcohol	0.5 g

Method of Preparation

- Take the required quantities of all ingredients in a dish, place over a boiling water bath until melt,
- Levigate thoroughly until the mixture becomes cold,
- Fill the ointment base in a wide mouth glass bottle and seal.
- Label the base.

Product: Zinc oxide Ointment

Standard for drug: It contains not less than 99%w/w of ZnO.

Standard for product: Content of Zinc oxide: 18.5 – 21.5%w/w, calculated as ZnO.

Composition

Each g contains

Zinc oxide 0.2%w/w in a non-aqueous ointment base

Use: Astringent, Protective.

Lot size: 10 g

Manufacturing Formula

Zinc oxide	IP	2.0 g
Liquid Paraffin, heavy	IP	1.5 g
White wax		0.325 g
Soft paraffin, white		6.175 g

Method of Preparation

- Transfer weighed quantity of zinc oxide into a mortar pestle, levigate with liquid paraffin until a smooth paste is formed,
- Take weighed amounts of white wax and soft paraffin in a dish, heat on a boiling water bath until these ingredients melt, mix well,
- Add melted base gradually to the zinc oxide paste, continue to levigate until uniformly mixed and desired smoothness is attained,
- Carry out the test,
- Fill the preparation in a suitable collapsible tube or wide mouth glass bottle, seal with a cap,
- Label the preparation properly.

Product: Salicylic Acid and Sulphur Ointment

Standard for drug: Salicylic Acid contains not less than 99.5 and not more than 101.05w/w of $C_7H_6O_3$, calculated on dried basis. Sulphur contains not less than 99.5%w/w of S.

Standard for product: Content of Salicylic Acid: 2.85 – 3.15%w/w, calculated as $C_7H_6O_3$,

Content of Sulphur: 2.85 – 3.15%w/w, calculated as S.

Composition

Each g contains

Salicylic Acid	IP	30 mg
Sulphur	IP	30 mg

In a suitable base

Use: Scabicide

Lot size: 10 g

Manufacturing Formula

Salicylic Acid	IP	0.3 g
Sulphur, precipitated	IP	0.3 g
Liquid paraffin, heavy	IP	1 g
White wax		0.4 g
Soft paraffin, white		7.6 g

Method of Preparation

- Take weighed quantities of precipitated sulphur and salicylic acid in a mortar pestle, levigate with liquid paraffin to make a smooth paste,
- Take white wax and soft paraffin in a dish, place it over a boiling water bath and stir with a glass rod until these ingredients melt completely,
- Add the melted base to the paste gradually with continuous levigation, continue to levigate till uniform smooth ointment is obtained.
- Carry out the test and fill in a suitable collapsible tube or in a wide mouth bottle, seal the container and label properly.

Salicylic Acid and Sulphur Ointment10 g

Each g contains	
Salicylic Acid IP 30 mg	Store below 25°C; Do not freeze.
Sulphur IP 30 mg	Keep out of reach of children.
In a suitable base	Use as directed by the physician
FOR EXTERNAL USE ONLY	Mfg. Lic. No. xxxxxx
Manufactured in India by:	Batch No. 1324
RCP Pharmaceuticals	Mfd. MM YYYY
Kohka, Kurud Road	Exp. MM YYYY
Bhilai. CG	M.R.P. Rs.

Creams

Creams are usually prepared for external use. These are viscous, homogeneous, semi-solid emulsions, may be either oil-in-water type(o/w, aqueous cream) or water-in-oil type(w/o, oily cream). Certain water miscible bases having a complex matrix-like physical structure are also known as *creams*, they are often anhydrous or contain only a small proportion of water and similar in appearance to traditional emulsion-type cream base.

Creams are used to apply solution or dispersion of medicament to the skin for therapeutic or prophylactic purpose where a highly occlusive effect is not necessary.

Bland creams may also be used for their emollient, cooling or moistening effect upon the skin.

Cream bases and Raw Materials

Aqueous creams are usually o/w emulsions. By the selection of anionic, cationic or non-ionic emulsifying agents it is possible to formulate aqueous creams which are compatible with most active ingredients.

The w/o emulsions, i.e. oily creams are usually used for their emollient and occlusive properties. These are formed by metallic soaps, beeswax, wool fat and its derivatives and some synthetic non-ionic substances. Non-emulsified systems having appearance and consistency of creams are generally used as topical vehicles for corticosteroids; they usually contain a continuous solubilising phase and a solid phase. The solvent in the solubilising phase may be propylene glycol and the solid phase a mixture of a fatty acid and high molecular weight macrogols.

Material used in creams and other semisolids are:

(a) Hydrocarbons (hard, soft and liquid paraffins)

(b) Alcohols (cetostearyl, cetyl, stearyl)

(c) Glycols (glycerol, macrogols, propylene glycol)

(d) Lanolin and its derivatives, fatty acids (oleic, stearic)

(e) Beeswax, vegetable oils (almond, arachis, castor, coconut, cotton seed, maize, olive)

(f) Esters (isopropyl myristate), and

(g) Emulsifying agents.

Preparation of Creams

Emulsified creams which contain waxes or fatty solids are prepared by heating the oil soluble or oil miscible constituents together with the emulsifying agents, if oil soluble, at 70° – 75°C.

Water soluble or water miscible constituents dissolved in or incorporated with the aqueous phase are heated to the same temperature. The two phases are then mixed. If the dispersed phase occupies only a small volume, it is usual to add this to the continuous phase, otherwise the order of mixing is of little importance. The important factors are that the two phases should be at similar temperature and addition should be steady to avoid entrapment of air. Subsequent cooling should be slow with stirring. Sudden cooling or excessive aeration can lead to a granular product. After cooling to 30 – 40°C, the cream can usually be homogenized. All apparatus used in preparation and the final containers should be thoroughly cleaned before use and rinsed with freshly boiled and cooled purified water before drying.

Microbial Contamination

O/w type creams provide suitable environment for growth of micro-organisms. Even when a preservative is included the efficiency of the system may be impaired due to partitioning of the preservative between the oily and aqueous phases of the cream, or due to the partial inactivation of the preservative by the emulsifying agent or a hydrophilic colloid present. Increased amount of preservative may cause undesirable side effects. Consequently, the concentration of the preservative is necessarily a compromise. Thus, a high standard of cleanliness during processing and handling is essential.

Packaging of Creams

Well-closed containers those can prevent evaporation and contamination should be used. The material of construction should resist absorption and diffusion of the content. Collapsible tubes of metal or flexible plastic tubes may be used for packing of creams.

If aluminium tubes or containers are used they either should have an inner lacquer coating or a mixture of 0.1% of Na_2HPO_4 and 0.2% of NaH_2PO_4 may be used as buffer in the cream, if no specific buffer is mentioned or recommended to protect aluminium from corrosion and to reduce the chance of formation of hydrogen. Particularly creams containing organic mercury compound should not be packed in uncoated aluminium tubes.

Storage: Unless otherwise specified the creams should be stored at temperature below 25°C; but, not in a refrigerator.

Labelling

Along with other information it should mention distinctly, *For external use only*; strength of the active ingredient in terms of %w/v or w/w and in case of diluted creams, it should also mention that unless otherwise mentioned, *the diluted cream should not be used after 2 weeks after preparation.*

Difference between Ointment and Cream:

Ointment	Cream
1. Ointments are semisolid preparations in which the active substance(s) remain either as soluble state or suspended. These are intended for external application.	Creams are aqueous or oily semisolid emulsions in which the drug is generally remains in soluble state. These are also intended for external application.
2. These are usually greasier than the creams. The extent of greasiness depends on the type of base used.	These are less greasy and are either o/w (oil-in-water) or w/o(water-in-oil) emulsions.

Table *Contd...*

Ointment	Cream
3. These are more viscous, and they exhibit plastic flow with a definite yield value.	These are less viscous and pseudoplastic in nature.
4. Ointments are sticky and less spreadable.	These are soft and they have good spreadability.
5. These are protective and soothing.	Creams of w/o type are emollient, soothing and cleansing. This type is preferred for better spreadability and less greasiness. The o/w type creams due to continuous evaporation of water leave a residue on the skin after evaporation of water.
6. They can adhere to the skin for longer time, they are not easily removable.	Creams of o/w type can be removed easily.
7. The occlusiveness depends on the type of base used. The extent of occlusion – oleaginous base> absorption base > emulsifying base > water soluble base.	The w/o type creams are less occlusive than ointment and o/w type creams are non-occlusive.
8. Cosmetically less attractive.	Cosmetic appeal is more. Non-medicated creams are used as cosmetics. Vanishing creams are of o/w type.
9. Occlusive ointments interfere with normal function of the skin.	Oil-in-water(o/w)creams have less interference with normal function of the skin.
10. Drug in ointments of hydrocarbon base is better absorbed.	O/w cream also promotes percutaneous absorption of drug.

Pastes

These are one type of semisolid preparation, the difference between ointment and paste is that the solid content in the latter is high even up to 50%. A large quantity of insoluble solid powder is incorporated into an ointment base for which the paste is found to be stiffer. A paste when spread over skin adheres in the form of a thick layer, it forms a protective and soothing coating over the inflamed and affected skin surface. For this these are useful for protecting the face and lips from the sun.

Pastes are usually less oily than the ointments and they form thick layer over the skin surface their cosmetic elegance is also less. Since the solid content is high, paste of a potent medicament may produce reaction on the skin also.

Pastes are prepared by levigating the fine powder of the solid with a portion of the congealed base till uniformly mixed, then the rest portion of the base is gradually added with continuous levigation until uniform dispersion of the powders is made.

Base used for preparing paste may be hydrocarbon base, e.g. emulsifying wax, glycerol; sometimes water-soluble base, e.g. macrogol base is used.

Comparison between paste and ointment:

Ointment	Paste
1. The ointments are soft due to less content of powders.	Pastes are stiff due to high content of powders, even up to 50%.
2. On application these leave a very thin layer Over the area of application.	On application these leave a thick coat over the area of application.
3. The protective activity is less compared to paste.	The protective activity is more due to formation of thick coat over the area of application.
4. Ointments have very good spreadability and free from grittiness.	Pastes do not have spreadability, these are also free from grittiness.
5. Ointment can migrate from its area of Application. Hence, a powerful drug can affect the normal and healthy skin also.	Due to thickness, paste cannot migrate from its area of application. Thus, there is no damage of the normal, healthy skin by a powerful drug.
6. Ointments are emollient and greasy in nature.	Pastes are emollient and less greasy.
7. Ointments being greasy, can affect 7. Perspiration through skin.	Pastes are porous due to high content of powders do not affect perspiration.
8. Ointment cannot absorb exudates.	Because of high content of powders, these can absorb exudates.
9. Ointments with hydrocarbon base are more macerating in their action.	Pastes even made with similar hydrocarbon bases are less macerating the ointments.
10. These are cosmetically attractive.	These are cosmetically less attractive, as they leave a thick layer on the skin.
11. These do not require any device to apply.	These are applied either with a spatula or Spreadon tint or with other dressing.
12. These can be easily removed from the skin and can be applied on the scalp.	These are not suitable for scalp treatment, as these cannot be removed easily from the hair.
13. These need not to be kept for long time.	Once applied, left for long period.

Packaging and storage: Pastes should be packed in glass or plastic containers fitted with screw caps having impermeable liners or with close-fitting slip-on lids to prevent the content from diffusion or absorption. Alternatively, these can be packed in collapsible tubes like ointments.

Formulations

Product: Aluminium Paste, Compound

Synonym: Baltimore Paste.

Standard for the product: Content of zinc oxide, 37.0– 42.0 % calculated as ZnO;

Content of aluminium, 15.8 – 20.0 % calculated as Al.

Use: Protective in burns.

Lot size: 10 g

Manufacturing Formula

Aluminium powder	2.0 g
Zinc oxide	4.0 g
Liquid Paraffin	4.0 g

Method of Preparation

- Take weighed quantity of aluminium powder and zinc oxide into a mortar pestle,
- Add measured volume of liquid paraffin and triturate until a smooth paste is obtained.
- Determine the content of aluminium and zinc oxide.
- Pack the preparation in a clean, dry, wide mouth suitable glass container,
- Seal with a pilfer proof cap and label appropriately.

Product: Magnesium Sulphate Paste

Synonym: Morison's Paste.

*Standards for the product:*Content of magnesium sulphate, 36 – 41% calculated as $MgSO_4$;

Content of phenol, 0.45 – 0.55% calculated as C_6H_6O.

Use: Dehydrating (drawing) boils and carbuncles.

Lot size: 10 g

Manufacturing Formula

Phenol	0.05 g
Glycerine	5.5 g
Dried Magnesium Sulphate q.s	

Method of Preparation

- Dry about 7 g of magnesium sulphate at 150°C for $1^{1}/_{2}$ hours or at 130°C for 4 hrs., keep it in a desiccator,
- Dry glycer^{i}ne at $1^{2}0_{0}$C for one hour a^{n}d cool in a desiccator,
- Dissolve phenol in measured volume of glycerine,
- Weigh 4.5 g of magnesium sulphate, transfer it into a clean, dry mortar pestle,
- Add phenol solution to the powder and triturate until a smooth paste is obtained,
- Determine the content of magnesium sulphate and phenol,
- Pack in a suitable glass container and label appropriately.

Note: The label should mention, *Stir well before use.*

Product: Resorcinol and Sulphur Paste

Standards for the product:

Content of resorcinol, 4.75 – 5.25% calculated as C_6H_6O;

Content of sulphur, 4.75 – 5.25% calculated as S;

Content of zinc oxide, 38.0 – 42.0% calculated as ZnO.

Use: Anti-acne.

Lot size: 10 g.

Manufacturing Formula

Resorcinol, finely sifted	0.5 g
Precipitated Sulphur	0.5 g
Zinc oxide, finely sifted	4.0 g
Emulsifying ointment	5.0 g

Manufacturing Method

- Transfer the weighed quantity of zinc oxide, precipitated sulphur and resorcinol into a clean mortar pestle, triturate these with a little of emulsifying ointment until a smooth paste is obtained.
- Add gradually the remaining portion of emulsifying ointment and continue trituration.

- When a uniform, smooth paste is obtained, determine the content of zinc oxide, sulphur and resorcinol.
- Fill the preparation in a suitable container, seal with a pilfer proof cap and label.

Product: Titanium Dioxide Paste

Standards for the product:

Content of Zinc Oxide, 23.7 – 26.3% calculated as ZnO;

Residue on ignition, 53 – 58%w/w.

Use: Sun burn protectant.

Lot size: 10 g

Manufacturing Formula

Titanium Dioxide	2.0 g
Chlorocresol	0.01 g
Red Ferric Oxide	0.2 g
Light Kaolin	1.0 g
Zinc Oxide, fine sifted	2.5 g
Glycerin	1.5 g
Purified water	q.s

Manufacturing Method

- Transfer the weighed quantity of titanium dioxide, ferric oxide, kaolin and zinc oxide and mix thoroughly and triturate.
- Dissolve the chlorocresol in the glycerine, add 2.8 ml of purified water.
- Add the solution gradually to the powder mix and triturate until a smooth paste is obtained.
- Determine the content of zinc oxide and residue on ignition.
- Fill the preparation in a suitable container, seal with a pilfer proof cap,
- Label

Gels

These are semisolid disperse systems containing polymers or long chain molecules in the internal phase. The long-chain molecules or the polymer cross-link and interact among themselves and form a weblike structure. Within this structure the external phase is entrapped. Such a system seems to be single phase. Hydrated gelatin is a classic example of gel. Sometimes, the suspensions, milks and magmas of inorganic hydroxides and clays are called as gels as they are highly viscous. The particles of bentonite form a three-dimensional structure throughout the gel. This is a real two-phase system where the particles of bentonite do not dissolve in water but only dispersed throughout the continuous phase. Reversible gels are semisolids and viscous at low temperature. These become liquids when temperature rises. Most of the aqueous and nonaqueous gels are prepared with the help of heat and high-speed mixing.

Now a days, gels are one of the widely used as drug delivery systems. Gels are most commonly used for oral, topical and ophthalmological, parenteral administration. A gel can be used for prolonged action of a drug when injected intramuscularly or implanted into the body. The cosmetic preparations in the form of gels may be shampoo, skin, fragrance and hair-care preparations, dentifrices etc. The gellants are used as binders in tablet formulations, as protective colloids in suspensions, as thickening agents in oral liquids and suppository base.

Based on the nature of the colloidal phase (gellants), gels are primarily of two categories, inorganic and organic. Organic gels may be of two types-natural and synthetic. The natural gums like acacia, xanthan, and carrageenan are anionic polysaccharides. Synthetic gellants may be cellulose derivatives, e.g. carboxymethylcellulose sodium, hydroxypropyl-cellulose, hydroxyethylcellulose, hydroxypropylmethyl cellulose, etc., polyethylene and its copolymers, acrylic polymers, metallic stearates and synthetic block copolymers.

Based on the nature of solvent gels may be divided into two types-aqueous (hydrogel) and nonaqueous (organogel). There is another type, xerogel. Xerogel are solid gels containing less amount of solvent. Dry gelatin, tragacanth ribbons, acacia tears are the common example of xerogel. These are frequently prepared by evaporating the solvent from the gel.

Some gels may contract on storage and the internal liquid comes out at the surface of the gel. This process, called as *syneresis*, may occur in organogels, organic and inorganic hydrogels. Mostly this is observed in gels containing less amount of polymer. The reason may be, the decrease in elastic stresses during setting of the gel, decrease in the space for the solvent, as a result the liquid is forced to come out of the gel matrix. The concentration of salts in the gel may have effect on syneresis.

Conversely a gel may absorb liquid resulting the increase in volume. This phenomenon is called *swelling*. This is due to the penetration of solvent into the gel matrix.

When the hydration of a gellant depends on temperature, gel is formed due to change in temperature and such gel is reversible. When due to a chemical reaction, e.g. salt bridging or cross-linking, a gel is formed, it is irreversible.

The viscosity of a gel directly related to the molecular weight of the polymer(gellant). That is lesser amount of a polymer of higher molecular weight can result the desired viscosity of the gel. Gels are pseudoplastic fluids and show non-Newtonian flow characteristics.

Commonly used gelling agents in the pharmaceutical preparations are given below in the Table 13.1.

Table 13.1 Commonly used pharmaceutical gelling agents

For Aqueous solution	For Non-Aqueous solution
Carbomers	Clays and organoclays
Gelatin	Colloidal silicon dioxide
Colloidal silicon dioxide	Modified cellulosics
Cellulosics	Low HLB surfactants
Natural gums(xanthans, aligns, carrageenans, pectins)	polyethylene
Non-ionic surfactants starches	

Formulations

Product: Diclofenac Gel

Standard for drug: It should contain not less than 99.0% and not more than 101%w/w of

Diclofenac Diethylamine, calculated as $C_{18}H_{22}Cl_2N_2O_2$ on dried basis.

Standard for product: It should contain not less than 90% and not more than 110%w/w of the

Stated amount of Diclofenac, calculated as $C_{18}H_{22}Cl_2N_2O_2$ on dried basis.

Composition:

It contains

Diclofenac Diethylamine	BP	1.10%
Equivalent to Diclofenac sodium	IP	1%
Linseed oil	BP	3.0%
Methyl salicylate	IP	1.0%
Menthol	IP	5.0%
Benzyl Alcohol	IP	1.0%

In a flavoured washable gel base

Use: Analgesic, anti-inflammatory.

Lot size: 10 g

Manufacturing Formula

Diclofenac Diethylamine	BP	0.11g
Linseed oil	BP	0.3g
Methyl salicylate	IP	0.1g
Menthol	IP	0.5g
Benzyl Alcohol	IP	0.1g
Sodium Alginate Gel Base	q.s	10 g

Manufacturing Method

- Take Diclofenac sodium, accurately weighed, in a mortar pestle,
- Add linseed oil and make a paste,
- Add benzyl alcohol and methyl salicylate, levigate thoroughly,
- Add menthol and sufficient gel base, mix thoroughly to make a uniform gel,
- Carry out the tests, fill the preparation in a suitable collapsible tube, seal and label.

Preparation of sodium alginate gel base

Sodium alginate	IP	1.0 g
Glycerin	IP	1.0 g
Methylparaben	IP	0.02 g
Calcium gluconate	IP	0.05 g
Purified water	IP	8.0g

- Take 8 ml of purified water in a 25 ml clean beaker, add methyl paraben and heat to dissolve, cool the solution, transfer into a clean mortar pestle,
- Add glycerin and mix,
- Add sodium alginate and levigate vigorously until a smooth slurry is formed,
- Add calcium gluconate and mix vigorously.
- Pack the gel in a clean, dry wide mouth glass bottle, seal and label.

Warning: To be sold by retail on the prescription of a Registered medical practitioner only.

Diclofenac Gel 5g

It contains

Diclofenac Diethylamine	BP	1.10%
Equivalent to Diclofenac sodium	IP	1%
Linseed oil	BP	3.0%
Methyl salicylate	IP	1.0%
Menthol	IP	5.0%
Benzyl Alcohol	IP	1.0%

in a flavoured washable gel base

Store in a cool place.
Do not freeze.

FOR EXTERNAL USE **ONLY**

Mfg.Lic.XXX

Manufactured in India by
XYZ Pharmaceuticals
Kohka - Kurud road, Bhilai

B.No. 1234
Mfd.MM.YYYY
Exp. MM.YYYY

Product: Zinc oxide Gel

Composition

Each g contains

Zinc oxide	0.2 g
Aqueous gel base	q.s

Use: Mild astringent and topical protectant.

Lot size: 5 g

Manufacturing Formula

Zinc oxide	IP	1.0 g
Sodium hydroxide	IP	0.016 g
Carbomer 934		0.04 g
Water, purified	IP	3.9 ml

Manufacturing Method

- Accurately weigh the carbomer 934, measure the required volume of purified water and transfer in a mortar pestle, add the carbomer to it.
- Weigh accurately 1.07 g of sodium hydroxide, dissolve in sufficient purified water to make 10 ml of solution. Pipette out 0.15 ml and add drop wise to the mortar with gentle agitation.

- Add the weighed quantity of zinc oxide slowly to the mortar with gentle stirring.
- Continue to mix slowly until a smooth, homogeneous gel is prepared. Air should not be entrapped.
- Take a sample and test for zinc oxide content.
- Fill the preparation in a 5 ml capacity collapsible tube and seal.
- Label the tube properly with a note, FOR EXTERNAL USE ONLY.

Product: Piroxicam Gel

Standard for drug: It contains not less than 97% and not more than 103%w/w of $C_{15}H_{13}N_3O_4S$, calculated on dried basis.

Standard for product: It should contain not less than 95% of the stated amount of Piroxicam IP,

calculated as $C_{15}H_{13}N_3O_4S$,

Composition

It contains

Piroxicam IP 0.5%w/w in water soluble gel base.

Use: Analgesic, anti-inflammatory.

Lot size: 5 g

Manufacturing Formula

Piroxicam IP	25.0 mg
Methylcellulose 4000 cps	40 mg
Carbopol 934	12 mg
Propylene glycol	0.8 ml
Methylparaben	0.75 mg
Purified water q.s	

Manufacturing Method

- Weigh accurately required quantity of piroxicam, transfer into a clean mortar pestle, crush to make fine powders,
- Weigh separately 4.975 g of gel base, add in portions to the powder and levigate thoroughly till a uniform mixture is obtained, avoid entrapment of air during levigation,
- Carry out the test, fill the gel in a clean collapsible tube and seal properly.
- Label the tube.

Preparation of 10 g of Gel base

Methylcellulose 4000 cps	80 mg
Carbopol 934	24 mg
Propylene glycol	1.6 ml
Methylparaben	1.5 mg
Purified water qs to make	10.0 g

Method

- Weigh accurately 120 mg of methylparaben, dissolve in 4 ml of hot purified water,
- Pipette out 0.5ml of this solution to a 10 ml clean beaker, add another 3 ml of purified water, heat to 90°C, disperse methylcellulose, keep it in a refrigerator for overnight,
- Take another 10 ml clean beaker, pipette 3 ml of purified water, disperse carbopol,
- Adjust the pH to 7.0 by adding 2% NaOH solution, about 0.6 ml shall be required,
- Add propylene glycol and mix thoroughly,
- Mix methylcellulose and carbopol fraction thoroughly, add sufficient purified water to make 10.0 g and mix well.

Product: Ibuprofen Gel

Standard for drug: It contains not less than 98.5% and not more than 101%w/w of $C_{13}H_{18}O_2$, calculated on dried basis.

Standard for product: It should contain not less than 90% of the stated amount, calculated as $C_{13}H_{18}O_2$.

Composition

Each g contains

Ibuprofen IP 0.02g in a gel base.

Use: Analgesic.

Lot size: 10 g

Manufacturing Formula

Ibuprofen	IP	0.2 g
Sodium alginate	IP	1.0 g
Glycerin	IP	1.0 g
Methyl Paraben	IP	0.02 g
Calcium gluconate	IP	0.05 g
Purified water	IP	8.0g

Manufacturing Method

- Take 8 ml of purified water in a 25 ml clean beaker, add methylparaben and heat to dissolve, cool the solution, transfer into a clean mortar pestle,
- Add glycerine and mix,
- Add sodium alginate and levigate vigorously until a smoothslurryis formed,
- Add calcium gluconate and mix vigorously.
- Add micronized ibuprofen with slow levigation until a uniform gel is obtained,
- Carry out the tests,
- Pack the gel in a clean, dry wide mouth glass bottle, seal and label.

Product: Sunscreen Gel

Composition

Each g contains

Glyceryl-p-amino benzoate	3%
Monoiso-propanolamine	0.09%
Ethanol	50 %

in a hydrous, flavoured gel base.

Use: Protection from sun burn.

Lot size: 10 g

Manufacturing Formula

Glyceryl-p-amino benzoate	0.3 g
Monoiso-propanolamine	0.009g
Ethanol	5.2 ml
Carbomer 940	0.1 g
Sandal wood oil	0.01 ml
Purified water	5.0 ml

Manufacturing Method

- Measure the required volume of alcohol and transfer into a clean and drymortar pestle,
- Disperse the weighed quantity of carbomer940, add weighed amount of Glyceryl-p-amino benzoate and dissolve in the solution,
- Add Monoiso-propanolamine to this slowly, add sandal wood oil and mix,

- Add measured volume of purified water slowly with slow stirring, care to be taken to avoid entrapment of air during stirring.
- Once the gel is formed, pack it in a suitable collapsible tube, seal well and label.

Evaluation of Semi Solid Dosages Forms

As per Pharmacopoeia the semisolid preparations in general are evaluated by conducting following tests:

- Description
- It includes color, odour, and physical appearance including texture. There should be no change in color, odour and texture of the preparation.
- Identification
- Identification test for drug and other ingredients as mentioned in the official monograph or testing protocol of a proprietary product.
- Assay
- The product should be tested as per standard or official method to determine the content of active ingredient per unit quantity of the product.

However, after development of a semi solid preparation following tests are conducted for evaluation of the product.

- Description

  As mentioned above
- Viscosity should be determined using s rotational viscometer suitable for measuring the viscosity of a non-Newtonian fluid. The viscosity should be within the expected limits.Viscosities of formulations were measured by using Brookfield DV-I (spindle T-D spindle code S94) at 10 rpm. As the RPM increases viscosity decreases. Only in case of gel spindle codeS93 was used.
- Spreadability

  This is not an official test. However, this property can be measured using a suitable method that can describe how much surface area can be covered by a limited amount of the product within a stipulated time. Unless otherwise mentioned sspreadability of the formulation can be determined by a modified apparatus suggested by Muttimer et al.It consists of a wooden block, which was provided by a pulley at a one end. A rectangular ground glass was fixed on this block. An excess of ointment (about 3 gm) under study was placed on this ground plate. The ointment was then sandwiched between this plate and another glass plate having the dimension of fixed ground plate and provided with the hook. A 1 Kg weight was placed on the top of the plates for 5 minutes to expel air and to provide a uniform film of the ointment between the plates. Excess of the ointment was scrapped off from the edges. The top plate was then subjected to pull of 80 gms. With the help of string attached to the hook and the time (in seconds) required by top plate to cover a distance of 10 cm be noted. A shorter interval indicates better Spredability. Spredability is given in unit gm.cm/sec Spredability of the formulation may be determined by the following formulation,

$$S = M \times \frac{L}{T}$$

Where, L = length moved by glass slide

T = Time in seconds

M = Weight in pan and

S = Spredability

- Extrudability

  This is another unofficial test carried out to assess the consistency of the product and to determine how much pressure would be required to expel the content from a collapsible tube.It is usual empirical test to measure the force required to extrude the material from tube. More quantity extruded better was Extrudability. The formulation under study was filled in clean, lacquered aluminium collapsible tube with nozzle tube of 5mm opening and applies pressure on tube by the help of finger. Tube extrudability was then determined by measuring amount of ointment extruded through the tip when the pressure was applied on tube.

- Draize skin irritation test

  A known amount of test material (product) is to be introduced under a one square inch gauge patch. The patch is applied over the skin of 12 albino rabbits, (6 with intact skin) and (6 with abraded skin). The patch is secured in place with adhesive tape and the entire trunk of the animal is wrapped with an impervious material for a 24 hourperiod, After 24 hours the patches are removed and resulting reaction is evaluated for erythema and oedema formation. The reaction is again scored at the end of 72 hours and the two readings are averaged.

- Uniformity of drug-content

  This is an official test carried out to determine whether the active constituent has been mixed uniformly with the bulk. Samples drawn from different zones of the bulk product or from randomly sampled packed products are evaluated to determine the content of active ingredient. The result must comply with the standard given in the individual monograph or in standards of a proprietary product.

- Uniformity of content

  Randomly drawn samples are examined by removing the content as completely as possible and weighed. The individual content of the product must comply with the limits.

- *In-vitro* dissolution

  USP Apparatus 4: Flow-Through Cell Apparatus. In the flow-through method, the test sample is in a small volume cell through which media is pumped at a constant temperature. Upon leaving the cell, the eluate is filtered and can then be analyzed directly or collected in fractions to calculate the percent drug release. Several other automated and flow-through methods have also been used. An "insertion cell" used in conjunction with a compendial flow-through cell (USP) has been described by Chatteraj and Kanfer where the release of acyclovir from semisolid dosage forms was monitored. The results were found to compare favourably with previous acyclovir release data using different diffusion cells and indicated that their "insertion cell" offered distinct advantages compared to VDCs in that it is easier to use and readily adaptable for use with the compendial flow-through apparatus

Exercise

A. Multiple Choice Question Carrying 01 Mark

1. Which of the following dosage forms is semisolid?

   (a) Elixir (b) Injection

   (c) Enema (d) Ointment

2. Which of the following is used to prepare semisolid dosage form?

   (a) Liquid paraffin (b) Starch

   (c) Magnesium sulphate (d) Lactose

3. Which of the following formulations provides emollient effect?

   (a) Capsule (b) Cream

   (c) Aerosol (d) None of the above

4. Which of the following statements is correct?

   (a) Creams are generally more greasy preparation

   (b) Creams are generally less greasy preparation

(c) Ointments are generally less greasy than creams
(d) Ointments are not greasy preparations.

5. Gels are commonly used for
   (a) Oral administration (b) Topical application
   (c) Parenteral administration (d) All of the above
6. Which of the following statement is correct?
   (a) Bentonite dissolves in cold water
   (b) Bentonite dissolves in hot water
   (c) Bentonite disperses in water
   (d) Bentonite does not dissolve in water
7. Which of the following statement is correct?
   (a) The cream should contain calcium hydroxide
   (b) The cream should contain a sodium phosphate buffer.
   (c) The cream should contain sodium acetate
   (d) The cream should contain potassium hydroxide.
8. Which of the following statement is correct?
   (a) The aluminium container should have inner lacquer coating
   (b) The aluminium container should have a lacquer coating
   (c) The aluminium container should have inner color coating
   (d) The aluminium container should have color coating
9. Unless otherwise mentioned creams should be stored at
   (a) 10°C (b) 30°C
   (c) 25°C (d) 40°C
10. In general creams are cosmetically
    (a) Not appealing (b) Poor appealing
    (c) Absolutely poor appealing (d) More appealing
11. Occlusiveness of oleaginous ointment base is
    (a) More than absorption base (b) Less than absorption base
    (c) Less than emulsifying base (d) Less than water-soluble base
12. Which polyethylene glycol is liquid?
    (a) PEG 200 (b) PEG 300
    (c) PEG 400 (d) All of the above

13. Which polyethylene glycol is solid?
    (a) PEG 300 (b) PEG 400
    (c) PEG 1540 (d) PEG 200
14. Which layer of the skin acts as most effective barrier for penetration through skin?
    (a) Stratum corneum (b) Stratumlutinum
    (c) Stratum granulosidum (d) None of the above
15. The antibacterial activity of quaternary ammonium compounds is reduced by
    (a) Water soluble base (b) Water removable base
    (c) Hydrocarbon base (d) None of the above
16. Macrogol ointments should not be packed in
    (a) Aluminium container (b) Glass container
    (c) Polythene container (d) All of the above

B. Question Carrying 05 Marks

1. Explain water-removable base used to prepare ointment and mention its limitations.
2. Write down how a drug can penetrate the skin.
3. Write down the general method of preparation of ointment.
4. Write down the method of preparation of creams.
5. Write down the factors involved in preparation of semisolids.
6. What are various types of materials used to prepare cream? Mention one example of each type.

C. Question Carrying 10 Marks

1. Explain various classes of ointment bases used to prepare ointment.
2. Explain the factors that influence penetration of drug through skin.
3. Enumerate the factors to be considered for preparation of cream.
4. Distinguish between salient features of cream and ointment.
5. Differentiate ointment from paste.
6. Write a note on gel preparation.

Answers

A. Multiple Choice Question Carrying 01 Mark

1. (d)	2. (a)	3. (b)	4. (b)	5. (d)
6. (c)	7. (b)	8. (a)	9. (c)	10. (d)
11. (a)	12. (d)	13. (c)	14. (a)	15. (b)
16. (c)				

www.ingramcontent.com/pod-product-compliance
Lightning Source LLC
Chambersburg PA
CBHW080935240926
51849CB00004BA/464
9789391910648